# Future Prospects for Music Education

# Future Prospects for Music Education: Corroborating Informal Learning Pedagogy

Edited by

## Sidsel Karlsen and Lauri Väkevä

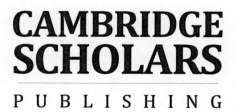

CAMBRIDGE
SCHOLARS
PUBLISHING

Future Prospects for Music Education:
Corroborating Informal Learning Pedagogy,
Edited by Sidsel Karlsen and Lauri Väkevä

This book first published 2012

Cambridge Scholars Publishing

12 Back Chapman Street, Newcastle upon Tyne, NE6 2XX, UK

British Library Cataloguing in Publication Data
A catalogue record for this book is available from the British Library

ISBN (10): 1-4438-3658-3, ISBN (13): 978-1-4438-3658-6

# TABLE OF CONTENTS

# INTRODUCTION

# THEORISING THE FORMAL-INFORMAL NEXUS: A CRITICAL EXAMINATION OF FUTURE POSSIBILITIES FOR MUSIC EDUCATION PRACTICE AND RESEARCH

In this anthology, we have collated articles that address in different ways what has come to be known as *informal learning pedagogy* within the music education field. Informal learning pedagogy refers to pedagogical approaches that build on strategies found within learning situations or practices outside formal settings, such as school lessons (Folkestad 2006). The aim of this book is to corroborate such approaches by subjecting them to a scholarly examination, hopefully strengthening and further developing the discussion of music-related informal learning in music education scholarship.

In our view, part of the maturation process of any scholarly field is to engage in discussion concerning its appropriate philosophical and theoretical underpinnings. It is also important to consider the areas of applicability and reciprocal relationships between the theory and practice of such frameworks. Thus, the articles selected in this book discuss ontological and epistemological frameworks, as well as both the potential and challenges that informal approaches entail for teaching and learning music.

## Informal Learning in Music Education

As musicians, music educators, and music scholars educated within the Nordic field of music education, we have encountered various forms of informal learning pedagogy during our careers. One area where these forms are prevalent is popular music. As of this writing, popular music has been part of Nordic compulsory school music curricula for at least 30 years. In 1971 a music teacher education programme (SÄMUS) was launched in Gothenburg, Sweden, embracing such musical styles as jazz, folk music, pop and rock (Olsson 1993). The programme quickly spread to Malmö (in 1973) and Piteå (in 1976). Similar programmes soon emerged in the higher music education institutions of the other Nordic countries— for instance, in Finland, popular music has been a part of music teacher training since the early 1970s (Väkevä 2006; Westerlund 2006).

The pedagogical approaches in Nordic school music often build on learning strategies that popular musicians employ when acquiring their skills and knowledge in informal situations or practices. This is reflected in the increase in empirical research on the learning styles, strategies and environments of popular musicians from the mid-1990s onwards (see e.g. Berkaak and Ruud 1994; Fornäs, Lindberg and Sernhede 1995; Gullberg 2002; Johansson 2002; Lilliestam 1995). Such research has encouraged further studies investigating and discussing musical learning in other types of informal learning settings (see e.g. Balsnes 2009; Karlsen 2009; Partti and Karlsen 2010; Salavuo 2006; Söderman 2007; Vestad 2010; Wingstedt 2008).

Since the appearance of Lucy Green's book *How Popular Musicians Learn* in 2001, music-related informal learning has also been a topic of major interest and debate in the field of international music education (see e.g. Rodriguez 2004). Green's subsequent research on the implementation of informal learning in "new classroom pedagogy" (2008) added yet another dimension to the discussion. It also provided something that the Nordic music educators had not yet been able to develop: a comprehensive, research-based popular music pedagogy. Green's work has engendered a new array of pedagogical possibilities, the value of which is acknowledged throughout the field of international music education (Lines 2009).

While the pedagogical significance of informal learning has been debated, sometimes critically, sometimes appreciatively, we find that only a few scholars have engaged in a thorough *theorising* of the formal-informal nexus, and in building a *philosophical basis* for research that further explores the possibilities for music education inherent in informal learning practices. It is this realization that motivates this book, with a hope that the debate will continue and bring forth new perspectives on how informal learning may be implemented in music education.

## Angles of Corroboration: a Brief Overview

The articles gathered in this anthology address informal learning pedagogy from different angles and through various theoretical perspectives. Taken together, they offer a multiplicity of points of departure for scholarly discussion and critique. In order to identify and highlight some main areas for debate, the articles are grouped according to what we consider to be their main angles of corroboration.

*Part I* of this book sheds light on the general challenges and consequences of transforming the field of music education through altering its pedagogy with modes of informal learning.

In her contribution, Ann C. Clements suggests that music educators, instead of following "ready-made" solutions for implementing informal learning practices, should focus on developing multiple models for such approaches and engaging in further experimentation. She points to culturally responsive teaching as one possible framework within which such explorations can be made.

Randall Everett Allsup and Nathaniel J. Olson call for a "second-wave" of research on the teaching of popular music in schools, in order to critically examine research on informal learning practices that are associated with the ways popular musicians learn. Drawing on a Deweyan pragmatist framework, they emphasize the ethical responsibilities of the teacher and the need to establish sound educational frameworks that build on informal learning.

The Deweyan pragmatist perspective is also evident in Lauri Väkevä's article, in which he problematizes the idea—derived from Green's work—that informal learning captures "naturally arising learning practices." He also unpacks Green's research on the informal learning of classical music and considers it in connection to digital musicianship and ICT-based music learning.

*Part II* focuses on earlier or parallel attempts to establish informal learning as part of formal music education, as well as on the experiences and implications of such efforts.

Greg Gatien conducts a historical reconstruction of the formalization of jazz education, an endeavour that he finds synergetic with Green's research. In particular, he discusses the challenges of upholding certain modes of transmission within academic structures.

In her article describing a Swedish higher music education programme for rock musicians, Sidsel Karlsen shows how educational environments that take account of popular musicians' needs might be developed through research and theoretical insights from within the framework of socio-cultural learning theories. She also critically examines this particular education's self-proclaimed "authenticity", and raises questions concerning its actual informality.

Eva Georgii-Hemming and Maria Westvall investigate the current discourses on music education in Sweden, which during the last twenty years have been dominated by popular music and informal learning pedagogy. They survey recent evaluations and studies that show how this approach may lead to a limitation of repertoire, content and teaching methods as well as to a general "lack of direction", and how it may in fact fall short in facilitating students' creative engagement with music.

*Part III* concentrates on informal learning within music teacher education and looks into different paths and possibilities, while also highlighting challenges.

Carlos Xavier Rodriguez discusses the problems with informal learning that he has encountered working as a teacher of both a high school rock band and of pre-service music educators at the university level. He pays particular attention to how, for formally trained students, informal learning pedagogy may provide inefficient tools for learning and even create a feeling of alienation.

Drawing on perspectives from critical theory and pedagogy, Panagiotis Kanellopoulos and Ruth Wright suggest that free improvisation could be used as a tool for helping student music educators acquaint themselves with modes of informal learning, and for fostering the qualities that are required in working with informal pedagogies in music education.

Finally, in *Part IV*, Lucy Green gives an account of the experiences and findings of a recent research-and-development pilot project focussed on informal and aural learning in instrumental music lessons. This project, building on her previous work, is an attempt to apply the strategies used and described in her book *Music, Informal Learning and the School: A New Classroom Pedagogy* (2008) in traditional one-on-one instrumental tuition. The findings are promising, as they chart possible paths for the renewal of this form of tuition, often characterised by practices inherited from the classical conservatoire pedagogy.

## The Exploration of Frameworks

As mentioned above, the articles of this collection examine informal learning pedagogy through different perspectives. The theoretical and philosophical perspectives we find most fruitful in this connection are (1) *culturally responsive teaching*; (2) *socio-cultural learning theory;* (3) *pragmatism*; and (4) *critical pedagogy*. In the following, we examine these four perspectives with regards to their implications for the scholarly discussion of future informal learning pedagogy.

## Culturally Responsive Teaching

The resources that people have access to in schools or in other formal environments, and also the kinds of learning environments and knowledge accessible to them in informal contexts, have proved to differ greatly with such social strata as race, ethnicity, class, gender and language group (Villegas and Lucas 2002). There is no reason to believe that music education is an exception. Hence, a music education scholar who wishes to engage in investigations of the formal-informal nexus would do well to educate herself as a culturally responsive researcher. This would necessitate being able to capture a variety of learning experiences, instead of focussing merely on those that are recognisable as being connected to persons with a similar background as that of the researcher. It would also necessitate the recognition of patterns of omission and exclusion. These patterns might be discerned, for example, in how certain modes of musical transmission correspond with those found within the social surroundings of a specific group of students, leaving the other students to learn in ways that are unfamiliar to them. Through their creation of a conceptual framework for educating culturally responsive teachers, Villegas and Lucas (2002) offer theoretical, research-based and practice-oriented perspectives that carry relevance for research into the formal-informal nexus of music transmission and learning. In the following, we will focus on their six strands of "essential dispositions, knowledge and skills" (xxi) needed in order to function successfully in multicultural and multilingual societies, as a point of departure for culturally responsive research within music education.[1]

In *strand one*, Villegas and Lucas (2002) affirm that in order to act in culturally responsible ways, aspiring teachers need to *gain socio-cultural consciousness*; that is, they need to become aware of how their life experiences, "as mediated by a variety of factors, chief among them race/ethnicity, social class and gender" (27), have shaped their worldviews. Tying this more closely to music education, we would like to argue that in order to work successfully in the realm of formal/informal music learning, researchers need to become aware of how their own teaching and learning histories have shaped their views of what constitutes knowledge and skills in music and the means by which these should be transmitted.

In *strand two*, the authors remind us of the necessity to *develop an affirming attitude toward students from culturally diverse backgrounds*. In other words, as educators or researchers who have grown up within the realm of the dominant cultural norms, we need to change the belief that our culture is "inherently superior to the cultures of marginalized groups in society" (35). While this should serve as a reminder to music education scholars, it could also be applied in a more practical way, helping the researchers working within the range of the formal-informal nexus to maintain an affirming attitude towards musicians who come from musical-cultural backgrounds different than their own.

*Strand three* presents the idea that culturally responsible teachers need to *develop the commitment and skills to act as agents of change*, an idea that should also be relevant for researchers in the field of music education (this idea is also clearly manifested in Green's work). Through the investigation of previously unexplored informal-musical territories, researchers could discover practices and ways of organising learning that could act as models for the transformation of classroom practices. Furthermore, they could employ action research in order to transform classroom music from within, through a collaborative negotiation between the researcher, teacher and students (see e.g. Rikandi 2010).

The *fourth strand* implies that teachers need to *embrace the constructivist foundations* of their framework. Central assumptions here are, for example, that knowledge is always "filtered through the knowers' frames of reference" (Villegas and Lucas 2002, 68), that the meanings given to educational content are always based on the learner's pre-existing knowledge and experiences, and that learning is an active process of constructing experience. Transferring these assumptions to the field of research entails that culturally responsive researchers build their work on paradigms that acknowledge research findings as something that is not "found" but, rather, "co-constructed" in the negotiation between the researcher and the other participants in the study. Such presuppositions are already implicit, for example, in ethnography, action research and narrative inquiry.

Stating that the overriding task of the teacher within such a constructivist perspective as outlined above is to "build bridges between [students'] prior knowledge and experiences and the new ideas to be learned" (79), Villegas and Lucas emphasise in *strand five* that the teachers need to *learn about students and their communities* so that they know their students and are able to help them feel connected. A similar attitude of curiosity might also be needed when trying to connect informal and formal music making as a music education researcher. In our rapidly paced multicultural society, new contexts and new ways of making music are constantly emerging. A researcher who wants to keep up with the times needs to ask herself such questions as: What, if anything, are the kids learning from playing e.g. Guitar Hero? Do Idols competitions have any educational value? What are the learning implications of participating in online music communities? What is happening at a private music school set up by an immigrant association (see e.g. Sæther 2010)? Furthermore, the researcher needs to linger on such matters as: Given that there are conditions of learning music that students already experience outside of school, how do they experience their formal music education?

In the *sixth strand,* the authors draw together the five previous strands in order to remind that it is necessary to *cultivate the practice of culturally responsive teaching* in order to provide good education and meet the needs of a changing student population. For music education researchers, this framework may serve as a basis for forming a new *attitude* towards research, and towards the process of constructing research-based knowledge; moreover, it can help them to establish a position from which they can interact responsively with their surroundings and thus collect rich and multifaceted data which opens up matters of inequality, exclusion and social justice. This would certainly be an asset in the future exploration of the possibilities for music education inherent in informal learning practices.

## Socio-Cultural Learning Theory

One of the paradigms underlying culturally responsive teaching is the socio-cultural perspective on development and learning. This perspective ranges from the work of Piaget and Vygotsky to recent developments such as Engeström's cultural-historical activity theory (Engeström 1987; North and Hargreaves 2008). In what follows, however, we shall focus on socio-cultural learning from the standpoint of *situated learning,* as found in the works of Lave and Wenger (1991; see also Wenger 1998, 2006), and in the related theories of Säljö (2000). We will put a special emphasis on how these ideas can be utilised for uncovering learning among the members of *communities of practice* and in the exchange of knowledge between different communities.

Lave and Wenger (1991) describe a "community of practice" as "a set of relations among persons, activity, and world, over time and in relation with other tangential and overlapping communities of practice" (98). Following Wenger's (1998) more explicit ideas of what characterises such communities,[2] it should be evident that many of the musical practices found on the informal side of the formal-informal nexus could be defined as communities of practice. What we usually think of as music-related peer or affinity groups (Gee 2001)—for example garage bands, music festivals, online communities, and local choirs—may be understood as communities of practice and analysed according to what is going on within them in terms of learning and distribution of knowledge.

Deliberately avoiding the acquisition metaphor of learning, Lave and Wenger (1991) describe how learning is integral to "generative social practice" and how the process of gaining knowledge can be explained as "legitimate peripheral participation" (35). In other words, acting within a community of practice, an individual gradually learns what the community is about and what she has to know in order to participate in it, in order to move from the peripheral position of a newcomer to the more mature stage of "full participation" (37). In order to capture the learning processes within such a community of practice, one must consider the relationship between the newcomers and the old-timers, as well as the relationship between the participants, activities, identities, and artefacts of the community. Hence, this theoretical framework allows investigation into the learning processes that occur, for example, when the newcomers and the more experienced members of an amateur brass band negotiate ways of exchanging information, or when amateur digital musicians stage, narrate and negotiate their musical identities in virtual space (Partti and Karlsen 2010). Another possible angle, elaborated by Säljö (2000), is to look into the role that communal artefacts play in the mediation of knowledge and how "human knowledge, insights, conventions and ideas [that] are built into apparatus" (82) are released when the artefacts are put to use. For example, one may investigate what role a mixing console plays in the act of creating and playing music in a rock band, and what kinds of music making it allows, supports or restricts.

In connection to the formal-informal nexus, socio-cultural theories of learning also provide tools for discussing the exchange of information that takes place between different communities of practice. For the purpose of describing the process of inter-community knowledge exchange, Wenger (1998) applies the concepts of *boundary objects* and *brokering*, which imply, respectively, the "artefacts, documents, terms, concepts, and other forms of reification around which communities of practice can organize their interconnections", and the "connections provided by people who can introduce elements of one practice into another" (105). Making use of these concepts, it is possible to define and understand the mediations and negotiations performed by a musician moving between different music-making contexts and bringing his or her artefacts, knowledge and skills from one arena to another. A recent example is mentioned by Partti (2010), who describes how digital musicians travel between different musical communities of practice and transfer their knowledge and skills, thereby also transforming them and the communities they become a part of.

Moreover, socio-cultural theories of learning can provide information on the routes that individuals use to move within specific learning contexts. Wenger (2006) refers to these routes as *learning trajectories*: personalised pathways through practices, communities, networks and institutions that together constitute the "*multi-scale social learning systems*" (4) of our time. For researchers setting out to explore how musicians are, for instance, enculturated into a specific musical style, the notion of learning trajectories may be useful because it can help them to map the whole range of the musicians' learning experiences as they make their way through contexts that provide various degrees of ownership and intentionality (Folkestad 2006).

As with most theoretical frameworks, socio-cultural theories have their limitations. One of the most obvious of these limitations is that they provide little information on how to design educational environments and how to teach within these environments. Lave and Wenger (1991) emphasise that "legitimate peripheral participation is not itself an educational form, much less a pedagogical strategy or a teaching technique. It is an analytical viewpoint on learning, a way of understanding learning" (40).[3] Another possible weakness is the rather positive belief that, among members of a community of practice, *learning will just take place*. Little effort is put into describing instances in which newcomers are denied access to knowledge, are interrupted in their efforts to strive towards full participation, or are subjected to an imbalance of power within the community. Hence, in order to discuss matters of exclusion, inequality and social justice, researchers of musical learning communities might want to look elsewhere.[4] As we shall see next, the philosophical perspectives of pragmatism and critical pedagogy may be useful in this quest for a normative framework.

## Pragmatism

One philosophical framework in which accounts of culturally responsive teaching and socio-cultural learning can be situated is pragmatism. Pragmatism has its roots in the late 19th century and early 20th century American discussion concerning the relevance of functional psychology and evolutionary biology to philosophy. Classical pragmatists formulated philosophical theories of knowledge, meaning and value based on the activity of human organisms in their biological and social-cultural environment. From an educational standpoint, the most important developments in classical pragmatism emerged from the work of John Dewey, who conceived philosophy as an endeavour to solve problems of everyday life (Dewey 1924/MW 12).[5] Dewey saw education as philosophy's laboratory, a practice in which the implications of philosophical ideas can be tested, and through which prevailing social habits can be transformed in ways that promote social life through the reconstruction of the shared realm of meaningful experience (Dewey 1916/MW 9).

For Dewey, the most important task of both philosophy and education was to alleviate problems brought along by modernity, problems that prevented the blooming of the positive freedom of individuals in democratic community life (Dewey 1946/LW 15, 154–169). The most severe of these problems was the alienation of the modern subject from her environment, a problem that, according to Dewey, had led to the separation of individual agency from the ethical needs of public social life. In his philosophy, Dewey vigorously attacked all dualisms that suggest a breach between the subjective and objective realms of values and science: he wanted to reconstruct philosophy as a holistic view of how different realms of experience can come together most constructively in social-cultural life.

Dewey's philosophy provides tools for immanent cultural critique, with education acting as its mediator. While education has an important role in the transmission of the social values of a culture, it also makes possible the critical examination of these values in terms of their future implications. Thus, education is not the mere presentation and reproduction of habits previously accumulated. By calling education a "laboratory" Dewey wanted to emphasize that its primary task, whether it takes place inside or outside school, is to provide tools with which to reflect on our shared cultural realm, so as to be better prepared to meet future situations of conjoint life. In a complex society, education becomes a necessary condition for social growth, or the expansion of the realm of meaningfulness that, according to Dewey, frames democratic life as a forum to negotiate different opinions, attitudes, and convictions as practical guidelines (Dewey 1916/MW 9).[6]

In philosophical research on music education, Deweyan pragmatism has been one of the frameworks that comprises diverse sets of ideas related to the meaning and implications of music in social life, especially as concerns the role of music education in promoting democracy, agency and equality (Bowman 2003; Väkevä 2004; Westerlund 2002; Woodford 2005). From this standpoint, there is no pedagogical meaning of music apart from the general meaning of education, and the general meaning of education amounts to growth. Growth is not just the accumulation of skills and ideas; it is the formation of an active ethical disposition, manifest in the ways in which we participate in conjoint efforts enhancing the conditions that make our shared lives meaningful. This necessitates active working, experimentation and negotiation with the subject matter of musical learning. Music education cannot be merely taken as the transmission of tradition, but it must also frame new possibilities for interpretation and ingrain new habits of thinking and action, and thus open new fields for agency in which musical traditions can be reconstructed and revalued in terms of their possibilities for enhancing the quality of future experience.

One of the consequences of applying the Deweyan pragmatist perspective to education is that it leaves the curricular framework open, by emphasizing the importance of learning situations. Because all learning (and thus, all teaching) is considered to be situational, it makes little sense to peg our pedagogical practices to established values, standards and norms, derived from bygone situations. Thus, as part of general education, music education can be seen as a practice constantly adapting to change, in which constant negotiations of meaning take place over the value and significance of what is learned, how and why. This implies that music is not seen as a collection of established musical practices or canonized masterworks, but as a constantly evolving cultural field, intertwining with other cultural fields through which we make sense of our lives as social beings. Pragmatism suggests that we heed the actual processes in which music is made and re-made, disseminated and enjoyed, and accept them as situational points of departure for pedagogical practices, always keeping the more extensive goal of social growth in sight.

In its openness and recognition of the challenge of constant cultural change, Deweyan pragmatism provides a normative basis on which we can justify the demand for cultural responsiveness and the related need to examine learning as sociocultural practice. For music educators, it can also provide a tool to avoid fixed notions of the function of pedagogical methods and goals. By emphasizing the dynamic nature of growth as a constant expansion of our meaningful relations to each other and to our environment, and by further underlining individual agents' ethical relationship to society, pragmatism puts agency in focus. From the pragmatist standpoint, music education aims at more than developing musical agency: musical agency is one way to find one's place in the shared reality of ethical life. With this recognition comes an enhanced awareness of the power relations that condition social relationships. By suggesting that education is immanent cultural critique, pragmatism also suggests that we take seriously the possibility of social change through acknowledging the power structures of the society.

# Critical Pedagogy

Critical pedagogy is an educational perspective, and a pedagogical program, that applies the ideas of critical theorists to the issues of becoming human in society. Critical pedagogy posits that education and growth are a constant negotiation of one's place in society, and that culture is the medium in which this negotiation takes place. From this position, critical pedagogy derives its two tasks: to examine how power relations work in education, and to suggest educational practices more conducive to emancipation.

There are several ways to specify what this approach means for educational research and teaching practice. According to Aittola, Eskola and Suoranta (2007, 6), critical pedagogy includes different theoretical perspectives, "united by the critical interest of knowledge and the quest for the possibility of change for a more just society that stems from the perspective of hope." In other words, the critical perspective is as much a political program of action as it is a theory. In this sense its agenda can be related to Freire's "pedagogy of hope", developed and applied in Anglo-American cultural settings by e.g., hooks (1994), McLaren (1995) and Giroux (Giroux and McLaren 2001).

Critical research on education can focus, for example, on issues related to gender, ethnicity, social strata and globalization. A constant subject of discussion in critical pedagogy is power, its distribution in society as well as its practices. One way to look at this distribution is to link power with knowledge and to argue that it is through ownership of knowledge that society defines access to its discourses (Foucault 1980, 2005, 2010). By recognizing the conditions of this ownership, critical pedagogues can suggest ways to empower the marginalized by providing conditions to develop their critical thinking. Thus, critical pedagogy implies the transformation of society through developing the awareness of how people come to know and understand themselves as agents of their own understanding.

In music education, critical pedagogy has been suggested as an alternative to music-centered philosophical and theoretical approaches. For instance, Regelski (2002) argues that critical theory can guide the focus of the profession to recognize the needs of marginalized groups. The solution to the problem of different perspectives and opinions in music cannot be found in rampant multiculturalism; we need a mutually accepted rational framework within which to negotiate the significance of different claims for power. Regelski suggests Habermas' communicative rationality as this kind of a uniting base.

Thus, it can be argued that a basic problem for critical music pedagogy is to mediate the needs of communicative reason and the multifarious cultural needs of a rapidly fragmenting society. As concerns the formal-informal nexus in music education, it becomes vital to create the means to bridge various situations of learning in a normative setting that provides a forum for developing the critical knowledge of the mechanisms and techniques used in society to distribute power. In communicative action, participants in negotiations do not just argue for the legitimation of their idiosyncratic views, but seek a common ground in which to recognize different lifeworlds. A key issue is to avoid the hegemonic determination of the pedagogical value of music before this common ground is established. From the critical standpoint, a major problem with Western institutionalized music education is its association with the "cultural patriarchy" of Eurocentric high culture and its techniques of skill mediation, knowledge and attitudes. The recognition of different ways of learning music outside of this system of mediation is an important step in expanding music educators' sensibility to communicative situations. This necessitates critical awareness in the form of a willingness to recognize the meaning potential of different lifeworld-related practices—not only for the practitioner but also on the part of the music education researcher.

## Concluding Remarks

In this introductory chapter, we have aimed at exploring four possible frameworks for the scholarly investigation of the formal-informal nexus in music education. Despite their obvious differences, these frameworks also display similarities, perhaps best explained as a need for researchers to be attentive and observant and to critically examine and constantly expand their own views and assumptions about what musical competencies and learning might look like, and where they could be achieved and enhanced. Moreover, all frameworks emphasise—in various ways and through using different metaphors and theoretical concepts—the significance of the "links of learning" that weave in and out of both informal *and* formal learning arenas, or Wenger's (2006) "learning trajectories."

By exploring the remaining chapters of this book, interested readers may discover more points from which informal learning pedagogy can be corroborated. For example, there seems to be a further need to examine how embedding informal modes of transmission into academic structures transforms not only the latter but also the modes of transmission themselves. More work is also needed on the matter of recreating students' experiences of authenticity. Another fruitful angle might be to perform a deeper investigation into formally trained students' resistance to or discomfort with informal learning pedagogy and ask how it could—or whether it should—be overcome. Overall, as hinted at in the beginning of this introduction, we believe in discussing the appropriate theoretical and philosophical underpinnings of such research, not just in order to engage in the general growth of the field, but also because there is a need to elicit such frameworks' specific ethical, moral and political implications and consequences through scholarly conversations. If, for example, our goal in focussing on the formal-informal nexus is to contribute to a democratisation of the music education field, then we ought to make sure that we build from frameworks and practices that will enable, not restrict, such efforts.

It is our hope that this book will guide future studies in directions that we, at the present, cannot foresee. It is hoped that the theorising of the formal-informal nexus both in this chapter and throughout the anthology, through the presentation of a wide range of experienced scholars' viewpoints, will provide fertile soil for such explorations.

# References

Aittola, T., J. Eskola, and J. Suoranta. 2007. "Johdanto [Introduction]." in *Kriittisen pedagogiikan kysymyksiä* [Problems in Critical Pedagogy], eds. T. Aittola, J. Eskola, and J. Suoranta, 5–8. Tampere: Vastapaino.

Balsnes, A. H. 2009. *Å lære i kor. Belcanto som praksisfelleskap* [Learning in Choir. Belcanto as a Community of Practice]. PhD diss., Norwegian Academy of Music. Oslo: NMH-publikasjoner 2009:6.

Berkaak, O. A., and E. Ruud. 1994. *Sunwheels. Fortellinger om et rockeband* [Sunwheels. Stories about a Rock Band]. Oslo: Universitetsforlaget.

Bowman, W. 2003. "Re-Tooling 'Foundations' to Address 21st Century Realities: Music Education Amidst Diversity, Plurality, and Change." *Action, Criticism, and Theory for Music Education* 2 (2). http://act.maydaygroup.org/articles/Bowman2_2.pdf

Dewey, J. 2003. *The Collected Works of John Dewey, 1882–1953. Electronic Edition.* Charlottesville: InteLex Corporation.

Engeström, Y. 1987. *Learning by Expanding: An Activity Theoretical Approach to Developmental Research.* Helsinki: Orienta-Konsultit Oy.

Folkestad, G. 2006. "Formal and Informal Learning Situations or Practices *vs* Formal and Informal Ways of Learning." *British Journal of Music Education* 23 (2): 135–45.

Fornäs, J., U. Lindberg, and O. Sernhede. 1995. *In Garageland. Youth and Culture in Late Modernity.* London: Routledge.

Foucault, M. 1980. *Tarkkailla ja rangaista.* [Surveiller et punir]. Helsinki: Otava.

—. 2005. *Tiedon arkeologia* [L'archéologie du savoir]. Tampere: Vastapaino.

—. 2010. *Sanat ja asiat: Ihmistieteiden arkeologia* [Les mots et les choses: Une archéologie des sciences humaines]. Helsinki: Gaudeamus.

Gee, J. P. 2001. "Identity as an Analytic Lens for Research in Education." In *Review of Research in Education 25,* ed. W. G. Secada, 99–125. Washington, DC: American Educational Research Association.

Giroux, H., and P. McLaren. 2001. *Kriittinen pedagogiikka* [Critical Pedagogy]. Tampere: Vastapaino.

Green, L. 2002. *How Popular Musicians Learn. A Way Ahead for Music Education.* Aldershot: Ashgate.

—. 2008. *Music, Informal Learning and the School: A New Classroom Pedagogy.* Aldershot: Ashgate.

Gullberg, A.-K. 2002. *Skolvägen eller garagevägen. Studier av musikalisk socialisation* [By Learning or Doing. Studies in the Socialisation of Music]. PhD diss., Luleå University of Technology.

hooks, b. 1994. *Teaching to Transgress: Education as the Practice of Freedom.* London: Routledge.

Johansson, K.-G. 2002. *Can you Hear What They're Playing? A Study of Strategies Among Ear Players in Rock Music.* PhD diss., Luleå University of Technology.

Karlsen, S. 2009. "Learning Through Music Festivals." *International Journal of Community Music* 2 (2/3): 129–41.

—. 2010. "Revealing Musical Learning in the Informal Field." In *Sociology and music education,* ed. R. Wright, 193–206. Aldershot: Ashgate.

Lave, J., and E. Wenger. 1991. *Situated Learning. Legitimate Peripheral Participation.* Cambridge: Cambridge University Press.

Lilliestam, L. 1995. *Gehörsmusik: blues, rock och muntlig tradering* [Playing by Ear: Blues, Rock and Oral Tradition]. Gothenburg: Akademiförlaget.

Lines, D. 2009. "Exploring the Contexts of Informal Learning." *Action, Criticism, and Theory for Music Education* 8 (2): 1–6. http://act.maydaygroup.org/php/archives_v8.php#8_1

McLaren, P. 1995. *Critical Pedagogy and Predatory Culture: Oppositional Politics in a Postmodern Era.* New York: Routledge.

North, A., and D. J. Hargreaves. 2008. *The Social and Applied Psychology of Music*. Oxford: Oxford University Press.

Olsson, B. 1993. *SÄMUS—en musikutbildning i kulturpolitikens tjänst? En studie om en musikutbildning på 70-talet* [SÄMUS—Music Education in the Service of a Cultural Policy? A Study of a Teacher-Training Programme during the 1970s]. PhD diss., University of Gothenburg.

Partti, H. 2010. "The Construction of Music and Technology Related Identities in Narratives of Digital Musicians." Paper presented at 3rd International Conference on Narrative Inquiry in Music Education (NIME3), Brisbane, Australia, November 2010.

Partti, H., and S. Karlsen. 2010. "Reconceptualising Musical Learning: New Media, Identity and Community in Music Education." *Music Education Research* 12 (4): 369–82.

Regelski, T. 2002. "'Critical Education', Culturalism and Multiculturalism." *Action, Criticism, and Theory for Music Education* 1 (1): 1–40. http://act.maydaygroup.org/articles/Regelski1_1.pdf

Rikandi, I. 2010. "Revolution or Reconstruction? Considering Change in Finnish Piano Pedagogy." in *Mapping the Common Ground. Philosophical Perspectives on Finnish Music Education*, ed. I. Rikandi, 162–77. Helsinki: BTJ.

Rodriguez, C. X. ed. 2004. *Bridging the Gap: Popular Music and Music Education*. Reston: MENC.

Salavuo, M. 2006. "Open and Informal Online Communities as Forums of Collaborative Musical Activities and Learning." *British Journal of Music Education* 23 (3): 253–71.

Säljö, R. 2000. *Lärande i praktiken. Ett sociokuturellt perspektiv* [Learning in Practice. A Socio-Cultural Perspective]. Stockholm: Prisma.

Sæther, E. 2010. "Music Education and the Other." *Finnish Journal of Music Education* 13 (1): 45–60.

Söderman, J. 2007. *Rap(p) i käften. Hiphopmusikers konstnärliga och pedagogiska strategier* [Verbally Fa(s)t. Hip-Hop Musicians' Artistic and Educational Strategies]. PhD diss., Lund University.

Vestad, I. L. 2010. "To Play a Soundtrack: How Children Use Recorded Music in Their Everyday Lives." *Music Education Research* 12 (3): 243–55.

Villegas, A. M., and T. Lucas. 2002. *Educating Culturally Responsive Teachers. A Coherent Approach*. New York: State University of New York Press.

Väkevä, L. 2004. *Kasvatuksen taide ja taidekasvatus. Estetiikan ja taidekasvatuksen merkitys John Deweyn naturalistisessa pragmatismissa* [Art of Education and Art Education. The Meaning of Aesthetics and

Art Education in John Dewey's Naturalist Pragmatism]. PhD diss,
University of Oulu. Acta Universitatis Ouluensis E Scienitae Rerum
Socialium 68.
—. 2006. "Teaching Popular Music in Finland: What's Up, What's
Ahead?" *International Journal of Music Education* 24 (2): 126–31.
Wenger, E. 1998. *Communities of Practice. Learning, Meaning and
Identity.* Cambridge: Cambridge University Press.
—. 2006. *Learning for a Small Planet.* http://www.ewenger.com.
Westerlund, H. 2002. *Bridging Experience, Action, and Culture in Music
Education.* PhD diss., Sibelius Academy. Studia 16. Helsinki: Sibelius
Academy.
—. 2006. "Garage Rock Band—A Future Model for Developing Musical
Expertise?" *International Journal of Music Education* 24 (2): 119–125.
Wingstedt, J. 2008. *Making Music Mean. On Functions of, and Knowledge
about, Narrative Music in Multimedia.* PhD diss., Luleå University of
Technology.
Woodford, P. 2005. *Democracy and Music Education: Liberalism, Ethics,
and the Politics of Practice.* Bloomington: Indiana University Press.

# Notes

[1] Villegas and Lucas' (2002) six strands concern teachers first and foremost,
however we believe that their points are also applicable to the world of music
education research.

[2] See Wenger (1998, 125) for a comprehensive list of indicators.

[3] This stand does not prevent Wenger (2006), in later writings, from expressing
strong opinions concerning how education should be designed in a globalised
world.

[4] See for example Karlsen (2010) on how socio-cultural theories, when combined
with perspectives borrowed from sociology, afford power-relations within music-
related communities of practice.

[5] Our references to Dewey (2003) are abbreviated EW for The Early Works, MW
for The Middle Works and LW for The Later Works, followed by part and page
numbers.

[6] Interestingly, Dewey also criticized the modern tendency to compartmentalize art
and the aesthetic into their own realm, distinct from everyday life. He argued that
aesthetic experience should be regarded as focal part of a humane way of life; in
turn, he saw art as a general attempt to deal with an ever-changing environment, at
best in ways that afford qualitative experiences that can be felt as consummatory,
or "esthetic" (Dewey 1934/LW 10). In *Experience and Education* (1938/LW 13)
Dewey also emphasized that it is the ultimate goal of education to contribute to the
quality of subsequent experience.

# PART I

# CHAPTER ONE

# ESCAPING THE CLASSICAL CANON: CHANGING METHODS THROUGH A CHANGE OF PARADIGM[1]

## ANN C. CLEMENTS

### Preface

Lucy Green's *How Popular Musicians Learn: A Way Ahead for Music Education* (2002) describes her research in the realm of popular musicians and music transmission. Through her more recent publication *Music, Informal Learning and the School: A New Classroom Pedagogy* (2008), Green has found many innovative ways in which to move from the realm of research and inquiry to the practical application and examination of that application through practice—a gap that many researchers fail to traverse. I feel that as we examine her work in a critical way and seek our own unique forms of implementation of the ideas she has presented, we must keep in mind that this latest text is an attempt to bridge the all too elusive gap between research and practice, and that in doing so there is room for experimentation. Through this publication she has exposed her research and teaching practices in a very intimate and personal way and we are indebted to Green for providing a model of "research to practice" that is so greatly needed in the field of music education.

### Introduction

First I would like to focus my attention on three strands that are apparent throughout Green's work: (1) student centered learning or students as source, (2) the role of teachers in informal learning, and (3) the organic nature of music learning. Each of these areas will be discussed in relation to popular musics and classroom music education. These conversations are a mixture of my personal response to her work and examples of practical applications of her work in American music classrooms, in the attempts to look beyond prior knowledge and practice towards new possibilities for the implementation of Green's work.

## Student Centered Learning

Key to Green's work is the concept of student centered learning. She constructs a good argument that it may be time to experiment with, or perhaps withdraw from, formal western music traditions of music teaching and learning—in which the teacher is often thought of as the end all be all of musical knowledge, and that to be successful as a teacher is to install knowledge upon the unknowing student. Green's experiment of application in *Music, Informal Learning and the School: A New Classroom Pedagogy* (2008) is an in-depth acknowledgement of students as sources of knowledge. Her methodology is based on partnerships of students, shared responsibilities among student-centered groups, and acknowledgement through the respect and valuation of students' pre-existing interests, abilities and preferences by the classroom teacher. In particular, student preference and knowledge become the primary starting points from which students expand outwards into different musical styles, genres and cultures.

Within the field of multicultural education the notion of culturally responsive teaching has raised awareness of students' individuality. "This approach to educational practice takes into consideration the needs, experiences, and perspectives of culturally diverse students, where its main purpose is to help students with their cultural and social identities in such a way that learning in any subject is made more relevant" (Abril 2008, 5). Culturally responsive teaching embraces constructivist views of teaching and learning, in which learning is viewed as an active process by which learners give meaning to new information, ideas, and principles and other stimuli, and in which teaching is viewed as inducing change in students' knowledge and belief systems (Villegas and Lucas 2002). While Green does not reference much literature regarding cultural diversity or learning practices for world musics in music education, which is rather disappointing, the practice of her evolving pedagogy is very much based on these principles. The consumption of music by youths, their musical preferences, and their musical knowledge can very easily be described as "youth culture" (or cultures), a generational and cultural grouping that is not often given serious consideration in a positive way. Youth culture, which is heavily comprised of musics and musicians, is a source that

Green acknowledges as legitimate and worthy of study for its own merits, including adolescents' culture and musical preferences and knowledge.

The largest portion of music makers in the United States cannot be found in professional or community bands, choirs, and orchestras. Instead, they are found in basements, pubs, garages, worship teams, computer labs, dance clubs, and recording studios. One can argue that lessons learned in one musical community—for example musical lessons from band, choir, and orchestra—can be transferred to other communities, but this is not necessarily true. Teachers frequently complain about students' inability to transfer knowledge from the general music classroom to the instrumental classroom or from the elementary music classroom to the middle school music classroom. If transfer between somewhat like musical idioms is difficult at best, how can we expect students to make the connections between musical systems that to them may have little-to-nothing in common? Transfer has to be taught, and unless you are teaching how to transfer to and from multiple musical cultures it has no lasting meaning or relevance.

It has been estimated that only 20% of high school students in the United States are participating in formal music instruction. Where are the missing 80%? The answer to this is quite simple, they're musicking (in Small's (1998) sense of the term)! Visit any local high school Battle of the Bands competition and you will see many students who may fall outside formal musical instruction but have musical skills and passion that are enviable by some of our best traditional singers and players.

How do we reach this missing 80%? Green believes that the time has come for music to be just that—music, unattached from our preconceived notions of "good" and "bad" and with an understanding that there is no hierarchy or superiority of particular genres; there is only personal preference. Music around the world is created, listened to, adapted, danced and moved to for the same reasons: it defines, represents, symbolizes, expresses, constructs, mobilizes, incites, controls, transforms, unites, and much more (Wade 2006). If we want to draw these students in and invite them to participate in an education that will bring them into adulthood and foster continued learning beyond and outside of classrooms, we must move towards pedagogies that are inclusive—and, shouldn't we pay more attention to their preferences than we do our own? It may be a balancing act, but I agree with Green that the time has come to tip the scales in their direction.

## Teachers and Formal Music Education

As Green expresses her created curriculum in *Music, Informal Learning and the School: A New Classroom Pedagogy* (2008) we begin to witness changes in the role of "teacher." Throughout the Musical Futures program (the curricular program that is the primary focus of this text) the teachers are asked to step back and allow for student centered learning. Green indicates that this was not always an easy role for teachers to adhere to. During each of the seven stages of this curriculum teachers were asked to "establish ground rules for behavior, set the task going at each stage, and then stand back and observe what the pupils were doing" (Green 2008, 74). Debbie, one of the teachers in this project framed her anxiety by stating "I'm terrified about the lesson today; just letting the students go off and jam. I'm actually scared of letting them do this . . . " (30).

I believe much of the disconnect between formal music education and learners' preferences and knowledge can be traced to institutions of higher learning. These institutions, serving as gatekeepers to the profession, generally reserve admittance to students whose training in Western art music qualifies them to continue such pursuits. Our institutions can be seen as an integral part of the reciprocal cycle of music teacher preparation—we only accept a portion of those for whom formal music education has "worked", and only if their voice or instrument is needed in a particular ensemble or studio. It is completely the wrong way to go about selecting the next generation of education hopefuls. While NASM has begun to make acceptations for the acceptance of a broader array of students (NASM Handbook 2007), very few programs are taking advantage of these changes—again, what can we do when there are no studios or ensembles to cater to various kinds of musicians?

Carlos Abril (2008), in a recent study of one teacher's journey to create a mariachi program in her central Chicago high school strings program, found that while she was willing to work for change, she felt she did not have the skills needed or perhaps even the confidence needed to risk change. While as a university musician she participated in the traditional string ensembles, she also played violin in a local Emo band (a style of emotional punk rock or heavy metal music). However, she was reluctant to even mention this band participation to the researcher as she thought he would be uninterested. Her participation in the band was a facet of her musical self that she claims did not inform her work as a university student or music educator years later. She never thought of them as being related. My own research (Clements and Campbell 2006) found a similar disconnect for teachers between what was required of them for the degree program and the other musical worlds in which they reside. If we want to prepare future teachers for success in teaching all forms of musics we, along with our colleagues in musicology, theory, and performance, must acknowledge all of the musics in which we are engaged. We all contain bi- or multi-musicality, but through formal education we begin to value some more than others, and this separation must end.

While Green takes a very strong approach to the role of teacher—or the lack of the role of teacher—I would like to suggest that music teachers play a role that is more similar to a facilitator and "sharer" in the learning process, and that their role be developed from the expression of their personal multi-musicality, their understanding of their students' needs, desires, knowledge and skills, and the musics and cultures that surround the school building within the community (both locally and virtually). I will address this more specifically in the next conversation.

## The Organic Nature of Music Learning

Green (2008) has created a fairly strict concept of how her research may be applied in classroom settings. The objectives and learning outcomes are created by the students with little to no involvement by the music teacher other than to set them on their way. While I fully support student centered learning, I can't help but have great faith in the intuitiveness, creativity, and ability level of music educators. To me any musical project + a music educator = a better musical project for "those musicians who can—teach." I know it is cliché but it is true.

The master-apprentice model is prevalent throughout most of the world's cultures; yet, it is strangely missing in Green's approach. While my own research on community musicians (Clements 2008; Clements and Gibbs 2007; Jones and Clements 2006) has shown me that music making among the popular realms may be constructed in solitude at times—a point that Green takes to extremes—the recordings they use are not the main instrument of teaching and learning. Musicians gather—it's what we do, the inexperienced alongside the more experienced. Even when recordings are used, the music is often brought to fruition not when it is copied or replicated but when it is arranged or created anew through organic means.

Another issue that I continue to struggle with is the very term "popular music and musicians." While I certainly do not mean to squabble, and defining terms is always a challenge, popular musics are individual, multidimensional, dynamic, and culturally and genre specific, not a large grouping. There is no such thing as "pan popular." A general term attached to a specific pedagogy would never fly in world music circles, for example, if someone where to develop a "Pacific Islands pedagogy"—it just does not work and it is not appropriate. Everything should be taught within its own terms. We also must keep in mind that popular musics are often popular because someone has paid big bucks for it to be that way, and often, popular musics, at least in a teen culture sense, are not fully organic. They are a deliberate attempt at profiteering and are frequently composed by professional, often non-recording or performing musicians, in a very traditional western way. While this is not universal, it is quickly becoming the norm.

The term "pedagogy" scares me and I am not completely sure where pedagogy ends and methodology begins. My research in community music making has led me to believe that the real beauty in the process is the way in which individuals engage in musical practices within the time, space, and location in which they find and develop their groove (in the full Charlie Kiel sense of the term; see Kiel and Feld 1994). I believe that on multiple occasions Green becomes too prescriptive—bordering on becoming a "the right way and the wrong way" curricular model, which is simply replacing traditional methods with a new one—one "soap box" to another. My wish for formal music education is to work to capture the freshness—the soul of the organic ways in which music is taught and learned in multiple avenues. These should be created based on a combination of student and teacher "know how" and should be instigated through personalized exploration and experimentation. The teacher, being an extremely knowledgeable resource of musical knowledge and capable of understanding their students, should create learning opportunities that will best meet the needs of students in their particular classrooms. Even with a base of student centered learning, it cannot be one-program-fits-all model as prescribed by Green (2008).

What the field of music education needs is a closer examination of what is out there happening in music classrooms at the grassroots level; an investigation of the kinds of programs innovative teachers found to draw in the multitudes of musicians within their school buildings. We need multiple single-case studies of these innovated programs to serve as models for future exploration and experimentation by the masses, both in prekindergarten through twelfth grade and in higher education.

Some teachers remain unaware or simply do not care to think about formal music education's relevancy in the lives of children, and Green does much to bring this topic to the table. But, in my opinion, many educators have already moved beyond Lucy Green and have found ways in which to keep the organic nature of music learning alive within the classroom. These organic forms of learning—deeply rooted in individual students and their preferences—intertwined with the musical skills and educational knowledge of teachers, will lead us into the new frontier of music education.

# References

Abril, C. 2008. "Culturally Responsive Teaching in Secondary Instrumental Music: Mariachi as a Case in Point." Paper presented at the Cultural Diversity in Music Education Nine Symposia 2008, Seattle, Washington, March 2008.

Clements, A. 2008. "From the Inside Out: The Case Study of a Community Rock Musician." Paper and poster presented at the Music Educations National Conference Bi-annual Meeting: Milwaukee, Wisconsin, April 2008.

Clements, A., and P. S. Campbell. 2006. "Rap, Rock, Race, and Rhythm: Music and More in a Methods Class." *Mountain Lake Reader* 4: 19–23.

Clements, A., and B. Gibbs. 2007. "Connecting 'In School' and 'Out of School' Musical Experiences." Paper presented at the Mountain Lake Colloquium for Teachers of General Music Methods, May 2007.

Green, L. 2002. *How Popular Musicians Learn: A Way Ahead for Music Education*. Aldershot: Ashgate.

—. 2008. *Music, Informal Learning and the School: A New Classroom Pedagogy*. Aldershot: Ashgate.

Jones, P. M., and A. C. Clements. 2006. "Making Room for Student Voice: Rock and Popular Musics in the School Curricula." Paper presented at the MayDay Group Colloquium: Princeton, NJ, June 2006.

Kiel, C., and S. Feld. 1994. *Music Grooves: Essays and Dialogues*. Chicago: University of Chicago Press.

NASM Handbook. 2007. Handbook for the National Association of the Schools of Music. http://nasm.arts-accredit.org/.

Small, C. 1998. *Musicking: The Meaning of Performance and Listening*. Middletown: Wesleyan University Press.

Villegas, A. M., and T. Lucas. 2002. *Educating Culturally Responsive Teachers: A Coherent Approach*. New York: SUNY Press.

Wade, B. 2006. *Thinking Musically: Experiencing Music, Expressing Culture*. New York: Oxford University Press.

# Notes

---

[1] Previously published in 2008 as "Escaping the Classical Canon: Changing Methods through a Change of Paradigm" in *Visions of Research in Music Education* 12. Reprinted by permission of the editor.

# CHAPTER TWO

# NEW EDUCATIONAL FRAMEWORKS
# FOR POPULAR MUSIC
# AND INFORMAL LEARNING:
# ANTICIPATING THE SECOND-WAVE[1]

## RANDALL EVERETT ALLSUP
## AND NATHANIEL J. OLSON

This chapter seeks to advance a critical examination of research on the informal learning practices that are associated with the way so-called popular musicians learn. It is our intention to theorize this practice with illustrations, seeking not to advance a particular operational platform or method, but to introduce responses to an ethical mandate grounded in our profession's obligations to diversify our curricula in an increasingly pluralistic and rapidly changing world. Our chapter begins with an appreciation of the pioneering work of Lucy Green. It can be argued that her seminal manuscript, *How Popular Musicians Learn,* helped to legitimize popular music as a field of music education research and smoothed the way for its inclusion in schools (Green 2001). Next, we will briefly outline new problems facing researchers as they move beyond a "first-wave" body of literature to a burgeoning "second-wave", where studies on popular music intersect with public education, curricular demands, and music teacher education. Early studies of popular music, from the fields of cultural studies (Frith 1996; McClary 1991), empirical research (Finnegan 1989; Fornäs, Lindberg and Sernhede 1995) and sociology (Frith 1988; Leblanc 1999) were rich in scope, but lacked grounding in educational theory or a strong interest in the public school mission. An anticipated "second-wave" calls for research studies that locate and problematize methods of teaching popular music. Looking forward to this second-wave, we will sketch our own model of teacher preparation based on the democratic potential of mutual learning communities, or what we fondly refer to as learning through "modified" garage bands (Allsup 2011).

It is hard to believe that it was only ten years ago that the field of popular music education research really took hold (Allsup 2002; Green 2001). Prior to the turn of the 20th century, there was only one published English-language research article that looked at popular music from the standpoint of teachers, schools, and applied instruction: this was Patricia Shehan Campbell's (1995) hard-to-find article called "Of Garage Bands and Song-getting." Today an expanding field of international scholarship is flourishing around the importance of popular music and the manner in which it is taught and learned (Green 2006, 2008; Folkestad 2006; Rodriguez 2004; Söderman and Folkestad 2004; Väkevä 2006; Westerlund 2006; Wiggins 2006; Woody 2007). Indeed, growth has been rapid. In five short years, the paradigm has shifted from descriptive research on what popular musicians are actually doing (Allsup 2002, 2003; Byrne and Sheridan 2000; Hebert and Campbell 2000; Green 2001) to heuristic investigations into the *whys* and *hows* of popular music and informal learning, especially as these domains intersect with schools, schools of education, methods of instruction, and our profession's efforts to diversify curricula (Abramo 2011; Allsup 2004; Davis 2005; Green 2006, 2008; Väkevä 2006; Westerlund 2006; Woody 2007). As Lucy Green also continues to play an important role in expanding this field of inquiry, writing and researching particularly around issues of informal learning and popular music, we turn now to a critical appreciation and critique of *Music, Informal Learning and the School* (2008), the contents of which frame increasingly complicated problems for researchers in this field. We will address four general concerns that spring from this work.

First, researchers must be careful not to make equivalent the notion of informal learning *ipso facto* with that of popular music.[2] Conflating informal learning with a genre-specific art form, as Green (2001, 12) does when she designed her Musical Futures curriculum around the practices of "Anglo-American guitar-based music makers" may lead to the unintended consequence of narrowing of musical possibilities rather than expanding them.[3] It deserves asking whether pedagogical inspiration from this mostly male, mostly White genre represents a step forward in our efforts to diversify classroom offerings. Are music lessons designed around "Anglo-American guitar-based music" a culturally responsive choice for all— especially considering the increasingly pluralistic makeup of public schools around the world? And if, as Green (2008, 110) is quoted as saying, the learning practices adopted "were based, not on a theory of child-centeredness or discovery-learning, but on an empirical investigation and analysis of the real-life, informal practices of popular musicians as they operate outside the educational environment", it is worth recalling that the empirical investigations referred to come from data she collected from a sample of fourteen all-White participants, twelve of whom were male, all of whom played what can be loosely described as White-ethnic rock (Green 2001).

Second, while Green (2008, 28–29) notes the reluctance and hesitancy with which teachers approached informal learning practices, little is said about how the training of these teachers could or should proceed. How will research studies inspired by the informal practices of popular musicians instruct the training of future music educators? What will changing approaches to teacher preparation look like? What new certification requirements will be asked of our student teachers? Second-wave research must empirically describe and philosophically justify that which it seeks to replace or modify.

Importantly, we must not conflate the term "school" with "schooling" or use these terms interchangeably. Should researchers fail, furthermore, to distinguish between "formal learning" and "*formalism*" and "informal learning" and "*informalism*", teacher educators will be left ill-equipped to imagine a role for teachers in which they do the business of educating, or schools as social laboratories in which students interact with all walks of life (Dewey 1916).[4] Ideally, teacher preparation will navigate a way for teachers to reap the pedagogical benefits of informal learning, while avoiding the negative consequences of succumbing to informalism.

Third, it deserves asking exactly what constitutes teacher quality in informal or popular settings? To outside observers, music teachers who apply informal processes in formal settings may appear to be doing very little. The children in Green's Musical Futures project decide the friends they wish to study with and the music they wish to learn. They spend most of their time copying what they hear from CDs and MP3s. In Green's (2008, 31) curriculum, professional educators are encouraged *not* to set explicit educational targets and learning objectives for their students, as "the free choice of the learners was one of the essential learning strategies that was drawn from the practices of popular musicians." As teachers become somewhat more involved in later stages of learning, even then their role seems limited to showing students "rough, simplified, or partial" forms and then "retreating", "not insisting on correct [instrument] hold or posture", and not "expecting accurate repetition" (35). If teachers are not helping to define educational outcomes or offering precise instruction, even a friendly critic is left wondering just how a music educator is trained in informalist teaching, to what uses are put a teacher's content expertise, and the degree to which an acquaintance with instructional theory is even necessary.

As the topic of teacher expertise bumps up against the values of informal learning, Green's research may have the unintended effect of fueling right-wing critics of education schools whose efforts to dismantle teacher certification—and public education in general—are advanced by arguing against the utility of training teachers, given the inherent ineffectiveness of teacher education programs on the one hand, and the inherent ineffectiveness of pedagogical theory on the other (Cochran-Smith 2002a; Kozol 2005; Will 2006). Her research likewise gives fuel to left-wing critics, those de-schoolers who see the public school as little more than institutional state apparatuses (to borrow from Louis Althusser) that reproduce conditions of hegemony and oppression. If music education researchers are now finding new favor in informalist learning as a reaction to a history of poorly trained music educators (Kratus 2007; Williams 2007), or if a profession's collective loss of faith in teachers and their capacity to educate is engendered, we may be sowing the seeds of our own demise. The music teachers in Green's book could easily be outsourced in favor of cheaper, less experienced, and under-educated labor. If the tenets of informal musical learning are to be adapted, second-wave research needs to provide broad and self-critical illustrations of what constitutes a qualified, indeed *highly* qualified, music teacher (Cochran-Smith 2002b; Darling-Hammond and Berry 2006).

Finally, are the methods and processes of informal learning equal to the unique problems that popular music brings to the classroom? How do students become media literate in informal settings (Buckingham 2003; Richards 1998; Vasudevan 2010)? Green worries, like many of us, that children are insufficiently equipped to defend against market exploitation. She claims, however, that children develop a "critical musicality" by learning the music they like (Green 2008, 83–85). Because they hear more, they will see more. We fear, in spite of this, that a curriculum based on the copying of MP3 recordings apart from adult interaction is educationally naïve, especially when faced off against the sophistication of predatory capitalism. No matter how beneficial investigations of popular music are, or how rewarding the processes of informal learning turn out to be, it seems prudent to provide formal spaces in which dialogue and critique can occur.

To this point, we turn to John Dewey, who like Green viewed informal learning as spirited and natural, but worried that its gains were too random, and its outcomes too narrow. Dewey imagined the school as a place of social experimentation, where the problems of home and neighborhood, or the musical problems of the garage, are worked out in common. In the following quote by Dewey, we have substituted a few words, garage for home, musical life for social life—but the reader will get what we mean. Dewey writes,

> The ideal *garage* has to be enlarged. The child must be brought into contact with more grown people and with more children in order that there may be the freest and richest *musical life*. Moreover, the occupations and relationships of the *garage* environment are not especially selected for the growth of the child; the main objective is something else, and what the child can get out of them is incidental. (Dewey 1915/2001, 24–25)

We know that young adults in informal learning environments, whether alone at a computer or with friends in a garage, are likely to work in isolation, away from the eyes and ears of adults (Finnegan 1989; Jewitt 2008; Putnam 2000). But we believe that the music classroom—the band room or choir room—is the ideal location for a critical sharing of values and perspectives, a community of diverse talents and powers, arguing and debating—indeed laughing and smiling—across differences. In this environment, the teacher will be a *critical* part of the community, coming as she will with experience and expertise gained from a lifetime of engagement with music. To stand on the sidelines and not invite students to consider that experience would indicate a less than full engagement from her, and consequently limit the learning potential of the shared community. As Westerlund (2006) describes her conception of garage band learning, she writes, "In knowledge-building communities, the teacher is a participator and co-learner, a more expert learner" (122).

This is the realm that we are most interested in working in. Purposeful, democratic spaces where teachers and students come together, not through the casualties of formalist or informalist ideologies, but through methods of living and learning where plausible human interests and diverse expertise intersect with shared desires. These are humble aspirations, not grand. But because they take many forms, they are not linked to a singular genre or method of instruction; they do not focus wholly on the teacher or exclusively on the student. Determinations of value—dare we say standards—are worked out in common. And growth—incidental and intentional—comes from interaction, not isolation. Concerning this chapter, we would have to say that we don't actually operationalize informal learning, or formal learning either. Rather, pressed, we would say that we operationalize democracy in the hope that by bringing the graduate students we work with to reach beyond narrow specializations to greater openness, they will do this for their own students in turn.

The problem, of course, is how to prepare teachers to comfortably interact in this arguably "idealized", always evolving classroom community. Older models of music teacher preparation focused primarily on mechanical skills like baton technique and woodwind fingerings, with the expectation of placing these *a priori* skills without reference into faceless schools in faceless neighborhoods. Today's music educator is often called upon to work in partnership with the particulars of location and context (Abrahams 2005; Custodero and Williams 2000). Looking outward, this is an interesting inversion of formal learning, where the teacher places skill at the service of student needs, rather than personal expertise. But neither should teacher expertise be hard to locate, only redirected or refocused toward a common good.

We are no more or no less inspired by the music that garage band musicians make than we are by the music of jazz, folk, classical, or hip-hop musicians. Resisting literal understandings of how garage bands are operationalized, we are inspired, rather, by how garage band communities are made and negotiated, the way problems get solved, and above all, the manner in which the music practiced and composed is personally meaningful and self-reflective. This focus leads to critical questions: *how* can the unique ways and qualities of garage band interactions be harnessed for positive educational outcomes? And, importantly, where is the teacher located in this dynamic? The questions that we ask are not "whether or not" or "why or why not", but *"how"* those very ways and qualities are formalized in a meaningful fashion. We must recognize this rather obvious fact, that anything we do in schools represents "formal" instruction. By choosing locations and contexts, providing instruments and opportunities, educators formalize formerly informal musical experiences and environments. The formal spaces of schools are different from the informal spaces outside, and they provide different opportunities and challenges for the learning communities that inhabit them.

The formalizing of informal musical practices does not come without hazard, to which the example of jazz music in the United States attests. Several authors lament that the improvisational, collaborative, and democratic culture of jazz became much more authority-driven, hierarchal, and score-centered as it was formalized in North American institutions[5] (Ake 2002, 2010; Prouty 2008). In addition to a proliferation of scored and notated pieces and a consequent de-emphasis on improvisation, Prouty (2008, 1) notes this formalization also carried "profound implications for the types of social relationships among practitioners [of jazz]." In other words, those who learned and played jazz in the secondary school or university-based conservatory have had different kinds of relationships as teachers and students than were present fifty years ago "on the street" or "on the bandstand." The authors conclude that jazz musicians coming out of American institutions today enjoy educational experiences that are essentially the same as their classically trained counterparts.

Both the audition-based classical-style study of music and the strict informalist experiences that Green advocates represent missed opportunities to invite (or even prod) students to engage with and across difference—to experience new ways of learning, creating, and making music—a critical role of a democratic mutual learning community. We worry that informalist facilitators, like their conservatory counterparts, may not be actively or purposefully engaged with diversity as an educational ideal, allowing the young people in their care—fans of a specific musical style, say—the disinclination to look beyond and listen beyond the performers and personalities that they like best or know best. Indeed, the students in Green's studies are essentially left on their own to explore the music they are most drawn to. In a setting that resists the false dichotomy of informal versus formal learning, nuanced educators can access the rich educational benefits of musical and social difference, and challenge their students to do the same. With an unfamiliar musical example to stir up discussion and debate, teachers will need to cautiously decide how that music is presented. It can be reduced to a superficial treatment that focuses only on how the music sounds different; or teachers can explore the multiple cultural aspects of that music, which will bump up against different kinds of values and signifiers. Such diversity-affirming learning communities put us in contact with others who understand and present the world differently—and teachers, through their role in these communities, will invite students to engage with one another, to wrestle with difference, and with musical practices to which they may not be initially drawn.

It seems then, that music teacher preparation must include experiences that ask future teachers to wrestle with the questions of both informal and formal learning while working with and across difference. Only in an experiential setting will students come to know where the questions are, and learn to navigate responses to those questions democratically, in particular settings with particular musics and particular individuals. The garage band classes at Teachers College are one attempt.[6] Beyond a mere theoretical engagement, students are placed in ensembles, randomly, with class members they may or may not know, and typically from a variety of national backgrounds and musical preferences. We ask them to consider seriously the unique perspectives and expertise of the members of their community (their garage band), and to explore musical genres with which they may be unfamiliar. Importantly, these students are asked to create music of their own, but they are not left on their own. As teacher-facilitators in this setting, and as part of this classroom community, we carefully design opportunities and invitations for these groups to take their experimentation further, to ask richer questions, and consider perspectives that they may not otherwise consider. It is in this interaction that our own expertise and experiences come into play. Our hope is that not only will these invitations enrich the experiences that these pre-service teachers bring to class, but that these future teachers will feel compelled to ask those same questions of their future students, as well as demonstrate the value and place of democratic expertise.

Questions, many questions, naturally arise, and these will be addressed by second-wave researchers in this new domain of inquiry. What does formal music teacher preparation look like in informal settings?—in popular music settings? What counts as teacher expertise? What does an informal learning-inspired curriculum look like? What adaptations are necessary? How do music educators adopt informal and popular music practices without losing their vitality and relevance? How do college music teacher educators with little or no experience in popular music prepare the next generation of music practitioners? What can Anglo-American music educators learn from Northern European schools, where popular music has been an integral part of public school for several generations?—what mistakes can we avoid?—what successes can we emulate? How can we embrace a diversity-affirming approach to popular music? What are the promises and limitations of ethnographic description in helping design instruction? What theoretical frameworks can we turn to?

The learning practices associated with popular musicians are sure to be operationalized through a multiplicity of means. We are convinced that the teachers best capable of managing such a task will be those music educators with a practiced democratic outlook. The foundation of democratic education rests on a diversity of ideas and their practical connection to a changing world. Now, on to the next wave.

# References

Abrahams, F. 2005. "Transforming Music Instruction with Ideas from Critical Pedagogy." *Music Educators Journal* 92 (1): 62–68.

Abramo, J. 2011. "Gender Differences of Popular Music Production in Secondary Schools." *Journal of Research in Music Education* 59 (1): 21–43.

Ake, D. A. 2002. *Jazz Cultures*. Berkeley: University of California Press.

—. 2010. *Jazz Matters: Sound, Place, and Time Since Bebop*. Berkeley: University of California Press.

Allsup, R. E. 2002. *Crossing Over: Mutual Learning and Democratic Action in Instrumental Music Education*. PhD diss., Teachers College Columbia University.

—. 2003. "Mutual Learning and Democratic Action in Instrumental Music Education." *Journal of Research in Music Education* 51 (1): 24–37.

—. 2004. "Of Concert Bands and Garage Bands: Creating Democracy Through Popular Music." In *Bridging the Gap: Popular Music and Music Education*, ed. C. X. Rodriguez, 204–23. Reston: MENC.

—. 2011. "Popular Music and Classical Musicians: Strategies and Perspectives." *Music Educators Journal* 97 (3): 30–34.

Buckingham, D. 2003. *Media Education: Literacy, Learning, and Contemporary Culture*. Cambridge: Polity Press.

Byrne, C., and M. Sheridan. 2000. "The Long and Winding Road: The Story of Rock Music in Scottish Schools." *International Journal of Music Education* 36 (1): 46–57.

Campbell, P. S. 1995. "Of Garage Bands and Song-Getting: The Musical Development of Young Rock Musicians." *Research Studies in Music Education* 4 (1): 12-20.

Cochran-Smith, M. 2002a. "Reporting on Teacher Quality: The Politics of Politics." *Journal of Teacher Education* 53 (5): 379–82.

—. 2002b. "What a Difference a Definition Makes: Highly Qualified Teachers, Scientific Research, and Teacher Education." *Journal of Teacher Education* 53 (3): 187–89.

Custodero, L., and L. Williams. 2000. "Music for Everyone: Creating Contexts for Possibility in Early Childhood Education." *Early Childhood Connections* 6 (4): 36–43.

Darling-Hammond, L., and B. Berry. 2006. "Highly Qualified Teachers for All." *Educational Leadership* 64 (3): 14–20.

Davis, S. 2005. "That Thing You Do!: Compositional Processes of a Rock Band." *International Journal of Education and the Arts* 16 (6). http://www.ijea.org/v6n16/index.html

Dewey, J. 1915/2001. *The School and Society*. Mineola: Dover.
—. 1916. *Democracy and Education*. New York: The Free Press.
Finnegan, R. 1989. *The Hidden Musicians: Music-Making in an English Town*. Cambridge: Cambridge University Press.
Folkestad, G. 2006. "Formal and Informal Learning Situations or Practices *vs*. Formal and Informal Ways of Learning." *British Journal of Music Education* 23 (2): 135–45.
Fornäs, J., U. Lindberg, and O. Sernhede. 1995. *In Garageland: Rock, Youth and Modernity*. New York: Routledge.
Frith, S. 1988. *Music for Pleasure: Essays in the Sociology of Pop*. Cambridge: Polity Press
—. 1996. *Performing Rites: On the Value of Popular Music*. New York: Oxford University Press.
Green, L. 2001. *How Popular Musicians Learn*. Burlington: Ashgate.
—. 2006. "Popular Music Education in and for Itself, and for 'Other' Music: Current Research in the Classroom." *International Journal of Music Education* 24 (2): 101–18.
—. 2008. *Music, Informal Learning and the School*. Burlington: Ashgate.
Hebert, D. G., and P. S. Campbell. 2000. "Rock Music in American Schools: Positions and Practices since the 1960s." *International Journal of Music Education* 36 (1): 14–22.
Jewitt, C. 2008. "Multimodality and Literacy in School Classrooms." *Review of Research in Education* 32: 241–67.
Kozol, J. 2005. *Shame of the Nation: The Restoration of Apartheid in America*. New York: Crown Publishing.
Kratus, J. 2007. "Music Education at the Tipping Point." *Music Educators Journal* 94 (2): 42–48.
Leblanc, L. 1999. *Pretty in Punk: Girls' Resistance in a Boys Subculture*. New Brunswick: Rutgers University Press.
McClary, S. 1991. *Feminine Endings: Music, Gender, and Sexuality*. Minneapolis: University of Minnesota Press.
Prouty, K. 2008. "The 'Finite' Art of Improvisation: Pedagogy and Power in Jazz Education." *Critical Studies in Improvisation* 4 (1): 1–15.
Putnam, R. 2000. *Bowling Alone: The Collapse and Revival of American Community*. New York: Simon & Schuster.
Richards, C. 1998. *Teen Spirits: Music and Identity in Media Education*. London: UCL Press.
Rodriguez, C. X., ed. 2004. *Bridging the Gap: Popular Music and Education*. Reston: MENC.

Söderman, J., and G. Folkestad. 2004. "How Hip-Hop Musicians Learn: Strategies in Informal Creative Music Making." *Music Education Research* 6 (3): 313–26.

Vasudevan, L. 2010. "Re-Imagining Pedagogies for Multimodal Selves." *National Society for the Study of Education* 110 (1): 88–108.

Väkevä, L. 2006. "Teaching Popular Music in Finland: What's Up, What's Ahead?" *International Journal of Music Education* 24 (2): 126–31.

Westerlund, H. 2006. "Garage Rock Bands: A Future Model for Developing Musical Expertise?" *International Journal of Music Education* 24 (2): 119–25.

Wiggins, J. 2006. "Compositional Process in Music." In *International Handbook of Research in Arts Education,* ed. L. Bresler, 451–67. New York: Springer.

Will, G. F. 2006. "Ed Schools *vs.* Education", *Newsweek*, January 16.

Williams, D. 2007. "What are Music Educators Doing and How Well Are We Doing It?" *Music Educators Journal* 94 (1): 18–23.

Woody, R. H. 2007. "Popular Music in the Schools: Remixing the Issues." *Music Educators Journal* 94 (4): 32–37.

# Notes

[1] This chapter is an extended version of an article previously published in 2008 by Randall Everett Allsup as "Creating an Educational Framework for Popular Music in Public Schools: Anticipating the Second-Wave" in *Visions of Research in Music Education* 12. Reprinted by permission of the editor.

[2] Not all popular music is learned informally; nor is informal learning solely derived from or derivative of popular musicians. Nor is the term "popular music" the ideal way to describe this multifaceted and overlapping genre. But at present, this is the term that has coalesced around this body of research.

[3] For information on the Musical Futures project, go to: www.musicalfutures.org.uk

[4] In this context, we define formalism as a teacher-directed doctrine in which students are trained to achieve predetermined outcomes. The doctrine of informalism is equally dogmatic; it is a form of self-directed learning that takes place solely through social intercourse, outside the school and without an assigned teacher.

[5] Today, an American teen can learn jazz in a private college preparatory high school and finish her music major in jazz studies at an Ivy League college. The same will soon hold true for rock and popular music.

[6] For a more thorough description of this course-work, see Allsup (2011).

# CHAPTER THREE

# THE WORLD WELL LOST, FOUND: REALITY AND AUTHENTICITY IN GREEN'S "NEW CLASSROOM PEDAGOGY"[1]

## LAURI VÄKEVÄ

## The "Real-World Music"

In her recent work, Green (2001, 2008) builds on the idea that there is a gulf between "real-world music" and classroom music (2). One of her main goals seems to be to pave the way for the former in the latter: to make the music in schools more in touch with reality. The learning practices of popular music are taken to bring the needed verisimilitude. As most students prefer popular music to other types of music, it is assumed that at least for this majority, its "naturally" arising learning practices appear as more real than other, more formal procedures (41).

While one can question if the pop/rock band procedures described by Green (2001) cover "nearly all sub-styles" of popular music, or whether they are really "natural", or even pedagogically the most interesting ones (Green 2008, 5; compare Väkevä 2006a; Allsup 2008),[2] it is significant that Green's point of departure is genre-independent. For instance, she does not insist that there should be more popular music in British schools at the cost of classical music—the latter having not exactly been in the cutting edge of school music in the last years at any rate (Green 2008, 153). Green's case is made more against the way music, classical, popular, or any kind has been taught; the reality she looks for relates to "the *processes* by which the relevant musical skills and knowledge are passed on and acquired" (3, italics original). She attributes the reason for the weak motivation and low take-up of music as a curriculum subject in the UK to the formal methods of instruction (2).

It is not surprising that popular music is preferred by many of the students, especially in Green's target group (13–14 year olds).[3] In fact, some of the students interviewed for Green's projects did not even seem to count classical music as "real" music! (154–158). This makes one wonder how music becomes "real" for someone; moreover, it makes one ask, how can a "musical world" be claimed for someone for whom it is "well lost"?[4]

In this chapter, my intention is to raise discussion rather than offer systematic critique. I also do not pretend to read Green's texts through neutral lenses: my interpretations are influenced by my background in the pedagogy of popular music and a pragmatist philosophy of music education, which makes my approach hermeneutic to begin with (Väkevä 2000, 2003, 2004, 2006a, 2006b, 2007). While I agree with many of the ideas that frame Green's books,[5] I think that a further elaboration of their underpinnings can encourage constructive discussion of the role of popular music based learning practices in music education (see also Frierson-Campbell 2008; Väkevä 2006a; Väkevä and Westerlund 2007; Westerlund 2006). I believe that this discussion is needed, not just for the obvious reason that popular music is becoming commonplace in many music classes around the world and calls for an elaboration of conventional pedagogical practices,[6] but also because this development might have more far-reaching implications. For instance, popular music pedagogy could indicate new ways in which music educators may conceive their subject in a society that accepts democratic participation and creative agency as its guiding key values (Westerlund 2006; Väkevä and Westerlund 2007).

This elaboration can perhaps also help us to investigate some issues that are not fully covered in Green's work. One of the practical aspects that invite new ideas is the rapid global proliferation of digital music culture.[7] Information technology has brought forth new, even radically new, ways of conceiving, manipulating, mediating, consuming, and recycling music, and these new ways suggest new ideas which might help us to reconsider music as art form, industry, and mode of communication (Born 2005; Mantere 2008; Taylor 2001; Väkevä 2006a). While Green (2008, 5, 41–42) frames the informal learning approaches as domain-independent in principle, the fact is that approaches that involve computers, social networks, and other assets of digital music and information technology are not really examined in her study, apart from an occasional hint of the use of digital instruments in conventional music making (48). Hence, there seems to be room for deeper meditation on Green's ideas from the standpoint of digital music culture.[8]

## Authenticity in Learning

Green's underlying idea seems to be that the authenticity of musical learning—the quality that makes it "real"—is based on the authenticity of the student's preferences: what really interests the student is "real" for the student, and thus worth learning from her standpoint.[9] This is easy to agree with: it is a commonplace in contemporary learning theory to treat intrinsic motivation as an important factor in learning, and it is best increased by means of engaging a student's active interest. One might also refer here to authenticity in learning (Petraglia 1998): learning is taken to be more effective when it is motivated by desires and needs that are original and genuine to the learner (Green 2006, 114–115). From this standpoint, a central condition for learning is a personal commitment, and this commitment is judged by the recognized practical value of what is studied. This idea has been the touchstone of educational philosophy since progressivism: it forms a central tenet of Dewey's pragmatist account of the role of interest in education and further frames student-centered ideas of constructivism.[10]

The motivational value of popular music may justify its place in music curricula. For instance, it can be argued that one can invigorate music classes with materials that students are already familiar with and to which they react positively. Thus, popular music may be used as an introductory device for music that is not so popular.[11] Popular music can also offer a gateway to further knowledge of music, musical literacy, and theoretical concepts. When popular music is taught in this way, a student-centered approach may become more a pedagogical device than an end result: student involvement is taken as a means to achieve ends that are not necessarily felt important by the learners. Authenticity, from this perspective, is something that may help teachers to achieve learning objectives that, from the student perspective, are "things remote", as Dewey put it (Dewey 1915/MW 8, 339, 1916/MW 9, 216).

However, Green does not subscribe to the idea that popular music should be taught only, or even primarily, for external goals (e.g, Green 1988, 2001, 138–139, 2006, 102). Like any music, popular music has its own "inherent'" or "inter-sonic" meanings, on which music education can focus (Green 2008, 87).[12] In fact, Green's need to map out the informal learning practices of popular musicians, and the ensuing need to experiment with the pedagogical application of these practices, seems to have risen from an urge to criticize the approaches by which popular music was taught primarily as a social and cultural phenomenon—more for its "delineations" than for its inter-sonic meanings (see also Moore

1993). According to Green, this approach may distort music's inherent (inter-sonic) meanings and let ideological conceptions dictate how these meanings are to be valued. At its worst, this distortion may lead to fetishization of the musical object, where music's inherent meanings are treated as autonomous essences (Green 1988, chap. 7). When this takes place, delineations may "appropriate the inherent meanings and become the means through which music appears to communicate its value" (86). For instance, the assumption that popular music is either indescribable or not worth studying for its inherent qualities may produce an ideological vacuum that is then filled up with extra-musical (e.g., sociological or cultural) meanings that are thought to better inform the students about what is worth learning in connection to this music. Against this, Green seems to argue that popular music, as any music, can also be an end in itself and thus can be studied for its own sake.[13] (Green 2008, 7; see also Green 2001, 2006)

Green also argues for a kind of means-value for popular music in school. By getting involved through the "natural" learning practices of music, students can learn to appreciate its delineations (Green 2006, 2008, 4). Learning to enjoy music for its inter-sonic meanings may encourage students to appreciate it in terms of its cultural references and further direct them to pay more attention to how the latter are situationally conditioned. This is based on the idea indicated above: that learning any kind of music in a "natural" way can make it "real" for its practitioners. Authenticity in learning can also spill over to new areas, widening the musical horizons of the students and introducing them to new musical worlds. Following Green's rationale, a sense of authenticity can thus transform enjoyment of one kind of musical expression into an appreciation of another.

One obvious problem in this account is the diversity of today's global music cultures, which tends to encourage more or less relativistic accounts of music's meaning and value. The inter-sonic meanings of music seem to evaporate into the variety of musical subject positions possible in contemporary mediated and networked culture—that is, the inherent meanings of music tend to be delineated in so many ways that the "natural" practices of learning music seem to always be conditioned by cultural conventions. Thus, it is entirely possible that one can never point out "natural" ways "to music", or to learn any music in its authentic terms, as musical cultures continuously influence each other and each other's indigenous procedures, intensified by global information networks (Vattimo 1992, 19–20).

Authenticity, one might further argue, may not be possible at all in a multifaceted culture: the most we can grasp are different cultural attitudes and approaches reflecting different discursive positions, always presenting musical values and objects in new light. As Rorty (1972) put it in his infamous attack on empiricist epistemology: a world outside of language is, for us, "well lost." Even if one does not subscribe to the extreme linguistic pragmatism of Rorty,[14] there is still something quite suspicious in the claims that one can discern an authentic way that music is, and could be, made and learned on the basis of its inherent qualities. Even if we grant a "virtual" autonomy (Green 2006, 104) to music, one might further argue that in education we could always do more than drill for authenticity. Is it not the goal of education to point out new critical possibilities and horizons of meaning in cultural processes, rather than just represent the ways in which music is "authentically" made or learned?[15]

Acutely aware of the discourses of multiculturalism, Green (2008, 41–42) still argues that while the variables making music authentic change along with the historical and social-cultural context, at least in principle it is always possible to hit upon the level at which people respond to music for its own sake, as a universally human expressive practice (see also Green 2006, 2008, 59).[16] Even if different musical cultures and sub-cultures articulate their own musical meanings, according to Green (2008, 42), in every case there lurks underneath a learning approach that is "fundamentally similar" in every culture and thus can be grasped by all learners. Moreover, as already indicated, the authenticity of involvement that makes learning one kind of music "real" to the student can spill over to other settings, as long as the teacher can distinguish the relevant learning practices in each case and establish learning environments where those practices can flourish. When students grasp music this way, they are empowered to make its terms their own regardless of its style, genre, or culture. Authenticity, from this standpoint, is not something that is an original property of the subject matter in music, but something that can be arrived at through internally motivated involvement with its inter-sonic properties. Channelled pedagogically, this can further lead to "critical musicality", a term that Green (83–85) advocates as a central goal of music education.[17]

## Authenticity In Situ

While one can be critical of the global applicability of the idea that all music has underneath a natural learning practice that is fundamentally similar in every cultural case,[18] Green's account of authenticity in learning seems to imply a pragmatic logic, which makes it especially inviting for music education programs that suffer a gap between school music and music outside school. One can perhaps open its logic further by considering how the locus of interest shifts from one learning situation to another.[19]

One of the most important teachings of Green's account here, pragmatically speaking, seems to concern the flexibility of musicianship. Given this flexibility, musicianship—taken as the capability to participate actively in the practices and processes of "musicing" (60)[20]—does not have to be restricted by the bounds of acquired musical habits; when a situation changes, new habits and attitudes can be developed that adapt to it. In pragmatist terms this also means that the musical self is not fixed: our selves constantly change along with our habits according to the needs and particulars of the situation, in music as well as in other realms of life. Authenticity is thus not something inherent to a static subject position, nor even something that is arrived at through a tedious project of individual self-realization (cf. Taylor 1989). If there is authenticity involved with learning, it must be somehow embedded in the continuing learning process. In fact, to prevent the self from changing would be to prevent growth, a pedagogical cardinal sin if one takes growth in Deweyan terms—as continuing expansion of the experienced realm of meaning (e.g., Dewey 1938/LW 13, 19–20).

What is crucial is that new habits are called forth by needs that emerge naturally from the situation—"naturally" indicating here that the need to learn stems from the tensions caused by the changes in environment that present new challenges to one's musicianship. For a practicing musician, this might simply mean that the need to learn is raised by practical musical problems-at-hand, as clearly happened in many of the cases described in *A New Classroom Pedagogy*. While new musical habits can perhaps be imposed from the outside to a certain degree, they serve future situations best when they are elicited by the practical needs of hands-on musicing, for this better guarantees their openness and flexibility in future applications. With informal learning, this implies that students should have a "say" about what they are expected to learn and how they will proceed in learning it; and, further, that the teacher be willing and able to provide them enough opportunities to try out different solutions to such emergent problems. This amounts to the Deweyan idea of experiential learning, and it also seems to apply to what took place in many of the projects described by Green (Green 2008, 91, 110).

In Green's frame of reference, room for students to navigate options is possible first of all because the students have inner motivation towards learning music of their own choice and in terms that they accept as authentic for it. Their need to learn more grows out of the practices to which the students are eagerly and free-willingly committed, inner motivation propelling them forward to adapt to new musical situations that arise as a result of their own initiating actions. Like Elliott (1995), Green (2008, 56–60) identifies this continuum of interest as a psychological state of flow, a condition that emerges when the student's ability is continuously contested by tasks challenging enough to call forth further involvement (Csikszentmihalyi 1990, 1996). In pedagogical terms, the teacher is first advised to stand by, observe, and at most help in the setting of the learning environment: she acts more as a facilitator than an instructor (cf. Clements 2008). Only later, when the situation has called forth new ways of adapting to change, she may suggest more focused practical solutions in order to guide the students towards more structured challenges.

## Authenticity in a New Key

It is in connection with these more structured challenges that a rupture seems to emerge in this logic of authenticity. In the projects of *A New Classroom Pedagogy*, the emphasis was eventually shifted from the autonomy of "haphazard" procedures to more systematic work with a pre-assigned piece of music chosen by the researcher.[21] Students were encouraged to apply their newly acquired skills in copying the song; as an aid, they were provided with a "broken-down" version on a CD (Green 2008, 26).[22] Thus, despite the relative freedom (e.g., in choosing instruments), the situation was now more formally controlled: students did not choose a piece of music to learn (and thus could not really contribute to its authenticity for their learning), nor were they given entirely free choice concerning the directions in which to proceed. Instead, the goal of this stage of the project was clearly articulated: the main undertaking was "to listen to and copy the song . . . using the tracks of isolated riffs as a guide if desired, in order to make up their own version of it as a band" (26).

While this can be interpreted as a break in the continuum of the informal approach, the pedagogical intent is clear: to provide the above-mentioned structuring that would guide the students' initiatives in the direction of "critical musicality" (84). In fact, after this more formal stage, the first, more freewheeling phase was repeated in most project schools, the idea being that the teacher-framed second stage helps the students to become more focused when working on the inter-sonic properties of the music of their own choice. Thus, the first stage of "dropping pupils in a deep end" (25) was established as a kind of a shock tactic to awaken students to the possibility that they can empower themselves to pay attention to the inter-sonic meanings of music, a skill more critically developed in the second stage.

It is noteworthy that in the second stage the critical attitude was evoked with the help of pre-designated lesson materials that partly dictated the focus of attention, and also by the programmatic choice of the song: the teacher's (and in this case, the researcher's) contribution was thus a determining factor in re-framing the situation for the critical approach. The method of establishing the learning situation was nevertheless similar in all three beginning stages, despite the relative differences in teacher input: in all stages, copying from the CDs was chosen as the launching procedure for preserving the authenticity of learning, an idea that was based on Green's earlier research on the learning of popular musicians (Green 2001). In fact, the procedure of copying music from the CD was deemed so crucial that it seemed to override some of the students' ideas of other possible ways of learning, such as using computers as an aid (Green 2008, 21, 25).[23]

After the first three stages, students moved into songwriting, with the idea that the learning from the first three stages could inform more creative activities. According to Green's report, songwriting turned out to be highly rewarding for the students. Here, again, informal work was the beginning phase, and more pedagogically structured tasks followed. In stage 5, the students were asked to follow models taken from the "'real' world of popular music" (27). The function of the models—professional bands and peer groups—was to provide an inside view of the songwriting process by demonstrating "how a song can be put together" (27). The "real-life" groups also acted in the role of teachers after the demonstrations, a procedure that gave extra encouragement to the students' efforts.

In both cases (viz. copying music from CDs and learning to write songs), the expectation was clearly that the "natural" situation provided the means of solving emerging problems, which were then to be applied to new, more pedagogically structured situations. After their inner motivation was raised, students would also find more structured tasks enjoyable, as they wanted to learn more and to put their newly acquired skills to new uses. Thus the sense of authenticity in learning would be preserved despite the formality of the more staged situations.

In pedagogical terms, this implies a reverse fading strategy: the teacher does not fade from the situation, but takes more responsibility as basic skills are internalized (compare Elliott 1995, 280). The relevance of formal teaching becomes apparent only after students are motivated to learn in a "natural" way, propelled forward by the inner rewards of manipulating the inter-sonic meanings according to (what they at least take to be) authentic musical practice. The disruption in the student-centered learning process is thus reframed as a natural development of the students' inner urge to learn more and to utilize their learning with the help of more formally established aiding structures and concepts. This idea brings to mind Green's (2001) observation that many of the informally trained musicians in her earlier study expressed their interest in learning music more formally after they had already gained a wealth of skills, knowledge and understanding from informal learning practices with the music of their own choice.

The idea that the teacher fades in, rather than out, does not have to be at odds with a pragmatist rationale that takes learning to be a function of changing situations. The teacher can become as much part of the learning situation as any other aspect, and formal pedagogy can ride on the students' flow established first in informal settings. However, the need for more structured teaching must emerge from the dynamics of the situation in order to build authenticity. One important aspect of this dynamic is the free interchange between the students when they negotiate the best ways to proceed in the task. Peer communication is also a central point of departure in Green's projects, based on her previous observation that, in informal settings, popular musicians both learn together and efficiently teach each other. The communicative and organizational habits that students acquire informally can also later turn out to be beneficial in more structured situations: in Green's research, groups were indeed able to act in a more integrated manner afterwards and to negotiate about their co-operative strategies and individual roles. (Green 2008, chapter 6)

Green's research suggests that as long as the more organized tasks are meaningfully connected to the earlier informal stages of learning, inner motivation can be preserved and the students' focus further targeted to new challenges. Authenticity, from this standpoint, is not threatened but transformed: it re-emerges as the quality of the pedagogically structured situation. In a way, it is transposed into a new key, as the sheer enjoyment of music encourages the students to pay more appreciative attention to its inter-sonic meanings. This critical attitude is supported by communicative skills, on the basis of which one can negotiate informed opinions of music's meanings. According to Green (88–91), this is required for a balanced, "celebratory" experience where both the inter-sonic and delineated meanings of music are taken positively.[24]

# Worlds Found or Made?

One can ask whether the transformation of authenticity in learning can also transform the musical content's conditions of authenticity—whether, in the informal practices of learning, "a music" may be changed to something different both in its inter-sonic and delineated meanings. It would be interesting to consider whether the practices of trying to reproduce "real-world music" in school can in fact produce new musical forms indigenous to the school setting, perhaps opening new musical realities along the way.

In this light, the most interesting phase of the research reported in *A New Classroom Pedagogy* was surely the last one (stages 6 and 7), where informal learning practices were applied to learn "Western classical music, broadly defined" (Green 2008, 149).[25] In this phase, the informal practices of popular musicians were used as exploratory vessels to carry the students to new experiences in musical styles to which they had previously paid little attention, at least in any positive sense—the music was, for the majority of them, "well lost" but, presumably, could be found again.[26]

Here we come back to the question of what guarantees the authenticity of learning when the situation is artificially changed. Earlier, the shift was rationalized by the notion that authenticity in learning was transformed to a new critical level. In order to be able to assume appreciative perspectives on the music one enjoys, one can benefit from a situation framed by the teacher for the needs of "critical musicality" without losing one's intrinsic motivation. In Green's study, the motivation developed in the first stage was preserved through the second stage by simply keeping the focus on music that the students liked. Live models further helped to target the students' attention in the fourth and fifth stage. Thus, authenticity was not really challenged by teacher or peer group intervention: meaningful musical engagement provided the impulse to learn more, and formal procedures were taken for their practical worth in helping further involvement. Authenticity of preference, even when transformed to a more critical level, still provided the red thread running through the continuum of interest.

However, in the "classical stages" of Green's research the situation was radically different. One justifiably wonders whether the music reportedly not preferred by the majority of the students really provided the needed authenticity in learning, especially when approached in a way that does not seem to be "natural."[27] This "litmus test" (Green 2006, 111) can also be seen as critical for Green's theoretical underpinnings: if it warrants the assumption that learning music can be internally motivated even in situations when its "content" alienates the students, one can further assume that authenticity in musical learning can be targeted methodically, regardless of the students' earlier preferences. These preferences, even if originally hostile, may give way to more critical attitudes that can be further channelled through playful hands-on involvement with the inter-sonic meanings of the music in question.

Even if the last stages in Green's research turned out to be more pilot studies than finished accounts (Green 2008, 151), she does report a change in the attitudes of many students. Music that was not originally "real" for many pupils appeared to become more "real" for them through tangible working with its inter-sonic possibilities in informal classroom situations (150, 168–175). Here the establishment of authenticity in learning seemed to be dependent solely on the carrying over of the motivation from working with music of the students' own choice established in the earlier stages. Hence, the students seemed to find the informal approach motivating in general, regardless of the "content" factor. The authenticity involved in this approach would not be restricted to any particular musical content, style, practice, or culture: it could be based on Green's global factor of musical involvement, which can rise in any kind of music as long as its "natural" conditions of learning are satisfied.[28]

Green's idea seems to be that even if this global factor is taken to be always "there", as a real-world possibility, ideological restrictions may hinder its emergence. The largely hostile or indifferent attitudes that the majority of the students projected towards classical music may be ideologically loaded with a set of negative delineations that replace the "inter-sonic" meanings of this music, presenting the latter more as a fetish than the real thing—not a natural situation from the standpoint of authenticity in learning (cf. Green 2003).

Not liking "a music" may actually be merely symptomatic of not liking what it brings to mind, and in these cases the music may not get the chance it deserves in its own right. The lack of critical appreciation may prevent a student from enjoying music on its own terms, and consequently get in the way of her enjoyment; in this case, the student would not have access to the flow channel that could be opened through an active involvement with manipulating and exploring music's inter-sonic relationships. This hidden, but nevertheless potential meaning can only be realized in an active dialectic of musicing that has been previously unrecognized due to the ideological lenses that distort one's perspectives. Such dialectic is behind all enjoyable involvement with music, and it also provides a "natural" way into its more critical appreciation.

Green (2008, 159) also mentions that, especially in stage 6 where the music was taken from British TV advertisements, its familiar delineations may have helped to open the door to its inter-sonic possibilities.[29] This seems to suggest that once music is identified in some way—once put on the cultural map—it is easier to access through methods that are motivating to students; that is, when students are able to put a positive (or at least neutral) "tag" on classical music, it is also easier to access it simply as music for its own worth.

Freedom in the use of musical instruments when arranging the pieces may also lower the ideological threshold. According to Green (161), the liberal choice of instruments in stages 6 and 7 made possible the use of sounds that allegedly carried more affirmative delineations for the students than the ones they heard from the CDs. For instance, the students could freely add a drumbeat to a classical piece—a procedure that many would probably say changes the idiom, even if the melodic and harmonic content of the music remained untouched.[30]

Despite of this room for maneuver, the need to preserve inter-sonic authenticity remained strong for many students. This was reflected in attempts to emulate the actual sounds they heard from the CDs, whether they preferred them sonically or not (perhaps reflecting their newly acquired critical musicality). This also made possible the use of classical instruments, which some of the students studied (c. 15%, according to Green, 150). However, the informal approach also introduced new ways of approaching these instruments: for instance, many classically-trained pupils had no previous experience playing by ear (163). Here again a striving for authenticity seemed to emerge, as there were cases in which it seemed to be difficult for the students to make a connection between formal and informal uses of these instruments (163).

Despite these attempts to be true to the sonic characteristics of the classical recordings, the results of applying the informal approach in learning the musical works distinguished the student versions from conventional classical performances. In a similar vein as when dealing with popular music earlier in the process, mistakes were tolerated, and the musical flow was kept uninterrupted even if someone was "lost"—not a commonplace occurrence in classical music rehearsals.[31] Green takes these observations as suggesting that the students achieved a psychological state of flow similar to the earlier stages: emphasis was not on details, but on the general "feel" of the music (163).

The students also took liberties in their arrangements. Omissions, inserts, melodic changes, even the composing of new sections were all signs of transformations by which the students adapted to the new situation (164). In fact, some of these changes were so radical that one may justifiably ask whether this was the same music any more: whether the students turned classical pieces into something else, more as result of their own inclinations, and more suitable to their own skills. According to Green (169), while some critics may take this kind of appropriation as submitting to a delusion that classical music is easier to learn than it is, it is also true that pedagogical simplification of difficult material has always been commonplace in music education.[32] One obvious way of carrying out this kind of simplification is the process already indicated above—the popular arrangement of a classical piece. One of the students interviewed in Green's study put it this way: "[A]ll you need to do is listen to the beats and stay with it really, and then you find it as easy as anything else. . . . All the other music things that we've been doing, like it's the same really, sticking with the beats." (169). As this notion was arrived at when discussing Beethoven, one may justifiably ask whether the idea was really to be true to the inter-sonic meanings of the piece, or whether new meanings were picked up from the reservoir that the students had earlier collected when working with popular music. Thus, at least some of the student arrangements discussed in Green's study seem to be instances of turning classical works into popular music. One can ask whether the students really learned to appreciate the inter-sonic meanings of classical works as they exist in the "real world", or whether they substituted meanings taken from music that they liked to the original inter-sonic meanings they did not like. The result could of course be called a hybrid style, and may be as justified as any artistic utterance, but the main point here is that identity and thus, presumably, the authenticity of the music was changed; if the ontological status of music can be transformed relatively freely without losing its authenticity, the ideal that school music should be made more like "real-world music" seems not to qualify as a necessary criterion for achieving authenticity in learning.

## In Media, *Res*

Be that as may, one of the most important findings of Green's research is certainly how easily ideological constraints may be mitigated when one is given a free hand to make music in a way that is intrinsically motivating.[33] It could be further argued that the music class in comprehensive schooling is one the few places where this is possible in a formal pedagogical setting. Especially when considering music education from an egalitarian standpoint (i.e. with the idea that music education should be accessible to all), the heterogeneous competencies aimed at in a general music class seem to demand that music should not be approached as a collection of pre-produced, autonomous, and immutable cultural formations, but as a dynamic process of creating new meanings from the resources at hand in a particular cultural environment. In the last decades, information networks have extended this environment immensely, opening a global network of creative possibilities. In principle, nothing prevents a properly equipped music class from utilizing this wealth, as long as it is acknowledged that almost anything can contribute to the creative process of learning music. If desired, a music class could be a place where musical worlds are not merely found, but also created.

The quotes of students cited by Green in the last part of her research reveal that many students interviewed were actually aware and proud of the musical transformations that took place in the "classical" stages. From this, one can infer that when the students were not inspired by the original music addressed in stages 6 and 7, they intentionally "made it better", manifesting creative agency and a degree of emancipation (170). One might also argue that in a contemporary multicultural, mediated, yet socially responsible democratic culture, where musical communication is so commonplace that most of it is not even acknowledged by teachers, students deserve to be given a wide range of possibilities for processing musical meanings in their own terms.

For Green, the freewheeling attitude towards transforming music reflects the above-mentioned play impulse at work. Rather than taking the classical pieces as authoritative cultural texts, the students handled the pieces with a sense of confidence, making them subject to their own musical interests. Instead of criticizing this procedure of appropriation as an inauthentic way of approaching music, the value of which depends on originality, Green takes the students' eagerness as a healthy reminder of how the lack of improvisation and playfulness in Western post-classical era music has made its learning "anti-musical" and distant to "why humans make music in the first place" (171; see also Green 2001, 3).[34]

Green (2008, 171) suggests that by transforming classical music to fit their own needs, students can empower themselves to become "less alienated from the music's inter-sonic properties and its delineated associations." This also helps them to rethink their relation to music. The newly found freedom in transforming music to better suit one's own situation thus relates to the goal of learning to appreciate it through "critical musicality." Some students in the study reported that their attitudes towards classical music changed as a result of the process: even if they would not necessarily listen to more classical works than before, they now seemed more willing to appreciate the workings of that repertory

(174). Thus, even if the students did not perhaps learn to enjoy classical works in their intended form (that is, as musical art works to be interpreted with precision and contemplated for their inherent qualities), through working with such literature, many learned to listen to music in general more critically. What seemed to emerge as an important idea was that classical music, as much as any music, can be adapted by anyone to her own expressive needs in whatever way she finds satisfying without losing the critical potential. This is surely an important lesson.

Despite the results of her empirical research, Green's more extensive rationale still seems to involve an underlying tension related to her theory of musical meaning. The summary at the end of *A New Classroom Pedagogy* leaves this tension visible. Green suggests that by paying more attention to authenticity in learning than to the authenticity of musical "content" and, further, by providing the students opportunities for developing critical musicality, a teacher can motivate them to learn any kind of music—"so long as it is 'real'" (176–177). While the first two ideas are clearly understandable in reference to the above-described emphasis on authenticity that can be transferred from situation to situation and aided by clever pedagogy, the "reality" part of the argument remains a bit troubling. On one hand, "reality" seems not to be judged according to music's authenticity, but according to how motivated the students are to learn it: what is "real" in music seems to be what students happily enjoy and want to learn more of. On the other hand the goal of the informal approach is to provide the students with "a doorway into the music's inter-sonic meanings", and these do not seem to depend logically on the students' inherent motivation or authenticity in learning (180).

Green is by no means a formalist: she clearly emphasizes the value of meaningful experiences that students can have when they approach music through "some amount of social action, which is both autonomous and co-operative" (180). This is the proper way for students to get involved in "direct production of musical inter-sonic meanings" (180). At the same time, she argues that students should be "stimulated by whole pieces of 'real' music" (180). The general challenge of "new music pedagogy" would be to "provide . . . curriculum content that authentically reflects the world outside the school": that is, "real-life music" (185). Hence, in Green's account, "reality" seems to be at the same time something that frames music in advance as an object of study and something that can be used as a criterion of the authenticity of its learning—that is, at the same time a property of musical content and its learning.

As a pragmatist, I wonder whether Green's empiricist point of departure, in which music is taken at the same time as objectively existing, carrying its own meanings for critical listeners to grasp through musical experience, and as something that is cognitively-culturally constructed in the process of its learning ("musicing"), is the best rationale to account for the ways in which the students actively transform music for their own situational needs (see also Väkevä and Westerlund, 2007). In the more creative situations described in *A New Classroom Pedagogy*, music's meanings seem to elude any clear-cut logical distinctions between its experienced content and the process of its meaning-formation (and, thus, of its learning). What the students do in the class seems to be as real as any song on a CD that they are listening to as long as they make it authentic—this authenticity being provided by their continuing interest in working out its possibilities. Musical reality seems to be transformed in this process: the subject is not just the "real-life music" represented. Music appears as a living practice that continuously claims new terrain in human life through the meaning-making processes of its transformation.

In this outlook, music's manner of being "real", and thus, the students' manner of representing it as subject to be learned, changes along with the process of learning: the musicing self is also transformed, continuously adapting to new creative situations. This change should not be dictated by any standard of authenticity alien to the needs of learning itself. There are no a priori limits for what counts as meaningful in musical processes, only socially and culturally (and thus, ideologically) framed conventions that can always be negotiated and argued about (but also accepted without critical consideration). Nevertheless, even if we accept that the ontological status (or "reality") of music may be transformed during the process of learning, this does not mean that musical meaning would reside entirely in the mind of an individual subject. There is still an objective locus of music's meaning, one related to the tangible social-cultural practice of its transformation, where real people act together in real ways, manipulating real-world tools and materials with expressive artistic goals for themselves and others to enjoy.[35]

Accepting this multi-faceted and mutable ontological status for musical reality does not imply that music education should be entirely haphazard, or that we should forget practical guidance in pedagogical situations, leaving all decisions to the students. As indicated above, teachers can be as much part of the learning situations as are other significant persons or things. The point is that music's meanings should be realized in the kind of musical practice that mediates between different phases of the continuing learning process, arising "naturally" from the needs of the situation. Music, as much as anything else that is experienced as meaningful, is objectified in this process as the situation is defined in some manner for future orientation: the "content" of music, or its material signifier, is examined in this process for its potential for raising new ideas to be interpreted as habits of action that help us to pass from a problematic situation to another and, thus, that can be applied to similar cases in the future.

For instance, when a student picks up the "feel" of the rhythm section from a CD or live model and learns to apply it to another musical situation (e.g., as a drummer or a DJ) what she learns is not something that is merely copied from the recording, as a "given" musical reality, but a tool she can use in future musical situations in order to realize more musical meanings: the tool is a new habit. The "feel" can be of course freely experimented with, mutated, reapplied, even torn apart and re-assembled in new expressive forms.[36] Here, the most important and authentic thing for the learner is the potential of the "feel" for realizing future reality, not its original status as a part of a recording by someone else.[37]

Nowhere is this experimental attitude on musical potentiality as lavishly experimented with as in digital music culture, at least if judged in terms of its accessibility. While musical appropriation has been commonplace in probably every musical culture in history, the possibility of using samples of real sound added a new layer of transformative potential to musical expression in the late 1980s. In the last decade, rapidly developing (and less expensive) digital technology has truly revolutionized the musicing (both music making and listening) of professional and amateur musicians alike; it has produced a wealth of new tools, which make possible new creative ways of reworking and transforming music. With these practices, the questions of the authenticity and ontological status of musical works changes, and new challenges are presented for theorizing about these matters. For instance, when someone produces a musical "mash-up", a collage assembled from commercially recorded, sampled and/or electronically produced sounds, freely circulating whatever assets she finds useful for her expression; when she utilizes online communities to distribute her ideas to anyone interested; when someone else, perhaps living on another continent, picks up her ideas and develops them further, thus making them part of her own expression; passing her music back to the earlier author, and to other potentially interested musicers; when new musical communication is built from such practices, perhaps culminating in an operative musical collective with a commercial recording contract, the members of which might continue to live in different parts of the globe—all of these instances exemplify the way ICT may revolutionize the common practices of musicing.[38] It also suggests new ways of thinking about the ownership and authenticity of music.[39]

Many more examples could be mentioned of the ways in which the "reality" of music can be transformed to suit the expressive needs of whoever has the access to and interest in digital music tools and communicative practices. Nevertheless, what counts here is the potential these practices have for our philosophies, theories, and methods of music education. I think that by paying more attention to these kinds of practices we might expand, even transgress, some of the common ways in which music has been learned, produced, disseminated, and enjoyed in the last decades. Moreover, and perhaps most significantly, they might challenge our conventional ways of thinking about the way music can be conceived, both as an art form and as an educational subject. At present, popular music pedagogy may offer the best forum for discussing this, but the more wide reaching general implications of digital music culture should also be acknowledged. General music education is definitely one of the settings for experimenting with its creative potential—and also for becoming aware of its ideological underpinnings.

The garage rock band procedures mapped out by Green (2001) have not disappeared, of course—surely they still constitute a major part of how pop/rock based music is made and enjoyed, even if the musicians no longer have to keep to traditional instruments and roles.[40] However, the new possibilities introduced by digital music culture suggest that garage band-based practices point to only one pedagogical approach to popular music today.

The critical lesson here seems to be that music education in school, at its best, does not have to merely reflect "real-world music." As Green shows, it can also create new musical realities, perhaps ones more empowering than rock bands have produced so far. Pragmatism reminds us that the "reality" of music education is a point of reference to further things, things that do not have to remain remote to the students, as long as the continuum of intrinsic motivation necessary to all authenticity in learning is guaranteed. This kind of authenticity would affix the students' attention to the potential meaning of the musical tasks at hand as they orient their musical thinking to the future. While this authenticity can lead to critical musicality, in the sense that the students may learn to form "balanced judgement[s], allowing considered responses and evaluation of different musics in relation to a variety of criteria" (Green 2008, 89), to really open the critical potential of music, music education has to acknowledge its transformative power. Conscious of this power, music educators should seize the potential for musical meaning making wherever it is found.

# References

Allsup, R. 2008. "Creating an Educational Framework for Popular Music in Public Schools: Anticipating the Second-Wave." *Visions of Research in Music Education* 12. http://www-usr.rider.edu/~vrme/v12n1/vision/1%20AERA%20-%20Allsup.pdf

Ashworth, P. 2007. *Electrifying Music. A Guide to Using ICT in Music Education.* http://www.musicalfutures.org.uk/rdProjects_inner_ict.html

Born, G. 2005. "On Musical Mediation: Ontology, Technology and Creativity." *Twentieth Century Music* 2 (1): 7–36.

Clements, A. 2008. "Escaping the Classical Canon: Changing Methods through a Change of Paradigm." *Visions of Research in Music Education* 12. http://www-usr.rider.edu/~vrme/v12n1/vision/3%20AERA%20-%20Clements.pdf

Csikszentmihalyi, M. 1990. *Flow: The Psychology of Optimal Experience.* New York: Harper and Row.

—. 1996. *Creativity: Flow and the Psychology of Discovery and Invention.* New York: Harper Perennial.

Dewey, J. "The Later Works: 1925–1953 (LW)." In *The Collected Works of John Dewey 1882–1953*, ed. J. A. Boydston. Carbondale: Southern Illinois University Press.

—. "The Middle Works: 1899–1924 (MW)." In *The Collected Works of John Dewey 1882–1953*, ed. J. A. Boydston. Carbondale: Southern Illinois University Press.

Elliott, D. J. 1995. *Music Matters: A New Philosophy of Music Education.* Oxford: Oxford University Press.

Frierson-Campbell, C., ed. 2008. "Beyond Lucy Green. Operationalizing Theories of Informal Music Learning." *Visions of Research in Music Education* 12. http://www-usr.rider.edu/~vrme/

Green, L. 1988. *Music on Deaf Ears: Musical Meaning, Ideology, Education.* Manchester: Manchester University Press.

—. 1997. *Music, Gender, Education.* Cambridge: Cambridge University Press.

—. 2001. *How Popular Musicians Learn. A Way Ahead for Music Education.* Burlington: Ashgate.

—. 2003. "Why 'Ideology' Is Still Relevant To Music Education Theory." *Action, Criticism and Theory for Music Education* 2 (2): 3–21. http://act.maydaygroup.org/articles/Green2_2.pdf

—. 2006. "Popular Music Education in and for Itself, and for "Other" Music: Current Research in the Classroom." *International Journal of Music Education* 24 (2): 101–18.

—. 2008. *Music, Informal Learning and the School: A New Classroom Pedagogy.* Aldershot: Ashgate.

Jackson P. 1998. *John Dewey and the Lessons of Art.* New Haven: Yale University Press.

Määttänen, P. 1993. *Action and Experience: A Naturalistic Approach to Cognition.* PhD diss., University of Helsinki. Annales Academiae Scientiarum Fennicae. Dissertiones Humanarum Litterarum 64.

—. 2008. "Pragmatismin näkökulma taiteen tutkimiseen [The Pragmatist Perspective to Studying Art]." In *Pragmatismi filosofiassa ja yhteiskuntatieteessä* [Pragmatism in Philosophy and Social Sciences], eds. E. Kilpinen, O. Kivinen, and S. Pihlström, 231–56. Helsinki: Gaudeamus.

Mantere, M. 2008. "Musiikin medioituminen [Mediation of Music]." In *Johdatus musiikkifilosofiaan* [Introduction to Philosophy of Music]. eds. E. Huovinen, and J. Kuitunen, 131–76. Tampere: Vastapaino.

Moore, A. 1993. *Rock, the Primary Text: Developing a Musicology of Rock.* London: Ashgate.

NUMU 2008. The Future of Music. http://www.numu.org.uk

Ojala, J., M. Salavuo, M. Ruippo, and O. Parkkila, eds. 2006. *Musiikkikasvatusteknologia* [Technology of Music Education]. Keuruu: Suomen musiikkikasvatusteknologian seura.

Petraglia, J. 1998. *Reality by Design: The Rhetoric and Technology of Authenticity in Education.* Hillsdale: Lawrence Erlbaum Associates.

Regelski, T. 2000. "Critical Education: Culturalism and Multiculturalism." *Finnish Journal of Music Education* 5 (1–2): 120–47.

Rorty, R. 1972. "The World Well Lost." *Journal of Philosophy* 49: 649–65.

—. 1980. *Philosophy and the Mirror of Nature.* Oxford: Blackwell.

Shusterman, R. 1997. *Taide, elämä ja estetiikka. Pragmatistinen filosofia ja estetiikka* [Art, Life and Aesthetics. Pragmatist Philosophy and Aesthetics]. Tampere: Gaudeamus.

—. 2000. *Performing Live: Aesthetic Alternatives for the Ends of Art.* Ithaca: Cornell University Press.

—. 2002. *Surface and Depth. Dialectics of Criticism and Culture.* Ithaca: Cornell University Press.

Small, C. 1998. *Musicking: The Meaning of Performing and Listening.* London: Wesleyan University Press.

Swanwick, K. 1988. *Music, Mind and Education.* London: Routledge.

—. 1996. "Music Education: Is There Life Beyond School? A Response to David Elliott." *Finnish Journal of Music Education* 1 (1): 41–46.

Taylor, C. 1989. *Sources of the Self: The Making of Modern Identity*. New York: Cambridge University Press.

Taylor, T. 2001. *Strange Sounds: Music, Technology & Culture*. London: Routledge.

Väkevä, L. 2000. "Naturalizing Philosophy of Music Education." *Finnish Journal of Music Education* 5 (1–2): 73–83. Also published in *Action, Criticism & Theory for Music Education* 1 (1). http://act.mayday group.org/articles/Vakeva1_1.pdf

—. 2003. "Music Education as Critical Practice: A Naturalist View." *Philosophy of Music Education Review* 11 (2): 33–48.

—. 2004. *Kasvatuksen taide ja taidekasvatus. Estetiikan ja taidekasvatuksen merkitys John Deweyn naturalistisessa pragmatismissa* [Art of Education and Art education. The Meaning of Aesthetics and Art Education in John Dewey's Naturalist Pragmatism]. PhD diss., University of Oulu. Acta Universitatis Ouluensis. Series E, Scientiae rerum socialium, 68. http://herkules.oulu.fi/isbn9514273109/isbn9514273109.pdf

—. 2006a. "Teaching Popular Music in Finland: What's Up, What's Ahead?" *International Journal of Music Education Showcase* 24 (2): 129–34.

—. 2006b. "What Can a Philosophy of Music Education Gain From Naturalist Pragmatism? A Deweyan Approach to Musical Semiosis." In *Music and the Arts. Acta Semiotica Fennica XXIII—Approaches to Musical Semiotics 10*, ed. E. Tarasti, 224–32. Imatra and Helsinki: International Semiotics Institute—Semiotic Society of Finland.

—. 2007. "Art Education, The Art of Education and the Art of Life: Considering the Implications of Dewey's Later Philosophy to Art and Music Education." *Action, Criticism & Theory for Music Education* 6 (1). http://act.maydaygroup.org/articles/Vakeva6_1.pdf.

Väkevä, L., and H. Westerlund 2007. "The 'Method' of Democracy in Music Education." *Action, Criticism, and Theory for Music Education* 6 (4): 96–108. http://act.maydaygroup.org/articles/Väkevä_Westerlund 6_4.pdf

Vattimo, G. 1992. *Läpinäkyvä yhteiskunta* [Transparent Society]. Helsinki: Gaudeamus.

Westerlund, H. 2002. *Bridging Experience, Action, and Culture in Music Education*. PhD diss., Sibelius Academy. Studia 16. Helsinki: Sibelius Academy. http://ethesis.siba.fi/ethesis/files/isbn9529658982.pdf

—. 2006. "Garage Rock Band: A Future Model for Developing Musical Expertise?" *International Journal of Music Education* 24 (2): 119–25.

Westerlund, H., and M-L. Juntunen 2005. "Music and Knowledge in Bodily Experience." In *Praxial Music Education: Reflections and dialogues,* ed. D. Elliott, 112–22. New York: Oxford University Press.

# Notes

[1] Previously published in 2009 as "The World Well Lost, Found: Reality and Authenticity in Green's 'New Classroom Pedagogy'" in *Action, Criticism and Theory for Music Education* 8 (2): 7–34. Reprinted by permission of the editor.

[2] For instance, they do not cover the various ways music is produced, disseminated, and reproduced in the digital domain, from home studios to remix internet sites where people offer their beats and loops for creative recycling. Not all pop/rock music is made in the band format, either, even if its sounds usually emulate band instrument sounds.

[3] This is confirmed by numerous surveys made in the UK and elsewhere, including those reported in Green's research. Of course, there are differences related to cultural background, age, previous education, and other factors. Moreover, as Green (2008, 156) acknowledges, social pressure might encourage those teenagers who do like classical music to say otherwise when interviewed by a teacher-researcher (the same might apply in their motivation to reveal eclectic popular tastes).

[4] While the analogue has appeared in Western literature at least from 17th century plays to modern science fiction, it echoes here one of the key images of Richard Rorty's (1972, 1980) pragmatist turn against the realistic mirror conception of knowledge, viz. the critique towards the common sense realist notion that truth consists of a one-to-one relation between an idea (or a concept) and its object. Here the phrase works as a leading idea that encourages probing deeper into the notion that music could be made "real" for someone who happily ignores it. It also raises the question of what is at stake when some part of the musical world is judged to be more "real" than another. While I do not want to make too far-fetched assumptions of Green's use of terminology, I think her work raises interesting ideas regarding the ontological status of music in education, and the different ways it could be made an object of learning.

[5] In fact, I learned to play rock music in the early 1980s in much the same way that Green describes in her studies, and found the informal approach of the "garage" a lot more motivating (and thus, "real") than the formal procedures of music education.

[6] There are of course differences between educational cultures. In the UK and some other European countries (including Nordic countries), popular music has been part of both general, vocational, and university-level music education since at least the early 1970s (Green 2008, 3; Väkevä 2006a; Westerlund 2006).

[7] By "digital music culture", I refer to the practices and procedures applied in making, disseminating, and consuming music with the aid of digital instruments

and tools, and through the information networks which revolutionized these practices in the late 1990s. While garage rock band practices have been influenced by digital music culture, the latter has also introduced entirely new approaches. Making music in a computer environment with virtual instruments, distributing one's music freely to others in online communities, remixing the music of one's peers and one's idols online, taking part in conjoint web-based musical projects, DJ'ing, even downloading music to listen to and to process further in one's personal computer or mobile device can all be taken as instances of this culture. These procedures are integral to current popular music and have been for some time; I also believe that they hold much unexplored pedagogical potential in conjunction with more traditional pop/rock band practices.

[8] I do not mean to indicate that the people involved with Green's research would be indifferent to this area. However, Green (2008, 48) mentions that only one teacher in her project "integrated and alternated the project strategies with ICT." Some of the challenges involved are addressed in the materials available at the project website, www.musicalfutures.org (Ashworth 2007). NUMU, the project's public platform "to engage and motivate students through music", is also an indication that digital music culture is taken seriously by the developers (NUMU 2008). I am also aware of the rapid expansion of the research in music education technology, a major portion of which centers on digital music culture (e.g., Ojala et al. 2006). However, in this chapter, my primary intention is to focus on the pedagogical issues introduced by this culture as pointers to more general concerns.

[9] This seems to resonate with William James' notion that reality (and thus authenticity) simply indicates "relation to our emotional and active life" (quoted in Shusterman 2000, 84). From this standpoint, what interests us, what we "conceive with passion", is affirmative (84).

[10] This tradition also informs Green (2008, 110), although learning practices tried out in her study were not based on "any theory of child-centeredness or discovery learning, but on an empirical investigation and analysis of the real-life, informal learning practices."

[11] E.g., when rock versions of classical works are taken as an introduction to the "real thing", as in some Finnish school music books.

[12] For an introduction to Green's theoretical standpoint on musical meaning, see Green (1988, 2006).

[13] Whether all inter-sonic meanings in popular music are worth studying is left somewhat unclear by Green. In any case, she distances herself from value relativism when she writes that there is "'better' and more worthwhile" music, even if this "cuts across styles" (Green 2008, 150–151).

[14] As many pragmatists writing in the arts and education do not (see, e.g., Määttänen 2008; Shusterman 1997, 188–194, 2002, 203–205).

[15] One expression of this idea is the critique of culturalism in music education; see Regelski (2000).

[16] In line with Swanwick, Green (2008, 58–59) considers music making universally as a "form of play" that depends on rehearsal of imagination towards

"pure sensory delight" in sounds, transcending cultures (Swanwick 1988, 71, 1996).

[17] Although Green derives the term partly from the theories of critical education, in *A New Classroom Pedgogy* she does not really elaborate it in the terms of ideological critique, except in the sense that analytical listening to inter-sonic meanings can "lead to a greater awareness of how the music industry works", examples being that the students can become aware that some popular musicians mime on their recordings when performing live, and that some of the musicians work behind the scenes, not taking part in the live performance (Green 2008, 83–84; cf. Green 1988, 1997).

[18] For instance, one might ask what is the "natural" way to learn Beethoven? If there is such a way, surely it is not based on copying from the CDs and arranging the music for rock instruments, even if the latter would produce fruitful results. Or, what would be the "natural" way to learn music that was originally made as a conglomeration of loops and breaks in a digital audio workstation?

[19] In what follows, I use as a background the Deweyan naturalist pragmatist notions I have examined in several earlier writings; see e.g., Väkevä (2000, 2003, 2004, 2006b, 2007). Again, I do not claim that Green's ideas are based on naturalist pragmatism; I use the latter as an interpretative framework. Nevertheless, I do believe that all practical and critical approaches to music education share at least some pragmatist underpinnings, such as locating the focus of music's meaning to musical agency (cf. Green 2008, 60).

[20] Green (2008, 60) refers to both Small's (1998) and Elliott's (1995) versions of the term. In my own writing, I use Elliott's term "musicing" to refer to such straightforwardly musical practices as singing, playing musical instruments, composing, arranging, conducting, dancing to music, etc. Small's term "musicking" opens the field up to more sociological interpretation. I think there is room for both meanings in the philosophical discussion of music education, but the difference should be kept in mind.

[21] This was the song "Word Up" by Cameo, a 1980s funk hit. The song was chosen because it was thought to be in a style "broadly familiar" to most of the students, and because, being riff-based, it was "easy to remember and to play" (Green 2008, 26).

[22] In the latter, the song's riff-based structure was divided into separate tracks; the students were also handed partial worksheets that indicated the note names. (Green 2008, 26.)

[23] In the more freewheeling stages, some of the students actually used online services to obtain lyrics for their chosen songs (Green 2008, 46). The use of sound loops, MIDI files, video lessons and podcasts was not reported, nor was the use of web communities.

[24] This claim for balance is perhaps not unlike the one framed by Dewey in *Art as Experience*. According to Dewey, "*an* experience", or "esthetic experience" [sic] emerges from the everyday practical background of experiencing, mediated through action, when the latter achieves a balance between its pragmatic and emotional dimensions: when, in other words, the self becomes so concentrated on

the task at hand that the inner constitution of the situation is pervaded by a complete, unique and unifying "felt" quality, an emotional representation of an artistic work is "consummated" (Dewey 1934/LW 10, chapt. 3; Jackson 1998, 7–12; Väkevä 2004, chapt. 3.3; Väkevä and Westerlund 2007; Westerlund 2002).

[25] Not all project schools chose to proceed to this phase: some were able to run it only for two or three lessons at the end of the term. Nevertheless, this part of the project represented a bold attempt to test an "extreme case" of trying to learn music that most of the students did not like by applying the practices they were already committed to in other kinds of music (Green 2008, 150).

[26] In the stage 6, the music was picked from British TV advertisements: the implication being that even if the pieces did not really interest the students, most had at least heard them beforehand. In turn, the repertoire studied in stage 7 was mostly chosen on the criteria that it would be unfamiliar to the students. The pieces in stage 6 were copied entirely by ear: in stage 7, the students were also provided a rehearsal record with "broken-down" parts, reminiscent of stage 2 (Green 2008, 151–153).

[27] Taken that for many of the students it does not really seem to be "natural", or authentic, to learn, for example, Beethoven's music by ear and to arrange his music freely for rock instruments. Of course, one might argue that these kinds of authenticity claims can—and even should—be contested by music education that strives for critical understanding of the workings of any music culture.

[28] I find this idea at least thematically related to Elliott's (1995) praxialist creed that all music is, at root, practice, and a musical practice can be learned by anyone who has access to its meanings, processed through active involvement with music in a social-cultural setting. For a pragmatist critique of some of the philosophical implications of this view, see Westerlund (2002), Westerlund and Juntunen (2005) and Väkevä and Westerlund (2007).

[29] Actually, the interviews revealed that only some of the pupils identified the pieces as music from TV (Green 2008, 158). Perhaps a more interesting case of delineations helping a student to tolerate classical music was that of a student called Justin (166). Despite his strong personal hostility towards this music, an attitude that did not really seem to change over the course of the project, Justin tolerated "Für Elise", and actually "produced good stuff" with it because of the personal delineations that remained for him (as with many other students, he had also played the piece before) (166). As Green suggests (167), another possibility might be that Justin did not actually assign this piece to the "classical" category because he actually liked it—the assumption being, that he classified classical music simply as music he did not like. This remark takes us back to reconsider the possibility that perhaps it is not just the identity of a particular work but an entire musical category that can change as a result of the approach taken.

[30] For instance, take the case of "Hooked on Classics", a series of albums released in the early 1980s. The genre can be called "classical disco", but few would probably really locate this music in the classical music category, as it was meant primarily for the disco floor. Of course, this raises a common issue in critical musicology: that music's identity may be defined by its function rather than by its

form. Green's argument is clearly that the inter-sonic meanings are an integral part of the identity of music and at least virtually autonomous of its delineations, including, I presume, its cultural uses.

[31] Also, the original speed of a recording was taken to be an integral part of the right "feel", as in popular music where it usually is marked by the beat (Green 2008, 163).

[32] The situation is similar when one first studies the "It is easy to play" versions of classical repertoire: the work may not be authentic, but the easier version may offer valuable first steps to the "real thing." The same practice is common in popular music where different "broken-down" versions often define the stylistic properties for a beginning student. As indicated, this procedure was also applied in Green's research. Of course, a significant difference is that classical music (or much of Western art music in general) is usually conceived as consisting of original works of art, the identity of which is for its most important parts relayed by notation, framing its status as an entity.

[33] A critical voice could remark that ideological constraints may not be mitigated, just neglected. Following Shusterman (2002), I would suggest that there might always be room for this kind of neglect, as the sheer somatic joy of practicing the art may in itself be transformative, even transgressive. However, to be conscious of the dialectic between what Shusterman indicates as art's "surface" and "depth"— viz. its aesthetic qualities and ideological conceptions—is more of a safe bet if one wants to be able to achieve any socially constructive critique through art education.

[34] While this might sound harsh, there may be a grain of truth in it, for Western tradition has certainly defined music ontologically in such a way that this kind of a free appropriation would be considered at best ignorant; at worst, a major transgression.

[35] This can be also argued on naturalistic premises, where the epistemological relation of a subject reflecting on an object does not suffice as a rationalization of meaning. Reality, from this standpoint, is not something we project on our mind's screen, and label with meaning, but something with which we are already entangled with as living organisms in innumerable ways, as meaningfully mediated by action. Meaning is from this standpoint a property of action, or more accurately a "habit of action" that refers to future possibilities (see, e.g., Määttänen 1993, 2008; Väkevä 2006b).

[36] This is what happens when breaks are sampled from records, sliced up with recycling software and reassembled (and often re-mixed) for further use as beats and loops. It is not only the order of the sound event that changes; often what is sought in this way is a new "feel", one recognized as a potential in the source material. Of course, this is what drummers and other rhythm section players have done for ages when composing new patterns: the logic of the creative transmutation remains the same. Nevertheless, digital tools have enhanced this creative potential vastly.

[37] However, the choice of the source material can also be a critical factor in musical expression based on recycling. For instance the common practice of circulating James Brown and Parliament/Funkadelic breaks in 1980s Hip-Hop

added an important layer of authenticity with crucial political allusions for those that wanted to take them—in addition to helping to establish a killer groove.

[38] This example is based on what I witnessed in the late 1990s when visiting a commune in the most northern part of Finland where my department was organizing distance learning. The issue came out of the preliminary discussions with the students; interestingly, the local teachers and parents seemed to be unaware of the fact that some of their young were involved with international online communities of music. The occasion definitely opened my eyes to the possibilities of musical globalization.

[39] An example of how tangled the issues of ownership and authenticity can get in the digital domain is when a professional act publicly encourages its fans to download its music freely, in a form of public domain (or Creative Commons) sound files, ready to be reworked in personal digital audio workstations—and when it further offers the fans a remix site where they can upload their own efforts for each other to listen to, discuss, and develop further. A famous promoter for this kind of open policy, and also a pioneer in the creative transformation of rock as a digitally produced, disseminated, consumed, and recycled art form, is Nine Inch Nails (aka NIN) , an industrial metal act built around the creative energy of Trent Reznor.

[40] NIN is again a good example of this, for Reznor produced its early records largely by himself, using digital instruments along with more traditional rock tools. This is especially notable in that the parent genre is heavy metal, often criticized for sticking to traditional models both aesthetically and ideologically. Digital tools have also influenced the use of guitars, basses and drums in recording and performing, opening a new wealth of possibilities in sound construction with these instruments. However, the most fascinating example of the creative dialectic between old and new ways of producing sound, and one that really "cuts" across historical authenticity is probably DJ'ing (or, rather, turntabling) with vinyl records and the re-appropriation of such practices with new digital turntables and DJ software.

# PART II

# CHAPTER FOUR

# CATEGORIES AND MUSIC TRANSMISSION[1]

# GREG GATIEN

Lucy Green's (2008) *Music, Informal Learning and the School: A New Classroom Pedagogy* gives rise to an interesting corollary. Does the manner of music's transmission inform our understanding of a musical category? While categories of music (Western classical, popular, jazz, etc.) can be difficult to define according to strict musical characteristics, a better understanding of musical transmission—of how a music is passed on and learned—may provide insight into the nature of a musical category itself. Green's work, which associates informal learning with popular music practice, presents this possibility. Such an understanding offers potential for music educators and students to become increasingly clear about what and how they are teaching and learning.

This essay uses the jazz tradition as a means of exploring the understanding of a musical category through its modes of transmission. The jazz tradition has synergies with Green's research because it is a music that has made the transition from informal to formal realms of learning.[2] The formalization of jazz education, within teaching institutions, has in recent decades focused more on "what" has been transmitted than "how" that transmission has occurred, affecting, among other things, our understanding of jazz as a category. This essay proposes that jazz and popular music can be linked through pedagogy by highlighting their shared cultural origins and overlapping communities in ways that further inform the idea of category as a pedagogically-driven construct.

Chronologically, I will begin at the end. Formal Jazz Education[3] has frequently been a controversial topic. Several scholars and performers have suggested that Jazz Education represents an adopted (or much adapted) method of transmission, which changes our understanding of the musical tradition itself.[4] The traditional ways of transmitting this music have been changed, compromised, or subverted to formal methods of instruction that fit more comfortably in the formal habitat, or are more efficient (perhaps even more effective, at least in achieving certain results) in the context of classroom or group settings. The discussion around how jazz is currently transmitted provides insight into how formal teaching and learning has affected our understanding of jazz as a musical category.

Jazz is a precursor to popular music as a music that has already shifted from informal to formal realms of transmission. In doing so, the jazz tradition has faced certain obstacles. These obstacles are informative in understanding how Jazz Education became framed as a valid course of study, and how its accompanying jazz pedagogies were developed. This context is particularly relevant in relating formal jazz pedagogies to both informal jazz pedagogies and the pedagogy developed by Green. Jazz is also an important precursor to popular music as the first music of the West African Diaspora to move into the "formal" (institutional) arena. It has become increasingly important to understand jazz's process of formalization as other musics from this Diaspora become introduced to "formal" music education. It is thus necessary to present some of the principal motivations behind the efforts to formalize Jazz Education—including establishing legitimacy—in order to ultimately view jazz as part of a broader musical tradition, and understand the potential of linking the modes of transmission to the music being transmitted

All of this will bring me to the chronological beginning, with a brief examination of how jazz was transmitted prior to its formalization. The modes of transmission employed by Green (developed through her study of popular musicians) are, as mentioned, similar to modes of transmission utilized by jazz musicians prior to Jazz Education. In showing these similarities, I focus on select musicians who have emerged as skilled and valuable jazz practitioners prior to the advent of Jazz Education.[5] This observation serves to demonstrate ways in which Jazz Education has changed the modes of transmission in the jazz tradition.[6] More importantly, it accounts for my strongest reaction to Green's work. By establishing the commonalities between the traditional transmission processes of these two types of music, the issue of musical category emerges. One side of this requires consideration of the possibility that the admission of jazz into formal structures was, in fact, the admission of a broader musical tradition. Another is the possibility that Green's work might suggest that a category can more aptly be defined by its modes of transmission than by its musical characteristics.

Attempts to define jazz as a musical category have proven difficult and prompted much debate. The difficulty of defining jazz has affected Jazz Education from its inception. As jazz became part of formal education (alongside its movement into other formal settings—concert halls, arts organizations), there became a need to develop an idea of what is to be taught and what kind of music counted as "jazz." Much of the controversy associated with the development of Jazz Education has resulted from the elusiveness of a categorical definition of jazz. Certain scholars and educators have viewed "jazz" as a relatively strict body of more-or-less canonical works ("America's classical music"[7]). Others viewed any attempt at strict definition as running contrary to their ideas of jazz (Deveaux 1998, 485–486, 504–505).[8] In order to frame the controversy, a brief description of the emergent and predominant pedagogies is useful.

The process by which jazz became an accepted part of music education curricula has resulted in some generally recognizable pedagogies that are supported by a wealth of published materials. Many of these pedagogies can certainly be viewed as emerging from a particular understanding of the jazz tradition. Equally important, however, are the ways in which these pedagogies represent a departure from that tradition. Many of the ways of transmission that have arisen in support of Jazz Education tend to focus on the "teachable" aspects of jazz. Among other things, this results in a premium being placed on an analytical understanding of canonical jazz improvisers that can be translated into print materials and play-alongs; a jazz ensemble repertoire that focuses on great works and is largely transmitted through notation; a history that focuses on a linear progression and stops when that progression becomes problematic, generally somewhere in the 1960s.

In North American public schools, these pedagogies typically involve the use of the "jazz ensemble" (big band) as the primary vehicle for jazz instruction. The jazz ensemble—the staffing of which generally adheres to the model provided by the Count Basie Band (among others)—supports enough students to make reasonable class sizes, and allows for certain aspects of jazz to be accessed and learned by students: history, theory, improvisation, certain kinds of reiterative pulse associated with jazz, and musical independence (when educators are able to follow the "one player per part" rule of jazz ensemble staffing). The bulk of teaching and learning takes place, however, through the rehearsing of repertoire. For better or worse, it allows music educators to function in ways that are often indistinguishable from rehearsing other large instrumental ensembles— pedagogies rooted in orchestral and wind band instruction can be used in jazz ensemble rehearsals, providing some level of comfort to non-jazz trained music educators (conducting, rehearsing notes and rhythms from a score, tuning, balancing, blending, and sight-reading all come to mind). In university-based programs, jazz instruction typically involves discrete courses in jazz history, jazz theory, jazz improvisation, jazz ensembles (often large and small), jazz pedagogy, private lessons, jazz aural skills, jazz composing and arranging, keyboard skills, and transcription and analysis.

In supporting these pedagogies, there has developed a sizable body of teaching materials: jazz theory books, jazz history/appreciation texts, jazz play-along recordings, jazz charts (many written with specific pedagogical aims: developing improvisational skill, accessing important historical works, or developing a sense of the "jazz canon", appealing to students through accessing popular tunes or grooves), and "how-to-improvise" methods. It has been asserted that these Jazz Education pedagogies, and their accompanying materials, are largely reflective of an unquestioning adoption of musicological practices in the codification of jazz practices and in the construction of a coherent jazz history. Music that is analyzable according to pre-existing academic methods and ideals receives the lion's share of attention in institutional settings (Walser 1993, 347–348).[9] The pedagogies are constructed along the lines of studying great works of great artists, or preparing students for this study, and the value in the study comes from the musical attributes of the music—those things that can be analyzed.

Writing in 1995, jazz pianist and scholar Ben Sidran provides a sense of this concern:

> In many ways, these are the best of times and the worst of times for jazz. On the one hand, music schools are turning out thousands of thoroughly prepared young players who, at an earlier age, are better versed in the grammar and idioms of jazz than ever before. The recorded evidence speaks eloquently of the "success" of our education system . . . On the other hand, most of the new jazz prodigies don't sound like anybody . . . Why doesn't today's education lead to the development of style? (Sidran 1995, 3)

Noted jazz performer, composer and educator Bob Brookmeyer echoed this sentiment in speaking of difficulties in writing for modern musicians: "All of us (jazz composers) have structural problems with solos, where to put them, how they belong, because the soloists have become so generic" (Ramsey 1999, 92). These two musicians speak to a broad concern that the creation of a canonical, codified way of understanding and learning jazz has led to a loss of individuality. Teachers using the same approaches, students learning the same music, the same patterns, and the same recordings in the same ways has led to an increasingly generic generation of musicians.[10]

From another perspective, jazz pianist and educator Michael Cain, writing in 2007, states that " . . . I found that jazz pedagogy in the academy and jazz pedagogy among practitioners, as I came to know it, often had very little in common" (Cain 2007, 35). Illustrating this observation, Cain compares the audition processes he has experienced as a professional jazz musician (processes which Cain rightly asserts can be understood through and rooted in jazz practices, jazz pedagogy, and jazz history) and those auditioning processes used in university-based jazz programs. His comparison results in the observation that the two processes, although linked somehow through a shared musical tradition, are not recognizably related. Cain states that:

> No jazz school would consider auditioning students the way Jack DeJohnette and Robin Eubanks audition their players, and yet they are two musicians most jazz schools would want their graduates to work with. (Cain 2007, 36)

Where Sidran asserts that institutions are training jazz musicians who are "thoroughly prepared" (Sidran 1995, 3), Cain illustrates that this preparation does not always line up with the expectations of the domain itself. This disconnect between the academic instruction of jazz musicians and the practices of tradition-steeped professional jazz musicians[11] can be interpreted as, at least in part, a result of the ways in which the study of jazz became "formalized." Implicit in this observation is the possibility that through adopting particular ways of teaching the jazz tradition, those musicians that study long enough have been prepared for a different kind of music and either need to retrain in the community of musicians, or make a different kind of music.

Historian Gary Tomlinson speaks of the formalization of jazz as having followed a European notion of high culture in the creation of a jazz canon, and that this notion of canon informs the majority of pedagogies associated with Jazz Education. He states that canonical construction, largely through its exclusionary function, results in a narrowing of what can be studied, what can be learned, and how we can teach. Furthermore, Tomlinson states that the canon, underpinning "jazz courses around the country" features,

> Exemplars of timeless aesthetic value instead of being understood—as the European works next door should also be understood but too rarely are—as human utterances valued according to the dialogical situations in which they were created and are continually recreated. (Tomlinson 1996, 76–77)

David Ake, also a pianist, scholar and educator, further articulates this concern. In examining the formalized study of canonical jazz saxophonist John Coltrane's music, Ake describes how certain aspects of jazz lend themselves to formal study, while others do not. In this case the earlier work of Coltrane is "teachable" (more easily lending itself to analysis and therefore can be systematized) while his later work, from his "avant-garde" period, is largely ignored. Ake attributes this decision to the ease with which Coltrane's earlier work fits into the mold of a "European" model of music education. Ake makes two observations that are pertinent to this discussion. The first is that through selectively excluding/ignoring the later work of Coltrane "a type of musical 'half truth'" is "passed on from teacher and institution to student" (Ake 2002, 145). The second is that ". . . jazz pedagogy's classical biases result . . . in a narrower understanding of what counts as 'jazz' in America today" (145).

Robert Walser, like Tomlinson, strongly questions the ways in which the construction of a jazz canon based upon Western European notions of analysis and the objectification of certain musical works, affects the musical tradition. Walser, focusing on the improvisations of Miles Davis, writes:

> The uneasiness many critics display toward Miles Davis' "mistakes", and their failure to explain the power of his playing suggest that there are important gaps in the paradigms of musical analysis and interpretation that dominate jazz studies. (Walser 1993, 345)

The jazz tradition, although having gained recognition as "a music worthy of study", has arguably reached a position where that study has become a study of past accomplishments deemed canonically significant. Guitarist Pat Metheny, in his keynote address at the 2001 IAJE Convention, expressed reservations about this model in stating:

> The attempts to make jazz something more like classical music, like baroque music for instance, with a defined set of rules and regulations and boundaries and qualities that MUST be present and observed and respected at all times, have always made me uncomfortable. (Metheny 2001)[12]

Keith Jarrett, a jazz musician of comparable achievement to Metheny, stated a similar concern towards viewing the tradition as a set of past accomplishments for study and preservation. In asking the question "When did jazz become a theory—a thing, not a process; a package, not an experience?", Jarrett suggests that canon-building changed the tradition (Jarrett 1996, 36). Jarrett furthers this assertion by saying: "Jazz is about closeness to the material, a personal dance with the material, not the material itself" (36, 102). While Jarrett's essay does not focus on the role of Jazz Education, Walser does make this connection. He argues that the dominant methods of analyzing and transmitting jazz, adopted from pre-existing practices of analyzing and transmitting Western art music, fail in helping us understand jazz (Walser 1993, 359).[13]

Jazz Education's adoption of formal modes of transmission has been criticized not only for its inadequacies in developing an understanding of jazz, but for failing to substantively change formal music education. Put another way, formal music education was viewed as a means of transmitting jazz rather than jazz viewed as a means of transmitting music. This is in contrast to Green, who investigates the inclusion of informal learning practices as a means to "recognize, foster and reward a range of musical skills and knowledge that have not previously been emphasized in music education" (Green 2008, 1). Wayne Bowman wrote in 2004 that: " . . . adding jazz to the curriculum did little to transform the way music educators conceptualized music, or curriculum" (Bowman 2004, 30). Bringing jazz into the fold of "formal" music has changed the kind of music we can study and practice, the kinds of ensembles we offer our students, the kinds of instruments, and the kinds of histories and theories we can learn. It has not substantially changed the ways in which we can study and teach music.

Based upon all of this, it is facile to conclude that Jazz Education got it wrong. This conclusion, however, would fail to articulate what Jazz Education represents to music education and how it has changed our ideas of formal music education. Instead, it is useful to understand the circumstances under which jazz became formalized. By looking at the ways in which jazz entered the academy, it becomes possible to see a larger and longer process at work. This process has not only provided continued scrutiny of itself and its own practices, but has established the possibility of a musical tradition other than Western classical music being accepted into our educational institutions.

The inclusions of "jazz" into the curricula of Western schools and universities undoubtedly required compromise. Formal Music Education was required to acknowledge that jazz was worth learning—an acknowledgment that was problematic in many ways, and took a considerable amount of time. In 1924, *The Etude*, the most popular American music teachers' journal, grappled with "the jazz issue" (in ways that seem remarkably similar to contemporary concerns over the inclusion of various popular musics). The magazine emphatically stated that addressing the "jazz problem" was not an endorsement of jazz. The only positive attributes of jazz that the magazine's editor seemed to acknowledge was that its popularity increased the number of students studying wind instruments (Walser 1999, 41–54). A popular textbook, published in 1941 and used in university music education classes, stated that:

> Jazz and art music are at opposite poles of the musical earth. In most respects they contradict one another . . . educationally they are antagonistic . . . [jazz] tears down what the music educator is trying to build up; and it is because the pupil hears so much more jazz than real music that his artistic tastes tends to deteriorate. (Dykema and Gehrekens 1941, 203)

There are many personalized accounts that point to the powerful resistance that jazz faced within academia. One example comes from Benny Golson, a renowned jazz saxophonist, composer and educator. In 1997, Golson stated:

> When I went to college, I could have been expelled for playing jazz. The official attitude about jazz was not good then. I had to practice my saxophone in the laundry room of the dormitory at night because I could not enter college and practice the saxophone as a part of the studies. I had to major on the clarinet. It seems to me that it was a European thing they were trying to uphold. (Fisher 2003, 11–15)[14]

While Golson did not offer a date, the experience he described would have occurred at his Alma Mater, Howard University, between 1947 and 1951 (Kernfeld 1994, 436). Somewhat ironically, Howard University's website boasts that in 1970 it became the first primarily Black university to institute a jazz studies program.[15] Jazz pianist and educator Bill Dobbins describes a similar experience, roughly twenty years after Golson's collegiate career:

> Those of us who formed the school's (Kent State University between 1964 and 1970) first ongoing jazz ensemble were thrown out of practice rooms, prohibited from signing out school instruments to play jazz and, in general, strongly discouraged from having anything to do with America's greatest musical contribution to world culture. (Dobbins 1988, 30)

The idea of including jazz in the practice rooms, classrooms, boardrooms, rehearsal halls, and performance spaces of educational institutions was clearly controversial. The University of North Texas, which is credited with having the first jazz major, would not initially use the word "jazz" in its calendar, calling it "Dance Band" instead (Gennari 2006, 213).

Wrapped up in these illustrations of the resistance that jazz faced (which are neither extraordinary nor universal) from formal music education are notions of art music, race, and values. For the purposes of this discussion, it is enough to recognize that these were significant obstacles for early jazz educators to negotiate. Not only does this partially account for ways in which the development of jazz education can be described as "haphazard" (Porter 1989, 137), but it also helps in understanding the ways in which it unfolded. Undoubtedly, those advocating the inclusion of jazz in formal education responded to specific obstacles in ways that must inform our understanding of the resulting emphases we now see in Jazz Education. Issues of cultural significance (legitimacy), racial equality and tolerance, and popularity emerge as central motivating factors.

Leonard Feather, whose work at New York's New School for Social Research in the 1940s is considered a landmark in jazz education, stated that one of his "principal, vital objectives in giving these classes was the inclusion in the students' minds of an acceptance and appreciation of the black man's central role in jazz" (Feather 1981, 21). Feather communicates an idea that gained currency over time: jazz was useful to schools because it provided a venue through which African-American achievement could be justly celebrated.

In late 1957 the Lenox School of Jazz was founded. The Lenox School lasted for four summers and was an outgrowth of an academically oriented lecture series (begun several years earlier) dedicated to a discussion of jazz. The intent of the lecture series was to demonstrate that "jazz is a significant contribution to American culture" (Niccoli 1951, 18). The Lenox School of Jazz retained this idea as part of its objectives, stating in its 1957 brochure that, among other things, it would offer students "a point of view toward jazz as a significant and vital art form of our time."[16] This is a good example of jazz making a case for it being worthy of study as high art, refuting deep-seated notions that it is some lower form of music. The Lenox School has been described as "a first of its kind institution aimed at establishing an academic basis for the study of jazz performance, theory, and history" (Gennari 2006, 210). The curriculum at Lenox, while involving small ensembles and a unique approach to private instruction (students were often deliberately assigned to master jazz musicians who played different instruments to avoid direct imitation), would be palatable to most music schools—that is to say jazz-specific classes in history, theory, composition, and improvisation were offered. Perhaps it is not coincidental that the 1967 Tanglewood Symposium also took place in Lenox. This symposium concluded, among other things (including that popular music ought to be studied in school), that jazz "should be an important component of American music education" (Porter 1989, 134).

Many of the current practices associated with Jazz Education can be linked with this need to legitimize the music, either as a form of high art or as a means of developing racial tolerance in a racially intolerant society, in order for it to gain acceptance. Western classical music tools of analysis were an obvious and highly effective way of demonstrating the intricacies of jazz in ways that were irrefutable to formal institutions. Walser writes that "it seems natural enough that people who are trying to win more respect for the music they love should do so by making comparisons with the most prestigious music around, classical music" (Walser 1993, 347). The fact that jazz instruction was being modeled upon a Western classical music framework must have also been just as obvious.

It is also demonstrable that factors of economics and popular demand were involved. Educational institutions could view jazz as a way to meet a particular demand, and thereby increase enrolment and revenue (Murphy 1994, 35). Jazz scholar John Gennari states that the societal changes of the 1960s—a shifting jazz audience, a shrinking jazz audience, fundamental changes to the ways in which Americans occupied their leisure time (television, for example), increasing awareness of issues surrounding civil rights, among others—was "a boon to jazz education" (Gennari 2006, 213). Professional jazz musicians, faced with these changes in the 1960s, could view "formal" education as a means of supplementing their income. Established musicians, aware that their music was popular among college-aged students, discovered that universities were among the most lucrative venues for their work.[17] Colleges and universities began meeting this demand—both through presenting jazz performances on campus and developing curricula that included some study of the jazz tradition.

Establishing the legitimacy and value of jazz took precedence over establishing the ways in which it would be/should be transmitted to students. The transfer of Western ideas regarding teaching method, canon construction, and analytical models into Jazz Education was largely unquestioned (Walser 1993, 348).[18] Establishing jazz as good for society, good for business, and as art music worthy of inclusion alongside the Western canon seems to have required the favoring of teaching methodologies that were familiar and accepted. This set of decisions lay the groundwork for the complexity and controversy that would surround the questions "what are we teaching?" and "why are we teaching this?"

If the social upheaval of the 1960s created favorable conditions for institutional jazz education, the 1970s is often seen as the decade in which jazz became an accepted reality in formal educational settings.[19] Given this timeline, along with the benefit and curiosity of hindsight, it is irresistible to ask why jazz was the African-American "other" music chosen for inclusion. While we have seen that considerable effort has been expended to confer the status of "art" music on jazz, it is reasonable to suggest that by the 1970s African-American music included other "types", and that jazz had been eclipsed in popularity by several of them. It is equally reasonable to suggest that the blues would have been considered of equal historical significance to jazz and therefore just as worthy of formal study.[20] Jazz was selected (instead of blues, soul, R&B, or rock) for reasons that seem to have included emergent concerns over its future as a musical tradition.

Cannonball Adderley, an alto saxophonist who gained prominence through his association with Miles Davis and continued leading his own groups into the 1970s, began his career as a music educator in Florida. In 1969, Cannonball addressed the question of why jazz would be the African-American music to enter formal music education.[21] In an interview with Leonard Feather, he stated that:

> Although there's more interest in performing music today than ever before, the standards for performance are probably lower than ever. When I was a kid, I knew I had to be a pretty good saxophone player to get a job . . . Today, though, a kid may be playing guitar just for his own enjoyment, then find that someone who doesn't play any better than he does has just earned $5,000,000 with a couple of records. There's not enough public admiration for truly great artistry. The only ones who are lionized and revered are the old men, like Pablo Casals. People select these institutions to idolize rather than the artistic level to emulate. We're hoping, with our college tours to stimulate young musicians into wanting to improve themselves. (Cannonball 1973, 32)

Cannonball expresses the widely held view that his musical tradition represented and required significant musical accomplishment. He also demonstrates that the very same upheaval that represented a "boon" to jazz education in the 1960s was a threat to the economics of being a jazz musician, and therefore a threat to the survival of his musical tradition. In dealing with these issues, Cannonball made the logical conclusion that the future of jazz could be secured through education. His desire to see his musical traditions and practices preserved can be read as a foreshadowing of the ideas presented by Wynton Marsalis, a jazz musician closely associated with the "neo-classical" view of jazz.

Neo-classicism arose after the 1970s. It clearly supposes a classicized tradition for its own referential existence, and therefore is committed to a canonical vision of jazz and its supporting Jazz Education. Marsalis, an eloquent and well-positioned jazz musician and educator, has served as a lightning rod for the neo-classical view of jazz based on statements like:

> People think I'm trying to say jazz is greater than pop music. I don't have
> to say that, that's obvious. But I don't even think about it that way. The
> two musics say totally different things. Jazz is not pop music, that's all.
> (Zabor and Garbarini 1999, 340)[22]

Marsalis would get more specific about his views in a piece written in
1988 for the New York Times, writing that "rock isn't jazz and new age
isn't jazz, and neither are pop or third stream. There may be much that is
good in all of them, but they aren't jazz" (Marsalis 1999, 335). Like
Adderley, Marsalis identified "popular" genres as threatening to the future
of jazz. Marsalis perceived the threat not simply as jazz being eclipsed by
more popular types ("easier" and more lucrative, in the view of Adderley)
of American-born musics, but also as a blurring of boundaries between
types of music. Pop musicians performing at jazz festivals capitalize on
the cultural cache of an association with art music while audiences are
misled into believing they have experienced quality art-music, all of which
serves to dilute and diminish the "real" music. Marsalis, often maligned
for presenting a narrow definition of jazz, presents a view of jazz that is
essential for a canonical understanding. He makes an emphatic case for
what gets included and what gets left out. As the focus of neo-classicism
and its associated controversy, Marsalis has instigated much valuable
debate.

Adderley is equally useful for jazz educators and scholars in rethinking
the idea of "what gets included." As examples of jazz musicians who
turned to educational settings as a source of work, members of the
Cannonball Adderley Quintet (in the late 1960s) developed a seminar on
"jazz and black-oriented music" that was delivered on university campuses
(Wilson 1972, 13).[23] Cannonball's seminar, while maintaining a focus on
jazz, was promoted as a "two-day program of lectures, seminars and
demonstrations on black music" (Wilson 1969). "Black music" was
defined as "music created by black people" and, because the seminar
explored the relationships between popular music and jazz, can be
interpreted as the American part of the West African Diaspora. Adderley
aimed to incorporate musicians from outside the jazz idiom as part of the
seminar, and considered jazz to be an aspect of a larger field of musical
study. In 1969 he expressed a desire that these seminars would "set a
precedent with jazz so that other areas of black music can be explored as
well" (Gleason 1969, 59). While it would be inaccurate to suggest that
Adderley would support the notion that jazz and popular music were the
same musical traditions (he stated the opposite on many occasions), these
seminars espouse a notion that jazz and popular musics have a shared
ancestry. This leads to the notion that while each type of American-born

Diaspora music (jazz, soul, funk, R&B, rock, country and western, pop, etc.) can be understood (and therefore taught) as a discrete tradition, each is also part of a larger, shared musical and cultural tradition. When the jazz tradition was admitted into the academic arena perhaps, as Cannonball had hoped and Green's work might indicate, jazz set a precedent by which this larger tradition also gained, even if tacitly, a foothold.

We can understand that the formalization of jazz pedagogies emerged out of utility and in ways that accommodated the prevailing values and priorities of the institutions involved. Jazz Education has ultimately functioned in ways that have substantively impacted our institutions and the music itself. While the impact of Jazz Education has often and justifiably been framed negatively, its very existence (along with the accompanying controversies) has likely informed the kinds of thinking about music and music education that lead to the sort of work Lucy Green has produced. Likewise, in order for Green's work to have greater meaning for Jazz Education, we must place formal jazz pedagogies into context with the modes of transmission relied upon by jazz before its "formalization."

Prior to Jazz Education, as mentioned above, jazz was transmitted in ways that are demonstrably similar to those described by Lucy Green. Students did not have access to books or printed music that codified the process of developing fluency, and therefore were left to their own devices. Sonny Rollins, in writing a foreword to John Fordham's book *Jazz*, states:

Nothing like this was available for my generation when we were growing up. We had to pick up what we could when we could and where we could. It was mainly recordings in those days until we were old enough to be admitted to nightclubs . . . (Rollins 1994)

The informal transmission of jazz is largely documented through oral histories and personal accounts. Interaction between jazz students and jazz teachers was not common or required (although by no means unknown), and tended to be in the form of one-on-one instruction often instigated by the aspiring youngster. There are many examples of young jazz musicians studying with older jazz musicians—Johnny Hodges getting lessons with Sidney Bechet; young bebop musicians receiving insights from Dizzy Gillespie; Lee Konitz's studies with Lennie Tristano; Sonny Rollins' and John Coltrane's experiences with Thelonious Monk—but fewer examples of study that occurred as either initial or regular instruction. Lennie Tristano, a rare jazz musician whose reputation is balanced between his accomplishments as a performer and as an educator, worked primarily with advanced students. There are numerous examples of celebrated jazz musicians who began with non-jazz music instruction, often in "formal" classroom settings, including many of the musicians mentioned or quoted in this essay.

Green states that jazz musicians have traditionally learned under the guidance of their elders—"'apprenticeship training'—whereby young musicians are introduced, and explicitly trained or just generally helped by an individual adult or a 'community of expertise'" (Green 2008, 6). Green's observation is intended to distinguish the learning practices of popular musicians from those used by jazz musicians. This is a commonly held view, and can be supported with several examples. As a distinguishing element between jazz and popular music, however, two points must be considered. The first is that this distinction often fails to account for initial learning processes that jazz musicians engaged in prior to their interactions with elder jazz musicians. The second is that the role assumed by the jazz elder often resembles the role of the teacher in Green's pedagogy.

As one example, Rollins refers to formative experiences he had with Thelonious Monk and Bud Powell. Rollins describes these experiences as taking place in the context of playing or rehearsing, but nonetheless ascribes formative educational value to them. Many jazz musicians speak of their interactions with elders in ways that, while not contradicting Green's statement, indicate an absence of "explicit" instruction in favor of an "experience" heavy approach to the sharing of expertise. The following exchange between Rollins and George Goodman provides one example: "I had wanted to ask Rollins what he learned from Monk. He answered me in a word: 'Everything'. What was it that Monk taught him? 'Nothing'." (Goodman 1999, 84). Rollins provided a more detailed description of his "apprenticeship" with Monk:

> Every day after school I would go to Thelonious Monk's place and practice with his band. He never really told me what to play, because I guess he respected my playing. But I learned a lot from Monk just hanging out with him (Nisenson 2000, 31).

On one level, it is clear that in order for Rollins to function in this kind of instructional setting, he needed to have certain fundamental skills in place—Monk did not need to teach him saxophone fingerings, for example. On another level, it is clear that working with Monk seems to have addressed all aspects of Rollins' musicianship. We can conclude that "learning through doing" was a guiding principle of this kind of pedagogical apprenticeship, reinforced by the experiences John Coltrane also had with Monk. According to Coltrane, Monk would simply start playing something, "maybe just one of his tunes", over and over again until Coltrane would "get it" (Porter 2001, 108). This instruction took place at a time in Coltrane's life when he was also musically advanced.[24] Most examples of "jazz apprenticeships" with which I am familiar (including Louis Armstrong with King Oliver, Coleman Hawkins with Louis Armstrong, Don Byas with Art Tatum, Miles Davis with Charlie Parker, and Cannonball Adderley with Miles Davis) seem to have required that certain fluencies be developed at an earlier stage and rarely account for the "beginning" stages of learning.[25] On the other hand, the role of the teacher in Green's pedagogy, largely removed from hands-on instruction, can be seen, at least loosely, in the role assumed by Monk. This kind of mentoring role is also common in the ways many other esteemed jazz musicians led (or continue to lead) their groups and interacted with younger musicians.[26]

How did jazz musicians acquire fundamental skills that allowed them to enter into productive learning situations with elder musicians? Coltrane, Rollins, and many other jazz musicians, seem to have acquired these skills largely through aural processes (primarily listening to and playing along with recordings), and often in the context of peer groups (along the lines described by Lucy Green). There is ample evidence of this, most of it anecdotal, scattered through a variety of source material—biographies, trade journal interviews, and histories. Including Johnny Hodges and Harry Carney, John Coltrane and Benny Golson, or Sonny Rollins and the rest of the "Sugar Hill Gang",[27] there are many examples of aspiring young musicians getting together outside of school to listen to and learn from the recordings they admired, as well as practice together. Benny Golson provides an articulate example of this practice:

And it was an empirical process, trial and error, bouncing off of one another. We imitated others, but that wasn't the total end. We were highly eclectic. How could there be anything else? You know, we bought the records. We listened to them. I copied solos. But we used that as a basis, intuitively. We didn't know what we were doing, but we set up our own infrastructure upon which we could build things in the future. (Golson and Merod 1998, 37)

Hand-in-hand with this kind of self-training came a broader—one might say cultural—study of the musical tradition. Following musical trends, adopting dress codes, language patterns, and sensibilities could be included, something that is evident in another quote from Sonny Rollins:

> We used to follow Coleman Hawkins all around. He was my idol and just
> being in his company was thrilling for me. He lived in elegant style,
> driving a new Cadillac and always dressing really well. I admired his sense
> of style almost as much as I did his playing . . . We learned a lot about
> what it meant to be a jazz musician. (Nisenson 2000, 30–31)

The role of the elder, therefore, can be expanded to include certain
ideas involving culture—imitation of dress, lifestyle, speech, character—
that would seem to be true for today's aspiring pop musician as much as it
was true for young jazz musicians. It also seems that whether
apprenticeship comes in the form of playing in groups with elders, or
playing along with recordings of those elders, the apprenticeship phase is a
key element to the transmission of both traditions. The jazz tradition may
well be distinct from popular music in that the learning process in jazz is
often overtly viewed as continuing well into a jazz musician's career, as he
or she moves into professional groups playing under the direction of older
musicians. Perhaps this is a result of a longer apprenticeship stage in jazz,
or the frequent intermingling of generations within jazz bands. Perhaps
even these observations are subtle and easily blurred distinctions.

The commonalities in the transmission practices of these two traditions
lead me to question the use of particular categories in discussing what
kinds of music we are teaching. In relation to jazz, pedagogical issues have
emerged as a result of the construction of a canonical vision of the
category. This category-building, made necessary by the institutionalization
of the music, forced the issues of not only what will be taught, but how
those things will be taught. If, for example, Keith Jarrett's idea is to be
considered—"jazz is not the material itself, but the musicians' 'dance'
with the material"—our constructs of category need reconsideration.

Of all the categories of music, "popular" seems the most clearly
described and therefore the least problematic. Its title allows for the
inclusion of music regardless of connotations of style or instrumentation
or culture. Berry Gordy Jr., the founder of Motown Records, called his
music "pop" in order to avoid being categorized (Robinson 2008, 310).
We ought to be able to identify popular music simply by asking the
question "is it popular"? Perhaps because of the inherent practicality of
this title, however, it falls short of being useful in identifying specific
musical practices and associated methods of teaching and learning. Issues
of what can be included and what cannot are not addressed by the
category.

Green's work is remarkably unaffected by this observation, as her
pedagogy, for the most part, does not rely on a prescriptive definition of
"popular music", but rather on the musical understandings of those

involved in the transmission-process. In her pedagogy, the connotations associated with the term "popular music" are left largely in the hands of the learners and teachers. Her pedagogy does, however, emerge from a study of pop musicians, so the methods of transmission that she uses are rooted in an interpretation of "what is popular music."[28] Jazz, and the impossibility of defining it based upon a set of musical characteristics, provides an example of how complex this issue can become. Rather than transfer these difficulties across genres, it may be useful, if not inevitable to rethink categories as they relate to music education.

"Jazz" and "popular music" are complex references that undoubtedly mean different things to different people. As Green demonstrates, the same holds true for "classical" music. She shows that students enter the classroom with definite sets of pre-conceptions regarding classical music that are often different than those held by their teachers and parents. Her work also illustrates that those pre-conceptions can break down through experience—largely in Chapter 7 (thinking of Justin's story on page 166 regarding "Für Elise", Madeline's heartwarming description of finding "a bit more joy in it" on page 170, but also the reporting on stages 6 and 7). Perhaps this is evidence that exposure to non-familiar genres of music leads to tolerance of those genres, but it also demonstrates that the categories might break down when listeners become "doers." This breakdown does not seem unusual. Duke Ellington is frequently cited as an example of a musician with little use for categories. On one occasion, Ellington stated: "I don't write jazz, I write Negro folk music" (Jewell 1986, 22). Other jazz musicians have expressed a similar sentiment. Max Roach, in a powerful essay written in 1972, stated that jazz, a term he ultimately rejected,

> is the cultural expression of Africans who are dispersed on this North American continent. It derives in a continuing line from the musical and cultural traditions of Africa. We must recognize what those traditions are, what it is we are doing musically, how we learn our music, how it pleases and has meaning, and what its significance is. (Roach 1999, 308)

Roach encouraged not only that the learning processes associated with his musical tradition need to be upheld, but that musicians needed to "cleanse" their minds of

> false categories which are not basic to us and which divide us rather than unite us. They are misnomers: jazz music, rhythm and blues, rock and roll, gospel, spirituals, blues, folk music. Regardless of what they are called, they are various expressions of black music, black culture itself, the expression of Africans in the diaspora. (309)

Roach uses cultural heritage, not racial propriety, as a means of establishing a category that has more meaning, more pedagogical utility, and can be more easily defined and understood. The ways of learning and understanding are included in his definition of the category. One might conclude that the category would not exist separated from its traditions.

Randy Weston, a jazz pianist, states that prior to knowing what being a musician was, he thought jazz was "the music of the black people: free, creative, and swinging." His understanding of this category seems to have changed with experience, in part noting that classical influences became increasingly apparent to him in jazz, but also in his own exploration of the cultural "roots" of jazz:

> I have decided to search for the roots of jazz, of gospel music, of calypso and of Latin music—all the different music by different people with dark skins spread out all through the New World, producing everything from Bossa Nova to Aretha Franklin, from Ray Charles to Charlie Parker. There is a definite link between all those people. They're all black, but there is another something else, too, and I think that other link between them is rhythm, a beat. (Taylor 1993, 29–39)

In the context of the above quotes, it makes a great deal of sense that popular musicians would have similar methods of transmission to those of pre-Jazz Education jazz musicians. While it is possible that these similarities are purely coincidental or the result of similar circumstances (having to learn music outside the walls of academia), the kinds of music being discussed, through a common heritage, also have substantial and fundamental links. First among these links would be a deep emphasis on groove. Others would include certain notions of function, social and cultural connotations/meanings, histories, and non-Western ideas of technique and timbre. The history of popular music would start at basically the same time, with basically the same people, and in basically the same place as the history of jazz. It is untenable to suggest that jazz and popular music are the same, but this is not really the point. They are part of the same musical tradition—maybe branches of the same family tree. Therefore, jazz and its relationship to the academy has meaning to popular music and Green's work can certainly have meaning for jazz.

I am inclined to give Jazz Education some credit for creating not only a space in our institutions for "other" music, but also for providing much needed discourse on the ideas of what counts, what we are teaching, and how we are teaching it. It seems possible, if not demonstrable, that Jazz Education and its accompanying controversies functioned as an earlier version of bringing "non-traditional" ideas into formal structures steeped in tradition, as Cannonball had hoped. This neither downplays Jazz

Education's other contributions nor diminishes Green's pedagogy. Green's work, from this perspective, seems to represent something significant: the inclusion of an "other" music (in this case a music from the West African Diaspora) primarily through the modes of instruction associated with that "other" music.

A cynic might wonder if certain modes of transmission can exist within our academic structures. Surely there are valid reasons why, to paraphrase Michael Cain, no jazz school would adopt the auditioning process or rehearsal techniques of working, even canonical, jazz musicians (Cain 2007, 36). Perhaps the kind of teaching and learning described by Green will be uncomfortable in institutions, which may prove poor substitutes for basements, garages, and clubs. Perhaps opening our schools to these ways of teaching these kinds of music will negatively affect our treasured yet commercially fragile musical traditions. All of these issues, and surely many more, will provide for interesting conversations, research, and decision-making.

Perhaps it's because I recognize and identify with her pedagogy that Lucy Green's work seems rich in common sense. Perhaps for these same reasons, I might be inclined to read too much into her work. It indicates awareness that the methods of transmission must now be considered a crucial part of the music being transmitted. From my perspective, this appears as a shift, as in jazz we have more focused on learning things that canonical jazz musicians seemed to know, rather than learning things in the ways that those musicians had learned. The later stages of Green's project—the classical music phase—demonstrates that the transmission of musical material can be viewed as more important than the material. This seems to resonate with ideas presented in this essay—notions that, at least within certain musical traditions, the process can take priority over the product. Taken into the difficult realm of category, all of this leads me to wonder if our notions of category can, in fact, be better dealt with through modes of transmission. Whether the piece is "Für Elise", "Take The A Train", or Cameo, the ways students approach learning the music might have more to do with its categorization than its composer. For educational purposes, what kind of music it is might be more accurately defined through understanding how it was learned and for what reasons.

Returning to my areas of jazz and Jazz Education, a wholesale return to pre-Jazz Education modes of transmission is clearly impossible. Nonetheless, Green's pedagogy offers worthwhile challenges and opportunities to Jazz Educators, which I expect will prompt further discussions around the jazz canon and the ways in which it is constructed, preserved and transmitted. These discussions, particularly those focused on and emerging from Jazz Education, may involve the challenge of broadening of our ideas of category, particularly as popular musics enter our formal institutions. In many ways, all of this seems a very long time coming as Cannonball Adderley and Max Roach, to name but two, were discussing the importance of studying music of the West African Diaspora almost forty years ago.

A broader understanding of categories for pedagogical purposes, linked to cultural systems of knowing and valuing music, where our more discrete categories are viewed as branches (branches that can intertwine) that inform our modes of musical transmission, in many ways (like Green's pedagogy), just seems like common sense. Many would agree with Derek Scott's preface to Green's book, in which he states that a "relativistic outlook has replaced the universal perspective of modernism" (cited in Green 2008, vii) and, as a result, we increasingly view music as deriving its meaning from its context. It seems entirely logical, and likely, that our pedagogies will be one of the crucial aspects that reflect this shift. What this could mean for jazz is impossible to predict, although it might present new ways of determining what counts and what doesn't count— practices might count more than the results of those practices. It might lead to a particular understanding of jazz that is not rooted in debates of definition, but in particular ways of making and learning music using a variety of materials, the diversity of which can be understood, transmitted, and linked through culture as much as through canon. Whatever might follow, Lucy Green, through her pedagogy, has given us much to consider.

# References

Ake, D. 2002. *Jazz Cultures*. Los Angeles: University of California Press.
Bash, L., and J. Kuzmich. 1985. "A Survey of Jazz Education Research: Recommendations for Future Researchers." *Council for Research in Music Education Bulletin* 82: 14–28.
Beale, C. 2000. "Jazz Education." In *The Oxford Companion to Jazz,* ed. B. Kernfeld, 756–65. New York: Oxford University Press.
Bowman, W. 2004. "'Pop' Goes . . . ? Taking Pop Music Seriously." In *Bridging the Gap: Popular Music and Music Education,* ed. C. X. Rodriguez, 229–50. Reston: MENC.
Cain, M. 2007. "Redefining the 'Other': Teaching Delight in Cultural Variety." *Journal for Music-in-Education* 1: 35–39.
Cannonball 1973. *Downbeat*, June 21, 13+.

Deveaux, S. 1998. "Constructing the Jazz Tradition." In *The Jazz Cadence of American Culture,* ed. R. G. O'Meally, 483–512. New York: Columbia University Press.

Dobbins, B. 1988. "Jazz and Academica: Street Music in the Ivory Tower." *Bulletin of the Council for Research in Music Education* Spring 1988: 30–41.

Dykema, P. W., and K. Gehrekens. 1941. *The Teaching and Administration of High School Music.* Boston: C. C. Birchard & Company.

Feather, L. 1981. "How Jazz Education Began." *Jazz Educators Journal* February/March 1981: 20–21.

Fisher, L. 2003. "A Conversation with Benny Golson." *Jazz Research Proceedings Yearbook.* Kansas: IAJE, 11–15.

Gennari, J. 2006. *Blowin' Hot and Cool: Jazz and Its Critics.* Chicago: University of Chicago Press.

Gleason, R. J. 1969. "The Rhythm Section", *New York Post*, July 29.

Golson, B., and J. Merod. 1998. "Forward Motion: An Interview with Benny Golson." In *The Jazz Cadence of American Culture*, ed. R. G. O'Meally, 32-61. New York: Columbia University Press.

Goodman, G. 1999. "Sonny Rollins at Sixty-Eight." *Atlantic Monthly* July 1999: 82–88.

Green, L. 2008. *Music, Informal Learning and the School: A New Classroom Pedagogy.* Burlington: Ashgate.

Jarrett, K. 1996. "The Virtual Jazz Age: A Survivor Manual." *Musician* March 1996: 36, 102.

Jewell, D. 1986. *Duke: A Portrait of Duke Ellington.* London: Pavilion Books Ltd.

Jones, L. (A. Baraka) 1967. "Jazz and the White Critic." In *Black Music*, 11–20. New York: William Morrow.

Kernfeld, B., ed. 1994. "Benny Golson." In *New Grove Dictionary of Jazz.* New York: St. Martin's Press.

Marsalis, W. 1999. "The Neoclassical Agenda." In *Keeping Time: Readings in Jazz History*, ed. R. Walser, 334–39. New York: Oxford University Press.

Metheny, P. 2001. "Keynote Address to IAJE Convention." http://www.patmetheny.com/writings.cfm

Murphy, D. 1994. "Jazz Studies in American Schools and Colleges: A Brief History." *Jazz Educators Journal* March 1994: 34–38.

Niccoli, R. A. 1951. "Stearn Conducts Jazz Panel Series." *Downbeat* 18: 18.

Nisenson, E. 2000. *Open Sky: Sonny Rollins and His World of Improvisation.* New York: St. Martin's Press.

Porter, E. 2002. *What Is This Thing Called Jazz? African American Musicians as Artists, Critics, and Activists.* Los Angeles: University of California Press.

Porter, L. 1989. "Jazz in American Education Today." *Journal of The College Music Symposium* 29: 134–39.

—. 2001. *John Coltrane: His Life and Music.* Ann Arbor: University of Michigan Press.

Ramsey, D. 1999. "Before and After: Bob Brookmeyer Searches for the Truth." *Jazz Times*, May 1999: 91–93, 213.

Roach, M. 1999. "Beyond Categories." In *Keeping Time: Readings in Jazz History*, ed. R. Walser, 305–14. New York: Oxford University Press.

Robinson, L. 2008. "It Happened in Hitsville." *Vanity Fair* December 2008: 304–315, 326–28.

Rollins, S. 1994. "Forward." In *Jazz*, ed. J. Fordham. London: Doris Kindersley Ltd.

Sales, G. 1984. *Jazz: America's Classical Music.* Englewood Cliffs: Prentice-Hall.

Scott, D. B. 2008. "General Editor's Preface." In *Music, Informal Learning and the School: A New Classroom Pedagogy*, authored by L. Green, vii. Burlington: Ashgate.

Sidran, B. 1995. *Talking Jazz: An Oral History.* New York: Da Capo Press.

Taylor, A. 1993. *Notes and Tones: Musician to Musician Interviews.* New York: Da Capo Press.

Tomlinson, G. 1996. "Cultural Dialogics and Jazz: A White Historian Signifies." In *Disciplining Music: Musicology And Its Canons*, eds. K. Bergeron and P. V. Bohlman, 64–94. Chicago: University of Chicago Press.

Walser, R. 1993. "Out of Notes: Signification, Interpretation, and the Problem of Miles Davis." *The Musical Quarterly* 77 (2): 343–65.

—. 1999. "Where the Etude Stands on Jazz." In *Keeping Time: Readings in Jazz History*, ed. R. Walser, 41–54. New York: Oxford University Press.

Wilson, J. S. 1969. *The New York Times*, November 12.

Wilson, P. 1972. "Conversing with Cannonball." *Downbeat*, June 22 1972, 12–13.

Zabor, R., and V. Garbarini. 1999. "Wynton vs. Herbie: The Purist and the Crossbreeder Duke it Out." Reprinted In Soul Craft, and Cultural Hierarchy. In *Keeping Time: Readings in Jazz History*, ed. Robert Walser, 339–51. New York: Oxford University Press.

# **Notes**

[1] Previously published in 2009 as "Categories and Music Transmission" in *Action, Criticism and Theory for Music Education* 8 (2): 94–119. Reprinted by permission of the editor.

[2] Largely following Green's example, I will use "formal" and "informal" simply to distinguish transmission practices that occur inside (formal) and outside (informal) of schools and universities. I do not intend the use of "informal" to imply "casual."

[3] I will use capital letters throughout this chapter to distinguish institutionalized, or formal, Jazz Education from informal jazz education.

[4] These scholars and performers include Ben Sidran, David Ake, Scott Deveaux, Michael Cain, and Robert Walser.

[5] This is to indicate that my examples should not be taken as definitive. My limited selection undoubtedly excludes many musicians that would better fit another model, and excludes other musicians who have come along in the post-Jazz Education world. I am only using some examples that account for my response.

[6] There are other factors that have undoubtedly affected and altered the transmission of the jazz tradition—the recording industry, being one example—but I will focus only on the role of Jazz Education.

[7] "America's Classical Music" is included in the title of Grover Sales' 1984 textbook, but is also closely associated with the celebrated jazz pianist and educator Dr. Billy Taylor.

[8] Also useful for grasping the implications of "definition" on jazz pedagogies are Eric Porter (2002, 287–334) and David Ake (2002, 112–145).

[9] Gary Tomlinson also addresses this in his article "Cultural Dialogics and Jazz: A White Historian Signifies" (Tomlinson 1996, 74–77).

[10] This idea is also briefly discussed by Charles Beale in his essay "Jazz Education" (2000, 757).

[11] Both Jack DeJohnette and Robin Eubanks are deeply rooted in the pre-Jazz Education jazz tradition primarily, though not exclusively, through their musical associations with "canonical" jazz musicians who pre-date Jazz Education.

[12] http://www.patmetheny.com/writings.cfm (Pat Metheny's official website).

[13] On this page Walser also states "the work of Miles Davis seems to repudiate conventional notions of aesthetic distance and insists that music is less a thing than an activity." This further supports the sentiment of Jarrett that jazz is more a "way" than a "thing."

[14] While taking place on March 1, 1997, this interview was not published until 2003.

[15] http://www.coas.howard.edu/music/academics/degree_programs/jazz_studies.html

[16] It's also interesting to note that the Lenox School, given its deliberate attempt to place students in contact with working professional musicians, in some ways is similar to stage 5 of Green's book. The brochure referenced can be seen at http://www.jazzdiscography.com/Lenox/brochure.htm.

[17] Gennari, on page 212 of his book (2006), points out that a 1966 *Billboard* poll found that Dave Brubeck, Miles Davis, Modern Jazz Quintet, Gerry Mulligan, Stan

Kenton, and Duke Ellington were among the most popular musicians for college students.

[18] As Tomlinson points out in his essay ("Cultural Dialogics"), critic and historian Amiri Baraka (LeRoi Jones) did question the transfer of Eurocentric notions into the jazz tradition in his 1967 article "Jazz and the White Critic." On page 18 of this article, Baraka wrote that dating back to the 1940s "the white middle-brow critic . . . was already trying to formalize and finally institutionalize it. It is a hideous idea. The music was already in danger of being forced into that junk pile of admirable objects and data the West knows as culture."

[19] Murphy (1994) summarizes a generally accepted reading of this history where the 1970s was the decade when the idea of including jazz in formal music education settings became generally accepted and acceptable. Another is found in Bash and Kuzmich (1985), who state that "Jazz Education is essentially a product of the 1970s and usually associated with the formation of the National Association of Jazz Educators (NAJE) in 1968" on p. 14.

[20] These ideas emerged from a long discussion of this essay with my colleague, Michael Cain.

[21] It would be impossible to fully answer "why jazz." Cannonball's comments and the following discussion of preservation and protection is only intended to raise one particular aspect of "why jazz", and lead into the idea of formal structures as protective of a canonical structure.

[22] The article from which this quote is taken is a fascinating exchange between Marsalis and Herbie Hancock. It should be noted that Marsalis quickly retreated from his assertion that jazz was superior to pop music.

[23] At the peak of his activity, Cannonball probably presented this seminar about 100 times in a year—by the time of this interview, Cannonball's group was noticing a decline in university interest due to an increase in the number of jazz programs at universities. Interestingly, Cannonball is asked if the teaching of jazz in academic institutions risks "over-formalizing" the music, indicating that this was a concern as early as 1972.

[24] My use of the term "elder" should be qualified. Monk was only thirteen years older than Rollins and nine years older than Coltrane. I'm using this term to connote both the experience of the older musician and the esteem in which he (and in this essay, they are all "he's") is held. Thinking purely in terms of chronology, this term can be misleading.

[25] I am not familiar with the sources used by Green to support her view of the "apprenticeship" model in jazz transmission. My examples are intended purely to demonstrate another interpretation of "apprenticeship" in the jazz tradition, not refute Green's.

[26] As examples, both Sonny Rollins and Miles Davis have been known to give very little direction to members of their bands, seemingly preferring musicians to develop their intuition, their ears, and their own sensibilities rather than through direct instruction. Nisenson (2000) mentions this on page 7, but it can be documented in other sources.

[27] "The Sugar Hill Gang" included Rollins, Jackie McLean, Walter Bishop, Kenny Drew, and Art Taylor (among others), who would all become notable jazz musicians.

[28] Wayne Bowman (2004), on pages 31–37, provides a very useful examination of the complexity of "popular music" as a category.

# CHAPTER FIVE

# BOOMTOWN MUSIC EDUCATION
# AND THE NEED FOR AUTHENTICITY:
# INFORMAL LEARNING PUT INTO PRACTICE
# IN SWEDISH POST-COMPULSORY MUSIC
# EDUCATION[1]

## SIDSEL KARLSEN

## Introduction

Whilst the inclusion of popular music and popular musicians' informal learning practices into formal, school-based music education is a quite recent topic on the international music education agenda, these issues have been debated for several decades within the music education communities of the Nordic countries. Efforts have been made to shed light on this area from theoretical, research-based and practical perspectives. For example, as early as the late 1970s and early 1980s, Benum (1978) and Ruud (1983) discussed formal and informal arenas for music learning in terms of intentional and functional music education. The discussion was, among other things, tied to the emerging popular music culture, and the potential overlapping and intersection of the two educational forms was studied. Furthermore, through early ethnographic studies of rock bands conducted within the fields of musicology, anthropology, and cultural studies (Berkaak and Ruud 1994; Fornäs et al. 1995), the level of general knowledge about popular musicians' musical development and modes of learning was increased. Likewise, a wide range of teaching material from the past 25 years serves to illustrate how popular music and its related ways of learning have been introduced into Nordic music education classrooms.[2]

Many of the topics that have been dealt with within the Nordic countries have recently been actualised and brought to the attention of an international audience by Green (2002, 2008), who, through her research into popular musicians' learning practices, and the subsequent development and implementation of a classroom pedagogy based on this research, has showed how knowledge about the learning of music in informal contexts can be utilised within music education in the lower and middle levels of the compulsory school system. While Green has generally been acclaimed for, among other things, developing a pedagogy that is responsive towards youth cultures (Clements 2008) and suited to strengthening already existing music education programmes (Heuser 2008), critical voices have also been raised, pointing to the dangers of absenting the role of the teacher (Georgii-Hemming 2009) and to the challenges of enhancing critical dialogue and consciousness in an approach that mainly takes the adolescents' own favourite music as a point of departure (Allsup 2008). Scholars have also debated whether informal approaches may still be considered or perceived as informal when being converted into a pedagogy and taking place within the framework of a school (Sexton 2009).

Although popular music has been included in compulsory school music education in the Nordic countries for decades, institutions for higher education have generally been slower in opening their doors for popular musicians and facilitating for their specific needs. However, in recent years, a more open approach to popular music within post-compulsory schooling has appeared, and in Sweden approaches related to those utilised in Green's pedagogy have been developed within the framework of a university-based higher music education programme, called BoomTown Music Education.

BoomTown Music Education (hereafter abbreviated BoomTown or BTME) is a 2-year higher music education programme for rock musicians, which is connected to the School of Music in Piteå, Luleå University of Technology, and situated in the southern part of Sweden in the town of Borlänge (BoomTown 2009). The programme is research-based in the sense that its working methods and pedagogical philosophy have been developed on the basis of the work of two Swedish music education scholars, namely Anna-Karin Gullberg and K.-G. Johansson. While Gullberg (2002) investigated the musical learning and socialisation of rock musicians, Johansson (2002) looked into such musicians' strategies when playing by ear (for further accounts of these studies, see below). Their knowledge and findings, combined with the practical implementation of a socio-culturally oriented view on learning (Lave and Wenger 1991; Säljö

2000), have provided the grounds for what has become a successful and steadily expanding popular music education programme.

The aim of this chapter is to problematise the BoomTown pedagogy, focusing especially on its self-claimed informality and authenticity. Further, I wish to relate this problematisation to one of the broader issues brought up in the current, international debate on the inclusion of popular music and informal learning practices in school-based music education, namely that of the informal approaches' ability to remain informal when included in formal education. In order to open up the field for the reader, I will first give a more detailed account of the research upon which BTME has been developed as well as a description of the education, its aims, philosophy and working methods. Furthermore, the education program will be analysed through Folkestad's (2006) four-point definition of aspects of formal and informal learning as well as Hargreaves et al.'s (2003) "globe" model of opportunities in music education, in order to expose some of the tensions between the formal and informal modes found within it. Next, I will report my own experiences from visiting BTME, and discuss my impressions in relation to theories of authenticity. Finally, an effort will be made to extract some of the findings from the analysis of BoomTown in order to, as mentioned above, contribute to the broader international debate.

## The Foundations of BoomTown—Research and Rationale

Despite the general acceptance of popular music and its related ways of learning found within the larger Nordic music education community from the late 1970s onwards, most research at the doctoral level continued to focus on more conventional forms of music education. According to Olsson (2005), the focus of the doctoral dissertations published in the period from 1995 to 2005 largely concerned "the interaction between learner, teacher and the educational subject-matter" (Olsson 2005, 22) within formal, rather "traditional" school contexts.[3] However, the research community at the School of Music in Piteå, Luleå University of Technology, Sweden offered two interesting exceptions, namely the works of Gullberg (2002) and Johansson (2002), mentioned above. In the following, I will give a further description of their studies by relating their respective research questions, design, methodology and findings.

## Strategies among Ear Players in Rock Music

As already indicated, Johansson's (2002, see also Johansson 2004) study concerned rock musicians' approaches to playing by ear, and the explicit aim was to "describe and explain strategies used by rock musicians to hear and play chord progressions when playing unfamiliar rock songs by ear" (Johansson 2002, 14). The study was designed using an experimental set-up in which six musicians, all accomplished players of typical rock-related instruments (bass, keyboard and guitar) and styles, were asked to play along to three different rock songs, which were unfamiliar to them and written and recorded especially for the study. The three songs were of increasing difficulty with respect to chord progressions, going from a very simple song "using chords in a way that would make it possible for an experienced ear player in the rock genre to play it by ear without problems" to a very difficult song "that would as much as possible avoid all harmonic clichés or conventions in rock music" (99). The participants' playing was recorded on tape and video and they were also interviewed after having played the songs.

By analysing the interviews as well as the audio and videotapes, the researcher was able to extract two main types of learning strategies, namely listening strategies and playing strategies, each with individual variations. For example, strategies could involve listening for well-known harmonic formulas or the bass part and deducing the chord from this, or playing chords or melodic figures or playing intuitively by means of "instant learning." In summing up his findings, Johansson concluded, perhaps not so surprisingly, that playing by ear is first and foremost learned through playing by ear. Furthermore, learning to play by ear also happens style by style, by becoming familiar with specific clichés, harmonic formulas and other style-related traits.

Johansson's research can in many ways be said to have built further on the work of Lilliestam (1995). While the latter was one of the first Nordic researchers to investigate processes of ear playing and to describe the three basic and equally important activities necessary for learning within this mode—namely listening, practising, and performing—the former (Johansson 2002) shows how the processes of learning to play by ear not only follow certain general steps, but are also style and genre specific and hence contextually dependent.

## Musical Learning and Socialisation among Rock Musicians

Gullberg's (2002, see also Gullberg and Brändström 2004) study focused on musical learning and socialisation among rock musicians, and the overarching aim of her study was to show how "different kinds of musicians have learned to play, understand and value rock music via informal as well as formal modes, and how this learning is related to institutional and non-institutional learning environments" (Gullberg 2002, 11). Her research was designed as three separate sub-studies, each with its own focus and methodology. While the first study was a studio set-up in which two different rock bands, one "institutional" (formed by students of a University School of Music) and one "non-institutional" (a more regular garage band), were asked to rehearse and record a song that was unfamiliar to them, the second study concerned how higher music education students, as well as "other student groups", valued the two recordings that were made in study number one (11). In the third sub-study, eight professional rock and pop musicians were interviewed about the learning processes they followed in becoming a musician and developing musical ideals—all seen in relation to institutional and non-institutional learning environments.

Overall, Gullberg's findings in many ways resembled those of Green (2002), showing that rock musicians' learning mainly took place through solitary listening, copying and playing, and also through collective, peer-based activities while playing in a band. While institutional settings were perceived by the interviewees as "good at offering training and knowledge on an intra-musical level" (Gullberg 2002, 202), a portion of the inter-musical and the majority of the extra-musical knowledge needed in order to become a rock musician were "primarily learned by active participation in the non-institutional music life." Consequently, the musicians interviewed in Gullberg's study who had made it into the University School of Music did not find that kind of "academic music education" satisfactory.

In summing up her findings, Gullberg wrote: "If knowledge of informal learning in music and a curious, open-minded and outgoing personality are not encouraged within the music colleges, these people will search for other pedagogical possibilities than the music teacher programmes" (201). Since the learning processes and strategies of the rock musicians she interviewed, and the context they needed for their further musical and professional development, seemed to differ significantly from what was allowed for and offered within the institutions of higher music education,

Gullberg predicted that change would be needed if rock musicians were to want to remain part of the Academies of Music.

Shortly after defending their dissertations in 2002, Anna-Karin Gullberg and K.-G. Johansson had the opportunity to contribute to developing an "alternative higher music education" that took rock musicians' specific needs into account through what has now become BTME.

## Introducing the BoomTown Music Education Programme

BTME is a 2-year-long higher education programme for young musicians playing rock and related genres such as pop, hip-hop and heavy metal. According to the school's website, it "combines the advantages of formal music education with the strengths of informal learning" (BoomTown 2009). The aims of the programme are presented as: (a) to offer a process-oriented university education for bands and musicians of rock music and related styles, on the music's own terms; (b) to emphasise music-making in groups and attend to peer-directed learning and aural traditions; (c) to welcome a multiplicity of musics and let the students, to a great extent, create their own learning environments, formulate their own knowledge and skill-related ends—and even choose the means by which to reach them; (d) to support the enhancement of musical knowledge by offering courses in songcrafting, sound engineering and entrepreneurship; and (e) to offer cognitive tools for understanding one's own operations and encourage creativity and autonomy in thoughts and deeds (BoomTown 2009).

Those applying to the programme are primarily already-existing bands, and during the entrance exams the focus is more on originality and personal expression than on technical skills or knowledge of a certain kind of repertoire. When accepted, each band gets its own rehearsal room, to which the band members have 24-hour access. However, this is not a rehearsal room of the old conservatory style, it is also a fully equipped recording studio, so that the students always have the chance to record, mix and remix their work. The importance of process is emphasised throughout the programme, and instead of having ready-made ends and means, these are, as pointed out above, decided by each student for him or herself.[4] With this freedom comes the responsibility for assessing whether or not you are progressing according to your plan, and to what extent you have reached your goals.[5] The opportunity for choosing one's own means and ends also implies that the musicians who are accepted into the program may decide to absorb themselves completely in one specific musical style. They can thus avoid becoming stylistically diverse, something which might otherwise often be required if attending more traditional performance-based or music-teacher training programmes. Furthermore, BTME employs no "regular teachers", and the selection of supervisors, speakers, guest musicians and pedagogues is customised according to the needs of the students.

## The Educational Philosophy of BoomTown

The educational philosophy behind BTME is built on a socio-cultural perspective (Lave and Wenger 1991; Säljö 2000) which emphasises the situated nature of learning and the development of knowledge as relational and contextual. Along with explaining in more detail the two interrelated theoretical perspectives underlying the BoomTown philosophy, efforts will be made to show how these perspectives are related to the research of Johansson (2002) and Gullberg (2002), and how the theory and research, combined, have been utilised for developing the BoomTown philosophy and environment.

In the epistemological perspectives of Lave and Wenger (1991), learning is seen to come about through individuals' "legitimate peripheral participation" in specific communities of practice. Learning is not perceived as "acquisition of knowledge", and the practices have no persons positioned as "teachers"; rather knowledge enhancement is assumed to happen when the communities' members relate to its activities, identities and artefacts. Furthermore, newcomers will often be introduced to the practice and little by little reach the stage of "full participation" (37) by observing the conduct of old-timers. A central task for the newcomer is to learn how to behave within a particular discourse and negotiate ways of being a person in a particular communal context. In Lave and Wenger's words, learning to become a legitimate participant in a community "involves learning how to talk (and be silent) in the manner of full participants" (105). In short, their epistemology emphasises learning as situated, in other words as "an integral part of generative social practice in the lived-in world" (35) and changing locations and perspectives, either by participating in several social practices or adopting several positions within one particular community of practice, is seen as part of actors' "learning trajectories, developing identities and forms of membership" (36).

As with Lave and Wenger (1991), Säljö (2000) emphasises the situated nature of knowledge and the necessity of participating in specific social practices in order to access the knowledge integral to and inherent in those practices. However, in more specific ways than the scholars referred to above, he shows how "human knowledge, insights, conventions and ideas are built into apparatus" (82), and hence how artefacts, including intellectual tools,[6] gain a crucial role in a community of practice's mediation of knowledge. Furthermore, Säljö considers language as humanity's "mediating tool" par excellence, and highlights its distinctive role in processes of knowledge development:

> Language is the most unique component in human knowledge-building and, more generally, in our ability to gather experiences and to communicate these to one another. Words and linguistic statements mediate the surrounding world to us and make it appear as meaningful. By communicating with others, we are introduced to ways of designating and describing the world which are functional, and which enable our interplay with fellow human beings in various activities. (84–85)

Consequently, in order for learning to take place, including within a community of practice, it is of utmost importance that its members are offered opportunities to communicate and share thoughts, feelings, ideas and experiences.

Johansson's (2002) research shows how playing by ear is situated knowledge in the sense that it can only be learned by doing it in context. Also, the clichés and formulas learned—the intellectual-musical tools— are style-specific and thereby contextually (and communally) dependent. As a consequence, the BoomTown students are offered opportunities for immersing themselves completely in the musical style of their choice. Since their ways of learning music are mainly ear-based, learning is probably also most effectively performed when each student is allowed to engage directly and heavily in his or her germane music. Furthermore, Gullberg's (2002) research emphasises the solitary as well as the peer and group-based development of knowledge among popular musicians, and also how much of their learning takes place in communities of practice, such as the band or bands to which they belong or the larger rock scene. Hence, instead of creating a more traditional educational practice, with ready-made classes and regular teachers, BoomTown is very much structured as an "educational community of practice." Old-timers, in the sense of professional and experienced musicians and producers, are brought in as examples of individuals who have reached the stage of "full participation" in the rock community, and the students learn by engaging with them—socially and musically. In addition, the students are allowed to use quite a lot of time in what is perhaps their most significant music-related community of practice—the band. The physical context of BoomTown is equipped with style-specific artefacts, in other words the electronic equipment needed to play certain popular genres, and the insight that language is crucial for the development of knowledge—individually as well as communally—is operationalised into making the regular writing of a diary the programme's most important obligatory task. The diary-writing serves two purposes: firstly, it is seen as a way of letting the students come to grips with their own thoughts, judgements and ways of approaching the world; secondly, it is utilised as a means and a point of departure for group reflection, in order to develop, jointly, awareness of how different forms of music-related learning and creative processes impact on the students' own music making.

## BoomTown as Seen in a Theoretical Perspective— Formal, Informal or Something in Between?

In an attempt to sum up the basic criteria of formal and informal learning situations, Folkestad (2006, 141–142) acknowledges four determining aspects, namely: (1) the situation—does the learning take place inside or outside institutional settings; (2) the learning style—is the music learned through playing by written notation or by ear; (3) ownership—who owns the decision of the activity, the learners or the teachers; and (4) intentionality—is the mind directed towards learning how to play or towards playing?

Applying these criteria to BoomTown, it is evident how this education, at least at first glance, may be claimed to function primarily in an informal mode, especially where the latter three aspects are concerned. Firstly, the most common learning style among the BoomTown students is, because of the stylistic traits and traditions of the music they play, to a great extent ear-based. While it of course can be claimed that the chord charts and different kinds of tab notation used for writing down and remembering rock music may count as "written notation", the music is not mainly learnt by playing, for example, notes written on a score, such as within the Western classical tradition, and the amount of time spent playing by ear is considerable.

Secondly, efforts are made throughout the programme to ensure that the students maintain ownership of the activities. This is evident in how the students choose means and ends as well as assess their own work, but is also seen in the decision to customise the staff according to the students' needs and thereby avoid having regularly employed teachers. The consequent lack of long-lasting teacher-student relationships might minimise the risk of teachers "owning" activities as well as students (the latter sometimes being a danger of more master-apprenticeship oriented teaching and learning practices). Nevertheless, BoomTown is still an educational program, which means that the students also have to meet certain criteria and participate in certain activities that are set and decided by administrators and staff. Hence, ownership is not entirely in the students' hands, even though it is perhaps more so than in many other kinds of higher music education.

Thirdly, while the aim of the BoomTown students is certainly to enhance their skills as musicians, it seems that the intention might be directed more towards playing and reflecting on playing within a musical framework rather than towards learning how to play through more traditional forms of rehearsing and within a pedagogical framework. Still, it is hard to say anything about students' intentions without having interviewed them with this in mind; and besides, what is the BoomTown educational philosophy if not a pedagogical framework?

Finally, although BTME, at least to a certain extent, facilitates informal learning practices, there is no doubt that when it comes to the first of Folkestad's four aspects—situation inside or outside institutional settings—this Swedish educational programme is formal and located safely within the framework of a university. The fact that it is a university programme is even utilised as part of its marketing to attract potential students.

When comparing BTME to Hargreaves et al.'s (2003, 158) "globe model"[7] of opportunities in music education, we arrive at approximately the same answers as above: BTME offers professional training of performing musicians, and, although the students assess themselves, there are examinations, among other means through public performances. Hence, the programme can be placed on the "formal" side of the globe leaning towards the statutory, "in-school" side. However, the learning that takes place within the framework of BoomTown can also be characterised as largely self-directed and "third environment"[8] related, something which places the programme on the "informal" and elective, "outside-school" part of the globe. Relating to the discussion above, a relevant question to ask in this regard is whether the learning is actually experienced by the students as informal and self-directed when someone has already decided for them, by designing the educational environment, that these should be the learning conditions. Nevertheless, from theoretical comparison BTME appears as it is marketed on its homepage, namely as combining the strengths of informal learning with the advantages of formal education: neither formal nor informal—rather something in between.

## Experiences from Visiting BoomTown

In the previous section, I discussed BoomTown's informality in relation to two different models or theoretical points of departure. In the following, I will provide the basis for a discussion of its authenticity by sharing my experiences from visiting the school.[9] In the spring of 2008, I had the good fortune of visiting BTME and meeting some of its administrators and students. I recall having two main impressions from this trip.

Firstly, I was immediately impressed by the quantity of "gear" that was available, understood as all kinds of technical equipment designed for the recording, making and mixing of music. Not only did each band have its own rehearsal room/recording studio—in addition, the school was about to build a large studio containing several sub-studios, with the ability to produce digital as well as analogue recordings. There was also a studio especially designed to meet the needs of hip-hoppers. All in all, these technological artefacts made the creation and performance of a vast variety of pop and rock-related styles possible.

Secondly, when I met the students, they were very keen to emphasise the way in which their education differed from the traditional conservatory style of educating musicians. Phrases like "this is something completely different", "I would never have chosen to attend the conservatory or any kinds of 'traditional' university music courses" or "this education allows me to do my own thing, musically speaking" were common. Curious to know more about their everyday lives as students, I asked them what an "ordinary day" would look like. Interestingly, they replied with examples that strongly reminded me of my own experiences as a student within the traditional conservatory system. Most of the time they practised their main instrument, either alone, in their regular band, or with other fellow students. They would then attend lectures, classes and instrumental lessons, and occasionally participate in larger performances organised by the school. In addition, they would keep up a busy musical life outside of the school itself. When I replied that their descriptions of "the everyday life of a BoomTown music student" reminded me very much of my own education as a classical singer, they sounded absolutely horrified: "No way, your studies must have been completely different, it cannot be compared to our form of education."

## BoomTown and the Need for Authenticity

In general, I consider bringing experiences from informal learning practices into post-compulsory music education as useful and necessary. However, from my own experiences as well as previous research (e.g. Kvale and Nielsen 1999; Nerland 2004) I know that such practices already exist within the more "traditional" conservatory system. Why is it, then, that the conservatory environment—despite having its own "informality"— did not seem meaningful to the BoomTown students?

In my opinion, the success of BTME lies not only in building on informal learning practices; it is also to be found in the way that the school is marketed as offering an "authentic", "alternative" and "non-institutional" education, and probably also in that the learning environment is experienced as such by the students who choose to enrol in the programme. Taylor (1991) reminds us that one of the most powerful discourses of modernity is that of authenticity and the necessity of cultivating an authentic self—an identity. He further connects authenticity with freedom: "Authenticity is itself an idea of freedom; it involves my finding the design of my life myself, against the demands of external conformity" (67–68). Furthermore, as Ruud (1997) points out, the notion of authenticity is inevitably connected to music and to the interrelationship between music and identity.

To the BoomTown students, the conservatory tradition obviously represented a most unwanted instance of "external conformity", while the BTME learning environment was something they could identify with, an "educational umbrella" under which they felt that they could freely explore and articulate their own musical identities and thereby learn music. Whether or not BoomTown really is authentic, or what a definition of authenticity in this regard might imply, is perhaps of lesser significance. The important thing for the students was that it fulfilled their need for authenticity and corresponded with their musical identities.

In a quite recent contribution, Wenger (2006) connects identity, learning, meaningfulness and education, or in his terms "social learning systems", in the following way: "I argue that when it comes to the production of meaningfulness, learning is subsumed under identity and [I argue] that social learning systems provide the context for this process" (17). In other words, in order to be experienced as meaningful, an educational context must exist, which takes into account the close and interwoven connections between identity and learning. This includes offering students the opportunity to be socialised into communities of practice which correspond with their identities—musical or otherwise.

Looking once again into the environment of BoomTown, it is evident how this programme enables such a socialisation, among other things by (1) letting the students participate in several "popular music communities of practice"—either the band or the larger group of students; (2) bringing in old-timers (experienced professionals) who can act as role models and guides for the newcomers (the students) on their way into the larger popular music community; (3) being equipped with popular music style-specific "gear"—also known as artefacts—which mediates much of the knowledge necessary for mastering the particular popular music practices; and (4) training the students in mastering the style and practice-specific language by letting them reflect, extensively, on their own music making and creative development.

In other words, BoomTown is a learning environment which is experienced as authentic and meaningful by popular music students because it takes into account their identity as popular musicians, and provides them with the tools to become such and to work efficiently within the wider popular music communities of practice.

## Conclusion

While the aim of this chapter was to problematise the BoomTown education from the perspectives of informality and authenticity, I will in this last section extract some insights gained through these efforts and address one of the key topics brought up in the debate surrounding Green's (2008) work, namely whether informal approaches will still remain, or continue to be perceived as, informal when included or converted into a pedagogy (Sexton 2009).

As can be seen from the application of the formal/informal criteria to the BoomTown environment above, this particular programme is situated somewhere in between these two poles, being mainly built on principles found within informal arenas, but still unable to escape its formality. Similar outcomes would probably have been arrived at if a parallel analysis had been undertaken on Green's pedagogy. However, in relation to the perceived meaningfulness and outcome of music education, whether on the post-compulsory or compulsory level, the question of formal or informal might be irrelevant—or at least not the right one to ask. Rather, we should ask how we might create meaningful learning environments in terms of fulfilling students' need for authenticity, and corresponding with as well as contributing to developing their identities. In this, mixing features from the formal as well as informal arenas for learning seems a fruitful place to start, trusting that they will complement and enrich, rather than defeat, each other.

# References

Adler, P. A., and P. Adler. 1994. "Observational Techniques." In *Handbook of Qualitative Research*, eds. N. K. Denzin and Y. S. Lincoln, 377–92. Thousand Oaks: Sage Publications.

Allsup, R. E. 2008. "Creating an Educational Framework for Popular Music in Public Schools: Anticipating the Second-Wave." *Visions of Research in Music Education* 12. http://www-usr.rider.edu/~vrme/v12n1/ vision/1%20AERA%20-%20Allsup.pdf

Balsnes, A. 2009. *Å lære i kor. Belcanto som praksisfellesskap* [Learning in Choir. Belcanto as a Community of Practice]. PhD diss., Norwegian Academy of Music.

Benum, I. 1978. "Musikkpedagogiske aspekter [Aspects of Music Education]." *Norsk Musikktidsskrift* 3: 121–30.

Berkaak, O. A., and E. Ruud. 1994. *Sunwheels. Fortellinger om et rockeband* [Sunwheels. Stories About a Rock Band]. Oslo: Universitetsforlaget.

BoomTown. 2009. "BoomTown Music Education." Accessed June 24, 2009. http://www.boomtown.nu.

Clements, A. C. 2008. "Escaping the Classical Canon: Changing Methods through a Change of Paradigm." *Visions of Research in Music Education* 12.
http://www-usr.rider.edu/~vrme/v12n1/vision/3%20AERA%20-%20Clements.pdf

Folkestad, G. 2006. "Formal and Informal Learning Situations or Practices *vs* Formal and Informal Ways of Learning." *British Journal of Music Education* 23 (2): 135–45.

Fornäs, J., U. Lindberg, and O. Sernhede. 1995. *In Garageland. Youth and Culture in Late Modernity.* London: Routledge.

Georgii-Hemming, E. 2009. "Informal Musical Practices in School? Some Critical Reflections from a Swedish Perspective." Paper presented at the 2nd Reflective Conservatoire Conference: Building Connections, London, UK, March 2009.

Green, L. 2002. *How Popular Musicians Learn: A Way Ahead for Music Education.* Aldershot: Ashgate.

—. 2008. *Music, Informal Learning and the School: A New Classroom Pedagogy.* Aldershot: Ashgate.

Gullberg, A.-K. 2002. *Skolvägen eller garagevägen. Studier av musikalisk socialisation* [By Learning or Doing. Studies in the Socialisation of Music]. PhD diss., Luleå University of Technology.

Gullberg, A.-K., and S. Brandström. 2004. "Formal and Non-Formal Music Learning amongst Rock Musicians." In *The Music Practitioner. Research for the Music Performer, Teacher and Listener,* ed. J. Davidson, 161–74. Aldershot: Ashgate.

Hargreaves D. J., N. A. Marshall, and S. C. North. 2003. "Music Education in the Twenty-First Century: A Psychological Perspective." *British Journal of Music Education* 20 (2): 147–63.

Heuser, F. 2008. "Encouraging Change: Incorporating Aural and Informal Learning Processes in an Introductory Music Education Course." *Visions of Research in Music Education* 12. http://www-usr.rider.edu/~vrme/v12n1/vision/4%20AERA%20-%20Heuser.pdf

Johansson, K.-G. 2002. *Can You Hear What They're Playing? A Study of Strategies Among Ear Players in Rock Music.* PhD diss., Luleå University of Technology.

—. 2004. "What Chord Was That? A Study of Strategies Among Ear Players in Rock Music." *Research Studies in Music Education* 23 (1): 94–101.

Karlsen, S., and S. Brandström. 2008. "Exploring the Music Festival as a Music Educational Project." *International Journal of Music Education* 26 (4): 363–73.

Kvale, S., and K. Nielsen. 1999. *Mesterlære: læring som social praksis* [Master-Apprenticeship: Learning as Social Practice]. Copenhagen: Hans Reitzel.

Lave, J., and E. Wenger. 1991. *Situated Learning. Legitimate Peripheral Participation.* Cambridge: Cambridge University Press.

Lebler, D. 2007. "Student-as-Master? Reflections on a Learning Innovation in Popular Music Pedagogy." *International Journal of Music Education* 25 (3): 205–21.

Lilliestam, L. 1995. *Gehörsmusik: blues, rock och muntlig tradering* [Playing by Ear: Blues, Rock and Oral Tradition]. Gothenburg: Akademiförlaget.

Nerland, M. 2004. *Instrumentalundervisning som kulturell praksis* [Music Instrument Teaching as Cultural Practice]. PhD diss., Norwegian Academy of Music.

Olsson, B. 2005. "Scandinavian Research on Music Education—its Scope of Ideas and Present Status." In *RAIME—Proceedings of the Eighth International Symposium,* ed. B. Olsson, 15–26. Gothenburg: ArtMonitor.

Ruud E. 1983. *Musikken, vårt nye rusmiddel?* [Music, Our New Intoxicant?]. Oslo: Norsk Musikforlag.

—. 1997. *Musikk og identitet* [Music and Identity]. Oslo: Universitetsforlaget.

Salavuo, M. 2006. "Open and Informal Online Communities as Forums of Collaborative Musical Activities and Learning." *British Journal of Music Education* 23 (3): 253–71.

Sexton, F. 2009. "Informal Learning: A Way to Raise the Attainment of Boys at Key Stage 3?" Paper presented at the 2nd Reflective Conservatoire Conference: Building Connections, London, UK, March 2009.

Säljö, R. 2000. *Lärande i praktiken. Ett sociokulturellt perspektiv* [Learning in Practice. A Sociocultural Perspective]. Stockholm: Prisma.

Söderman, J. 2007. *Rap(p) i käften. Hiphopmusikers konstnärliga och pedagogiska strategier* [Verbally Fa(s)t. Hip-Hop Musicians' Artistic and Educational Strategies]. PhD diss., Lund University.

Taylor, C. 1991. *The Ethics of Authenticity.* London: Harvard University Press.

Väkevä, L. 2006. "Teaching Popular Music in Finland: What's Up, What's Ahead?" *International Journal of Music Education* 24 (2): 126–31.

Wenger, E. 2006. *Learning for a Small Planet.* http://www.ewenger.com.

Westerlund, H. 2006. "Garage Rock Bands: A Future Model for Developing Musical Expertise?" *International Journal of Music Education* 24 (2): 119–25.

Wingstedt J. 2008. *Making Music Mean. On Functions of, and Knowledge about, Narrative Music in Multimedia.* PhD diss., Luleå University of Technology.

# Notes

[1] Previously published in 2010 as "BoomTown Music Education and the Need for Authenticity—Informal Learning put into Practice in Swedish Post-Compulsory Music Education" in *British Journal of Music Education* 27 (1): 35–46. Reprinted by permission of the publisher Cambridge University Press.

[2] Most of the scholarly contributions in this area as well as the teaching material have been written in Nordic languages and have therefore been largely unavailable to an international audience. For earlier attempts at communicating this "Nordic approach" internationally, see for example, Folkestad (2006), Väkevä (2006) or Westerlund (2006).

[3] In later years, the scope of Scandinavian music education research has been widely expanded, and nowadays studies can be found which investigate, for example, hip-hop musicians' educational strategies (Söderman 2007); learning among music festival attendees (Karlsen and Brändström 2008); musical online communities as an arena for development of musical skills and knowledge (Salavuo 2006); the learning of musical conventions and codes through computer games (Wingstedt 2008); and the local choir as a medium for socialisation (Balsnes 2009).

[4] The ends and means are not only related to the students' individual goals, but also to the shared goals of the musical group to which they belong—the band.

[5] Similar approaches are also utilised in a popular music programme in one Australian conservatorium (Lebler 2007).

[6] Säljö (2000) defines as "intellectual tools" models that constitute "resources for thinking" (102). Examples of such tools in a musical context may be clichés, scales or fixed harmonic formulas.

[7] In an article about music education in the 21st century, Hargreaves et al. (2003) draw up a "globe" model of opportunities in music education with three main bipolar dimensions. The vertical dimension "distinguishes between formal and informal opportunities" (158) so that the "northern part" of the globe is reserved paths that lead to qualifications and careers while the "southern part" represents informal opportunities. The horizontal dimension distinguishes between "statutory and elective provision", in other words the "western side" is dedicated to "in-school provision in all its forms" (158) while the "eastern side" denotes all opportunities selected by the students themselves. Finally, two circles exist, an inner and an outer, which represent "generalist" and "specialist" opportunities respectively.

[8] The authors define "third environment" as "social contexts in which musical learning takes place in the absence of parents or teachers" (Hargreaves et al. 2003, 157).

[9] I was not visiting BoomTown for the purpose of conducting research. Hence, the experiences and observations made were informal and not subject to any strict methodological procedures. However, explained in research terms, the observations made could be classified as conducted by a "peripheral-member-researcher" (Adler and Adler 1994, 379).

# CHAPTER SIX

# MUSIC EDUCATION: A PERSONAL MATTER? EXAMINING THE CURRENT DISCOURSES OF MUSIC EDUCATION IN SWEDEN[1]

## EVA GEORGII-HEMMING AND MARIA WESTVALL

## Introduction

There has been a trend in a number of countries over the last 10 years to develop pedagogical strategies for the classroom informed by musical learning and engagement in informal contexts, usually beyond the school. Informal pedagogical strategies have been regarded as a tool for increasing students' motivation for, participation in, and inclusion within music education in schools. However, experiences from music education in Sweden, stretching back over a considerable number of years, suggest caution in making such assumptions.

One objective with an informal pedagogical approach is to emphasise the individual student's personal experiences and his/her freedom to choose. Although Swedish music teachers' general intention is to take account of the students' "own" music, studies have shown that this purpose is not fulfilled, since not all students' musical lifeworlds are represented. Swedish students generally enjoy music in schools, but at the same time they find the subject to be old-fashioned and lacking in range of genres (Skolverket 2004a, 2004b). Accordingly, not all students feel their musical preferences are included in music education.

Studies concerning music education in Sweden also reveal that there is a focus on musical activities, skills and reproduction, rather than on the development of artistic and creative competencies by means of activities such as composition and improvisation (Georgii-Hemming 2005; Georgii-Hemming and Westvall 2010).

In addition, recent studies demonstrate that music teaching often lacks direction (Georgii-Hemming 2005; Georgii-Hemming and Westvall 2010). It could be debated whether this is due to a sharp focus on individual students' interests and personal development, supplemented with an openly formulated curriculum. This raises questions concerning the role of the teacher in learning processes.

Although educational researchers and national evaluators of education agree that a variety of students' personal experiences should be included in the school context, questions are raised concerning whether music education has become too limited in relation to repertoire, content and teaching methods. For that reason, the main issue in the ongoing debate on a national level is whether the objectives of participation, inclusion and democratic values are achieved through the current Swedish approach to music education (Georgii-Hemming and Westvall 2010).

## Music Education in Sweden: A Brief History

Over the past 40 years the music curriculum in Sweden has undergone major changes. These have been described as a transition from "School Music" to "Music in School" (Stålhammar 1995). This transition represents a shift from music as being a distinctive school subject towards a subject with a significant inclusion of students' own musical experiences and preferences from outside of school. The shift does not exclusively concern music education, as there is an increased emphasis on democratic values and students' participation in the general curriculum.

Music as a school subject achieved its subject status in 1955. Prior to this the subject was called singing. Singing was dominated by hymns and aimed at strengthening church singing, morale and national identity (Sandberg 2006; Stålhammar 1995). In the 1960s, a 9-year compulsory comprehensive school education was introduced for all children. Previously, in the 1946 School Commission's report (SOU 1948:27), which laid the foundations for this reform, the role of education to support democratic values was emphasised. Advocating a progressive interpretation of "citizenship education", it was said that school had to pay attention to children's participation and inclusion. At the same time the School Commission claimed that democratic teaching should have an objective and scientific basis. Therefore the primary focus of music education, according to the first curriculum, was on aesthetic education with the starting point in Western classical music. The subject focused on sight-reading music, singing in harmony and knowledge of Western music history (Lgr 62; Stålhammar 1995).

As a result of the emergence of popular music and youth culture during the 1960s, the curriculum was revised in 1969. The new curriculum took the first step away from "traditional" music education and music teachers were encouraged to use "teenage music" (Lgr 69; Sandberg 2006). The repertoire was further widened in the subsequent national curriculum (Lgr 80). This curriculum was designed around three main themes: To play together, To create music, and Music in society and the world. The latest curriculum was introduced in 1994 and revised in 2000 (Lpo 94; Kursplan 2000). In this curriculum, the role of music as a means of creating identity and for personal development is emphasised, and the core of the subject is defined as the act of playing together.

Since the 1990s, a decentralised education system has been introduced. This means that teachers can teach in a variety of ways based on centrally defined criteria. Thus, there can be a great deal of variation in music education between schools, resulting from differences in resources in individual schools, individual teachers' knowledge, or prioritisations (Englund 2005; Forsberg 2000).

## Music Education in Sweden Today— Content and Design of Lessons

Large group singing and playing in pop and rock bands dominate Swedish music education, according to both research studies (Georgii-Hemming 2005) and the national evaluation from 2003 (Skolverket 2004a, 2004b, 2005). The musical material is derived from pop and rock genres, and teachers are striving for as much authenticity as possible in their teaching. One can never escape the fact that a school is an institution with some, more or less, defined frameworks and conditions. Despite this, it appears that music teachers in Sweden are striving to create an experience of music and playing music which is as close to the musical practice outside of school as possible.

Usually, the students are relatively free to choose which songs they wish to play, and with which students to play or "form a band." The process resembles as far as possible the methods of pop and rock bands; basically listen, test and play. Students have the opportunity to make their own musical decisions and cooperate with one another, and the music learning is mainly peer-directed. Singing and playing can be said to be the content, the method as well as the objective (Lilliestam 1995, 2001; Georgii-Hemming 2005).

The teaching reflects the aims of the curriculum, which emphasises practical skills in singing and playing (Kursplan 2000). The importance of teaching and learning being rooted in the individual student's needs and motivation is reinforced in openly formulated documents that do not regulate teaching strategies and curriculum content in detail. The idea is that the teacher should, together with students and according to local conditions, plan and implement the teaching and learning that goes on in the classroom. Recent research studies reveal that the implementation of music education varies greatly between individual schools. Furthermore, there are few music teachers that use the texts available in different guidance documents, which are supposed to form the starting point for teaching. Instead, they design "their own curriculum" based upon openness towards students' leisure music and the individual competencies of the teachers (Ericsson 2001; Georgii-Hemming and Westvall 2010; Skolverket 2007, 34).

## Music Education in Sweden Today— Music Teachers' Goals and Ambitions

When music teachers are asked what their teaching should give to the student, ideas of personal and social development dominate, rather than musical communication and experience. The teachers want musically engaged students who extend this interest beyond the scope of an educational institution and apply it to individual or cultural needs (Georgii-Hemming 2005, 2006; Skolverket 2004a, 2004b). The function and use of music is playing, a skilled process with its foundation built upon practice (Elliott 2005; Varkøy 2001).

Music as a phenomenon is not a focus, and music is certainly not seen as an autonomous object. However, the meaning of music is perceived as a unique source for personal and social development. Therefore every student must be respected, learn to cooperate, be given opportunities to find their identity and become a fulfilled human being with self-confidence. They must also be made aware of—and take responsibility for—what he or she learns, and discover their own abilities and the potential value of aesthetic knowledge. Music is the uniting link between these ambitions. Music and human experiences belong together; through positive musical experiences human beings can feel joy and solidarity, develop self-esteem and discover that different forms of knowledge have a value (Georgii-Hemming 2005; Skolverket 2007).

# Music Education in Sweden Today—
# What is Not Being Prioritised?

It appears that singing and playing mainly pop and rock music dominates music teaching in Sweden. Western Classical music, jazz, folk music or music from other cultures is only marginally integrated into the curriculum. The selection of styles within the pop and rock genres is also limited.

Popular music today is a large and global musical field that can contain both old and new music, from traditional bands to music produced through different types of digital technology. Regardless of whether students or teachers choose the repertoire, it often involves music that students know well. Despite the intentions of the curriculum, few teachers actively work towards teaching in a way that reflects several cultural and musical fields—irrespective of whether they work in a school in a larger or smaller city or in a school with or without ethnic diversity (Kursplan 2000). A new form of school music based on easy-to-play pop and rock songs seems to have emerged. This includes both current hits (e.g. "I'm Yours" by Jason Mraz), traditional songs (e.g. "Tom Dooley") and also songs by groups such as Creedence Clearwater Revival, Kiss and Oasis (Karlsson and Karlsson 2009).

Even though some music teachers utilise computers in their classes (e.g. sequencer programmes) and allow students to mix music or work with DJ equipment, these instances are mainly an exception. Particular teaching strategies for creating music with the help of digital media are rare, as are discussions about the role of music in advertisements, films, dance and movement. Activities where music listening is the focus are also scarce.

Creative work involving music is emphasised in the compulsory comprehensive school curriculum (Kursplan 2000). One can of course argue that playing covers based on existing music is a creative process, but the artistic aspects of music in terms of creating new music, using sounds for interpretation, composing or improvising have had little impact on the teaching (Skolverket 2007; Thavenius 2002). Teachers provide students with opportunities to create their own music, and the teaching schedules are flexible enough to allow sufficient time for this. However, few students actually take advantage of this opportunity and few teachers apply it. Creating is not a central goal (Georgii-Hemming 2005, 2006). Repertoire, content and teaching methods are thus relatively limited. The reasons given by music teachers for why music creation does not occur include: that groups are too large, a lack of time, space, instruments, and, chiefly, a lack of computers. Teachers also argue that it is a matter of prioritisation (Skolverket 2007). These perceived barriers often do not exist in upper secondary school (for students aged 16–19), but studies suggest that lessons are still similar to those of compulsory comprehensive schools (for students aged 7–16). However, the reasons given for why there is often a lack of inclusion of music from various cultures and music listening are expressed differently. It seems that the primary goal is for every student to be offered the opportunity to discover his/her own musical preferences rather than widening their knowledge about different forms of music and different ways of engaging with music. Teachers speak of music lessons as the students' "breathing space" in the everyday school environment. The central aspect expressed is that students should be able to experience joy and comfort, that they are shown respect, and that they will be given opportunities to succeed in their attempts. Positive experiences in a comfortable environment are therefore seen as more important than encouraging students to play music from other cultures or to compose their own music (Georgii-Hemming 2005, 2006).

## General Principles behind the Implementation of Informal Music Pedagogy

Motives for implementing informal pedagogy in schools often stem from a desire to compensate for limitations in the content or methodology of the formal curriculum (Jeffs and Smith 1990). Furthermore, informal music pedagogy may be a way to address some students' lack of engagement with music education in schools.

The idea is that through informal music pedagogy, students will be empowered to influence and control the content, as well as the pace, of their own learning. The students choose the music they want to practise and perform, and it is learnt by listening and aural copying rather than from notation. This form of education takes place through self-directed learning, peer-directed learning and group learning, yet with moderate involvement from the teacher. This is considered to provide the students with a sense of recognition and a greater ownership of their learning experiences. The expectation is also that students will gradually become aware of other music genres outside their own experience. Therefore, informal education aims to offer students opportunities to try out new things, take risks and extend their experiences (Green 2008).

So far, these objectives mainly concern what is happening in the schools. In the general debate concerning informal learning practices, there are, however, also issues and objectives discussed which go beyond school (Green 2008). This has also been discussed by Wright (2008), who—with reference to Freire (1972) and Folkestad (2006)—argues that through drawing on informal learning and inclusion in music pedagogy, students will have the potential to develop their social consciousness. In line with the principles mentioned above, informal music pedagogy has a broader range and scope which stretches beyond the classroom. It intends to provide students with opportunities to participate in their societies as active citizens, both on a musical and more general level. This is a part of the students' life-long learning processes, including a preparation for democratic decision-making. It emphasises the importance of recognising other people's views and opinions respectfully, and equally of being treated with respect by others. If informal music pedagogy will in practice facilitate these aspirations, students have the potential to benefit from personal, musical as well as social development within the framework of compulsory music education.

## Opportunities and Issues with Individualised and Informal Music Pedagogy

There are significant issues related to the inclusion of informal practices in school. Experiences from music education in Sweden today raise questions regarding the process of learning, the roles and functions of music and education, as well as the role and function of the teacher in the students' learning processes.

The thoughts and reflections that are currently arising in music education in Sweden can be described as originating from an ambition to acknowledge students' musical interests and experiences. What are the musical, pedagogical and democratic consequences of this? Who and what are included in the reality of this pedagogy? Is this music pedagogical strategy leading to participation, inclusion and emancipation?

Opinions among music pedagogues and music researchers are many and varied, but no one argues that schools ought to re-introduce a curriculum which is entirely teacher-directed or excludes popular culture. Rather, questions arise concerning whether education has become too individualised and informal, and—if this is the case—whether there may be a more useful balance between the informal and formal learning situation; between the everyday and the unfamiliar. Can there be a teaching context that can include children's and young people's lifeworlds as well as broaden them, without becoming normative? (Boman 2002; Zackari and Modigh 2000).

# Music Education in School and Students' Motivation

A highly legitimate motive stated for the use of informal teaching strategies is to increase students' engagement with and motivation for music education in school (Folkestad 2006; Green 2001, 2008).

The image of Swedish students' motivation that has emerged through the national evaluation and previous research is partly contradictory. Students enjoy music as a subject and appreciate being able to play music in groups (Skolverket 2004b). Music curricula have increasingly become characterised by current music culture, and—at least parts of—popular music are being integrated into the subject (see above Karlsson and Karlsson 2009). Despite this, it appears that students experience the subject as old-fashioned and as lacking breadth of genres (Skolverket 2004a). Variations between different schools are large, but it can equally be assumed that variations within the subject in a school are small (Skolverket 2004b).

# The Role of the Teacher in Individualised
# and Informal (Music) Pedagogy

Connecting with students' experiences is a difficult task in a time of a multitude of norms, values, symbolic codes, and cultural and social backgrounds. Variations become endless (Giddens 1991). Many argue that in order to facilitate students' personal development as individuals and to nurture them towards responsible citizenship, which are the main aims of schools, supervised and individualised pedagogy appears to be the only solution. Individualisation in terms of individual projects has had a major impact on schools in general. This demands that teachers possess a wide range of knowledge in order for the supervision of projects to be adequate. If there is a lack of knowledge and competence, students risk being left to their own perceptions and experiences (Madsen 2002).

Madsen (2002) argues that the idea of "teachers as supervisors" and students as seekers out of knowledge leads to teachers simply becoming "administrators" of students' work. Teaching is not simply about the transmission of information, but also about individuals actively constructing ideas of the world through interaction between the known and the unknown. In order to create new knowledge, an active dialogue— between teacher and student, between student and student—based upon awareness and understanding is required. Teachers must therefore be able to comprehend students' experiences, understanding, and thinking in order to be able to deliberately challenge them (Madsen 2002).

Sociologist and youth researcher Ove Sernhede (2006) also argues that the necessary abstraction and reflection processes of knowledge development are made more complicated if boundaries between school and everyday life become too blurred. Instead, he states that school must be allowed to become a designated space for learning, if it is to be a place where young people feel that their realities are being taken seriously. School must be an arena for vital discussions concerning life where students, teachers and experienced adults meet, discuss and challenge preconceived beliefs, opinions and prejudices. The teacher's task is to make the classroom a platform for democratic discussion and equal participation and to ensure that everyone's voice will be heard, considered and recognised.

In a recently conducted study of student music teachers' perceptions of their ongoing teacher education (Georgii-Hemming and Westvall 2010), some criticism of music education in compulsory comprehensive school emerged. Student teachers who participated in the study had, at the time of data collection, undertaken placement in schools on six occasions. As a result of these experiences, student teachers argued that music education in school lacked progression of knowledge. The perceptions of the student teachers were that teachers "plodded along" without awareness of goals and without considering the curriculum. Instead, what actually happened during the lessons appeared to be influenced by what the teachers "had always done" and by spontaneous conversations with students (Georgii-Hemming and Westvall 2010).

The opinions that music lessons were characterised by temporary solutions and improvised discussions, influenced by makeshift trends and a kind of "what shall we do today?" methodology, have been confirmed in the results from the national evaluation. The evaluation stated that teaching tended to be short-term in character, as well as unplanned and populist (Skolverket 2004b).

As discussed earlier, the curriculum for music education is open as well as non-linear in character. Goals related to social and personal development are emphasised ahead of musical knowledge. This makes local variations possible, which is also one of the aims with the decentralised education system. This chapter does not allow sufficient space to discuss the political and ideological reasons behind this development. However, it is impossible to completely ignore the fact that the character of music is situated and that every educational situation is unique. The scope for local influence and variation can be viewed as positive in a school where the music subject has strong traditions, is a part of the local identity, and is an appreciated and integrated part of a wider context (Ericsson 2002). The fact that teachers and students can select working methods and educational content according to their own situation can increase general satisfaction.

A counter-argument to the above is that development of musical knowledge and skills demands repetition, continuity and practice aligned with deliberately well-structured material that gradually increases in complexity. An open and non-linear curriculum also results in difficulties with grading and issues with creating a nationally comparable education, which complicates student mobility. A student who wants or has to change school should be able to recognise teaching methods and content, as well as have the relevant knowledge required to participate in the activities (Skolverket 2007).

## Participation and Inclusion

Teaching methods, activities and educational strategies that belong to ideas of informal learning are not only aimed at connecting with students' experiences in everyday life. Participation and inclusion—in and beyond school—are important goals of informal learning (Green 2008; Wright 2008).

Previous cultural hierarchies between "high" and "low" have, if not entirely dissolved, at least adopted a different shape (Sernhede 2006). Many music teachers in Sweden are connecting with students' music preferences, leisure-related knowledge and interests (Bergman 2009; Stålhammar 2006). The problem is that this mainly appears to benefit those students who play instruments during leisure-time (Skolverket 2004a, 2004b). The national evaluation has not investigated the instruments, genres or experiential contexts to which this applies. However, experiences from pop and rock bands were partly useful in school, whereas skills in creating music with the aid of computers or mixing music were not at all reflected in the grading. The national evaluation also stressed that the majority of those who missed computers for music-making were boys from an ethnic background (Skolverket 2004b).

Thus, the ambition to connect with students is not inclusive of all groups of students (Stålhammar 2006). These issues have ethnic as well as socio-economic dimensions (Lundberg et al. 2003).

This problematic situation has been confirmed, complicated and amplified in a recent thesis within musicology (Bergman 2009). In this ethnographic study, a group of youths were studied both in school and during leisure time from 2002 to 2005, as they attended the Swedish school years 7–9 (aged approximately 13–15). During this period music lessons occurred in uniform gender groups and were based on students forming bands and rehearsing songs. Experiences from informal contexts, e.g. playing in bands, were thus nurtured. However, it is problematic that these experiences were valued considerably higher than skill in playing an instrument which did not belong to a traditional rock band setup, e.g. saxophone or violin.

The music teacher in the study aimed for working in accordance with informal strategies, and to connect with student interests. This strategy led to vaguely structured lessons designed by questions along the lines of "who wants. . .?" or "what do you want. . .?" The result was that dominant students controlled content and design, and they also had the courage to try out different instruments. Quiet students, on the other hand, remained quiet, and furthermore those who did not have experience in playing an instrument did not dare to try. Differences and problems also increased as the years went on.

In addition to ethnic, socio-economic and social issues, the study also highlights gender-related problems. According to Bergman (2009), boys who did not play electric guitar, bass or drums lost interest and started skipping classes during the last year. The uniform gender groups led to the girls developing a traditionally feminine position during the classes. Although they had a "go get it" kind of attitude in other mixed gender groups in school, they appeared insecure and with low self-esteem during the music lessons.

A critical reflection of whom and what is included in music education should contain topics that encompass students with a personal interest in music, as well as those lacking such interest. It is not necessarily a positive thing that students with a personal engagement in music have their experiences included in the lessons. Music can represent and give rise to identities (Bennett 2000; Frith 2002), as well as be a way to explore and visualise life experiences (Ruud 1996). Music has a strong connection with independence and personal integrity (Ericsson 2002; Stålhammar 2006). For those young people to whom certain music is an important and active part of these processes, a teaching strategy connecting closely to students can turn students' private projects into school projects. What was previously private, and perhaps also secluded, could instead become valued as a public qualification (Skolverket 2004b).

# Future Music Education: Emancipation and Multiculturalism

So far, this chapter has highlighted the conception that informal and individualised strategies do not necessarily result in motivation, participation and inclusion. There have been music education issues closely related to the knowledge development and content of the subject, and misgivings about progression, as well as concern that the areas of music creativity, composition and music listening are not highly prioritised in music education in Sweden.

We have also stressed the fact that decentralisation and an increase in individualisation have resulted in large differences between schools. As a result of a sharp focus on individual students' interests and an openly formulated curriculum—as well as where (music) education is situated, i.e. the context and traditions of the individual school combined with the participants' experiences—it is possible to speak of music education in Sweden in terms of local cultures.

Sernhede (2006) draws a parallel between this development trend and a general increase in ideas of distinctiveness, as well as what is sometimes referred to as "tribalisation" (Maffesoli 1988), which can lead to problems like marginalisation and class segregation. Sernhede argues that it is unfortunate if schools are contributing to a strengthening of these segregating tendencies.

Furthermore, this relates to considerations of the democratic task of schools to develop tolerance and understanding between geographic, ethnic, social and musical cultures; to facilitate meetings between people of different generations, genders, and between those who have different interests. Young people in today's society neither adopt nor grow without reflection into their parents' life choices, cultures or a particular traditional canon. Meaning and goals must be created and reconstructed by the individual (Sernhede 2006). If schools succeed in their democratic task they will not only develop responsible, aware and unprejudiced citizens; students will also be able to find alternative and multiple identities, lifeworlds and choices—referred to as emancipation in critical pedagogy (cf. Freire 1972; Wright 2008).

The problems associated with an individually or locally rooted music education are connected with the relationship between local, global and media functions in these processes. Media is an important inspiration in young people's identity construction. Media "teaches" people what values are considered to be important, and what lifestyles are possible and desirable. It is sometimes said that young people live in a global music culture, where through media they both encounter and can "conquer" different genres and cultures (Skolverket 2004b).

Even though we cannot, in this context, further examine this complex issue, it is necessary to stress that cultural multitude and the role models it produces has actually decreased through globalisation (Bauman 2000, 2001; Giddens 1990, 1991; Lundberg et al. 2003; Smiers 2003). It is therefore necessary for schools and teacher education to develop a professional awareness concerning issues related to the role that media plays in young people's lives. Undoubtedly, music education needs to address and include popular culture, but it should also contain a critical and sound discussion concerning popular culture and media. In that way, music learning has the potential to contribute to a thriving community and will encourage solidarity, acceptance and awareness within the framework of compulsory music education (Georgii-Hemming and Westvall 2010). School is undoubtedly a part of society, as is popular culture. Consequently, schools need to strive towards an understanding of this culture. Students also need to be able to have their own experiences of music—physically, intellectually and emotionally—and be given opportunities to understand cultural processes and structures in society, as well as in educational settings (Ruud 1997). Thus, a central issue is what functions and roles music education, as part of compulsory school, will and can have in the future.

It may no longer be productive to strive for schools to become more informal, and further parallel students' everyday lives (Sernhede 2006). Personal development and construction of meaning both occur through encounters between the known and the unknown (Gadamer 1997; Ziehe 1993). Sernhede argues that young people lack confidence in the current school system. Not because of too much alienation, but because schools "let them do whatever they want" (Sernhede 2006, 15). Instead of deliberately structured and formalised learning, large parts of music education are currently characterised by informal pedagogical strategies. The original development that influenced current Swedish education had democratic ambitions, but Sernhede (2006) argues that the resulting practices today do not lead to liberation and emancipation. In order to contribute to young people's identity processes and to provide opportunities to construct coherence and meaning, schools need to represent a meeting place where questions can be asked from different perspectives.

## Conclusion

Music is a personal matter, in the sense that music is created, perceived and experienced by individual humans. In schools, there are students with many and various—as well as few and limited—musical experiences. Students may have stronger or weaker personal relationships with music, in many different ways. Professional music educators can and must respect, understand and relate to this. Teachers have an ethical, moral and democratic responsibility to help students to construct meaning and develop their social and cultural foundations so that they will be prepared to meet, understand and collaborate with other people from a multitude of cultures in the broadest sense. If the responsibility for music education content and activities is left completely to the students, we risk failing not only these students, but also music itself and the meaning that music can have for people.

Informal pedagogy can be "a way ahead" for music education. However, informal learning in schools is a part of formal education and must therefore be supplemented and supported by formal learning. Schools are, and should be, an active arena for democratic processes in the broadest sense. It is an important challenge for music educators to reach out and include students in active musicianship within the framework of compulsory music education. The functions and uses of music should no longer mean simply a socialisation into a dominant culture—either lofty or everyday—but should instead contain a dialogue, and an exchange organised, initiated and guided by the teacher. This dialogue between different experiences should be respectful, critical, playful, musical and educational; musical creativity in different forms could contribute to the development of individuals as well as the development of society. Music education could be an exciting encounter between the familiar and the unfamiliar, between the individual and the collective, and an opportunity for the local and the global to meet. Music education is both a personal as well as a collective matter.

## References

Bauman, Z. 2000. *Globalization. The Human Consequences.* New York: Columbia University Press.
—. 2001. *The Individualized Society.* Cambridge: Polity Press.
Bennett, A. 2000. *Popular Music and Youth Culture: Music, Identity, and Place.* Basingstoke: Macmillan.

Bergman, Å. 2009. *Växa upp med musik: ungdomars musikanvändande i skolan och på fritiden* [Growing Up with Music. Young People's Use of Music in School and During Leisure Time]. PhD diss., University of Gothenburg.

Boman, Y. 2002. *Utbildningspolitik i det andra moderna. Om skolans normativa villkor* [Educational Policy in Second Modernity. On the Normative Conditions of Education]. PhD diss., University of Örebro.

Elliott, D., ed. 2005. *Praxial Music Education: Reflections and Dialogues.* New York: Oxford University Press.

Englund, T. 2005. *Läroplanens och skolkunskapens politiska dimension* [Curriculum as a Political Problem]. Göteborg: Daidalos.

Ericsson, C. 2001. "Skolans musikverksamhet som offentligt rum: en diskussion av Thomas Ziehe's begrepp i ljuset av en empirisk studie [The School's Music Activities as Public Space: a Discussion of Thomas Ziehe's Concepts in the Light of an Empirical Study]" *Nordisk musikkpedagogisk forskning* 5: 63–73.

—. 2002. *Från guidad visning till shopping och förströdd tillägnelse: moderniserade villkor för ungdomars musikaliska lärande* [From Guided Exhibition to Shopping and Preoccupied Assimilation: Modernised Conditions for Adolescents' Musical Learning]. PhD diss., Lund University.

Folkestad, G. 2006. "Formal and Informal Learning Situations or Practices *vs* Formal and Informal Ways of Learning." *British Journal of Music Education* 23: 135–45.

Forsberg, E. 2000. *Elevinflytandets många ansikten* [The Many Faces of School Student Impact]. PhD diss., Uppsala University.

Freire, P. 1972. *Pedagogy of the Oppressed.* Harmondsworth: Penguin.

Frith, S. 2002 [1996]. *Performing Rites. On the Value of Popular Music.* Cambridge: Harvard University Press

Gadamer, H.-G. 1997 [1960]. *Sanning och metod. I urval.* [Wahrheit und Methode. Grundzügeeiner philosophischen Hermeneutik.]. Göteborg: Daidalos.

Georgii-Hemming, E. 2005. *Berättelsen under deras fötter: fem musiklärares livshistorier.* [The Story Beneath Their Feet. Five Music Teachers' Life Histories]. PhD diss., Örebro University. http://urn.kb.se/resolve?urn=urn:nbn:se:oru:diva-109.

—. 2006. "Personal Experiences and Professional Strategies." *Music Education Research* 8: 217–36.

Georgii-Hemming, E., and M. Westvall. 2010. "Teaching Music in Our Time. A Study of Student Teachers' Reflections on Participation,

Inclusion and the Right to Musical Development in their School-Based Music Teacher Education." *Music Education Research* 12 (4): 353–67.

Giddens, A. 1990. *The Consequences of Modernity*. Cambridge: Polity in association with Blackwell.

—. 1991. *Modernity and Self-identity. Self and Society in the Late Modern Age*. Cambridge: Polity.

Green, L. 2001. *How Popular Musicians Learn. A Way Ahead for Music Education*. Aldershot: Ashgate

—. 2008. *Music, Informal Learning and the School: A New Classroom Pedagogy*. Aldershot: Ashgate.

Jeffs T., and M. Smith, eds. 1990. *Using Informal Education: An Alternative to Casework, Teaching and Control?* Milton Keynes: Open University Press.

Karlsson C., and S. Karlsson. 2009. *Lagom svåra och hyfsat moderna. En undersökning av spelrepertoaren i skolar 7–9* [Not Too Difficult and Quite Modern. A Study of Repertoire in Compulsory Music Education Amongst 13 to 15 Year-Old Pupils]. Bachelor thesis in Music Education, Örebro University.

Kursplan 2000. *Kursplan och betygskriterier i musik för grundskolan* [Syllabus and Assessment Criteria in Music for Compulsory School]. Stockholm: Skolverket. http://www3.skolverket.se/ki03/front.aspx?

Lgr 62. *Läroplan för grundskolan 1962. Allmän del* [Core Curriculum for Compulsory School 1962]. Skolöverstyrelsens skriftserie 60. Stockholm: SO förlaget.

Lgr 69. *Läroplan för grundskolan 1969. Allmän del* [Core Curriculum for Compulsory School 1969]. Stockholm: Liber Utbildningsförlaget.

Lgr 80. *Läroplan för grundskolan 1980. Allmän del* [Core Curriculum for Compulsory School 1980]. Stockholm: Liber Utbildningsförlaget.

Lilliestam, L. 1995. *Gehörsmusik. Blues, rock och muntlig tradering* [Playing by Ear: Blues, Rock and Oral Tradition]. Göteborg: Akademiförlaget.

—. 2001. *'En dödsmetall-hardcore-hårdrocksgrej, det är jättesvårt att förklara'. Göteborgska gymnasister tänker och talar om musik.* [A Deathmetal-Hardcore-Hardrock-Thing, it is Really Difficult to Explain. Upper Secondary School Students from Gothenburg Reflect on and Talk about Music]. Gothenburg: Institutionen för musikvetenskap, Gothenburg University.

Lpo 94. *Läroplan för det obligatoriska skolväsendet 1994* [Curriculum for Compulsory School 1994]. Skolverket. Stockholm: Fritzes.

Lundberg, D., K. Malm, and O. Ronström. 2003. *Music, Media, Multiculture: Changing Music Landscapes.* Stockholm: Svenskt visarkiv. http://www.visarkiv.se/mmm/

Madsen, T. 2002. "Återupprätta läraren! [Reestablish the Teacher!]" *Pedagogiska Magasinet* 3: 54–59.

Maffesoli, M. 1988. "Jeux De Masques. Postmodern Tribalism." *Design Issues* IV (1 & 2, Special Issues): 141–51.

Ruud, E. 1996. *Musikk og verdier. Musikkpedagogiske essays* [Music and Values. Music Educational Essays]. Oslo: Universitetsforlaget.

—. 1997. *Musikk og identitet* [Music and identity]. Oslo: Universitetsforlaget.

Sandberg, R. 2006. "Skolan som kulturell mötesplats [School as Cultural Meeting Place]." In *Uttryck, intryck, avtryck. Lärande, estetiska uttrycksformer och forskning* [Expressions, Impressions, Imprints. Learning, Aesthetic Expression and Research], ed. U. P. Lundgren, 35–65. Stockholm: Vetenskapsrådet. http://www.cm.se/webbshop_vr/pdfer/Rapport%204.2006.pdf

Sernhede O. 2006. "Skolan och populärkulturen" [School and Popular Culture]." In *Uttryck, intryck, avtryck: Lärande, estetiska uttrycksformer och forskning* [Expressions, Impressions, Imprints. Learning, Aesthetic Expression and Research], ed. U. P. Lundgren, 11–19. Stockholm: Vetenskapsrådet. http://www.cm.se/webbshop_vr/pdfer/Rapport%204.2006.pdf

Skolverket [Swedish National Agency for Education]. 2004a. *National Evaluation of the Compulsory School in 2003. A Summary Main Report.* http://www.skolverket.se/publikationer?id=1404

—. 2004b. *Nationell utvärdering av grundskolan 2003. Bild, hem- och konsumentkunskap, idrott och hälsa, musik och slöjd* [National Evaluation of the Compulsory School in 2003. Subject Report]. http://www.skolverket.se/publikationer?id=1385

—. 2005. *Grundskolans ämnen i ljuset av Nationella utvärderingen 2003* [Subjects in Compulsory School in the Light of the National Evaluation]. http://www.skolverket.se/publikationer?id=1497

—. 2007. *Musik – En samtalsguide om kunskap, arbetssätt och bedömning* [Music—a Guide for Conversations about Knowledge, Ways of Working and Assessment]. http://www.skolverket.se/publikationer?id=1889.

Smiers, J. 2003. *Arts under Pressure: Promoting Cultural Diversity in the Age of Globalization.* London: Zed Books.

SOU 1948:27. *1946 års skolkommisions betänkande med förslag till riktlinjer för det svenska skolväsendets utveckling* [The 1946 School

Commission's Suggestions for Guidelines Regarding the Development of the Swedish School System].

Stålhammar, B. 1995. *Samspel. Grundskola – musikskola i samverkan: en studie av den pedagogiska och musikaliska interaktionen i en klassrumssituation.* [Interplay. School and Music School in Collaboration: A Study of Pedagogic and Musical Interaction in a Classroom Situation]. PhD diss., Gothenburg University.

—. 2006. *Musical Identities and Music Education.* Aachen: Shaker.

Thavenius, J. 2002. *Den goda kulturen och det fria skapandet: diskurser om "kultur i skolan"* [The Good Culture and the Free Creation: Discourses on "Culture in School"]. Malmö: Malmö Högskola, Lärarutbildningen.
http://www.lut.mah.se/publikationer/utbrapp1302.pdf

Varkøy, Ø. 2001. *Musikk for alt (og alle): Om musikksyn i norsk grunnskole* [Music for Everything (and Everyone): On the View of Music in Norwegian Compulsory School]. PhD diss., University of Oslo.

Wright, R. 2008. "Thinking Globally, Acting Locally: Informal Learning and Social Justice in Music Education. Music Education as Liberatory Education." Paper presented at the International Society of Music Education, World Conference, Bologna, July 2008.

Zackari, G., and F. Modigh. 2000. *Värdegrundsboken. Om samtal för demokrati i skolan* [The Book of Values. On Conversations for Democracy in School]. Stockholm: Utbildningsdepartementet, Regeringskansliet. http://www.regeringen.se/sb/d/108/a/22393.

Ziehe, T. 1993. *Kulturanalyser. Ungdom, utbildning, modernitet* [Cultural Analyses. Youth, Education, Modernity]. Stockholm/Stehag: Symposion.

# Notes

[1] Previously published in 2010 as "Music Education—a Personal Matter? Examining the Current Discourses of Music Education in Sweden" in *British Journal of Music Education* 27 (1): 21–33. Reprinted by permission of the publisher Cambridge University Press.

# PART III

# CHAPTER SEVEN

# INFORMAL LEARNING IN MUSIC: EMERGING ROLES OF TEACHERS AND STUDENTS[1]

## CARLOS XAVIER RODRIGUEZ

It was a pleasure to read Lucy Green's new book *Music, Informal Learning and the School* (2008), in which she consolidates many ideas presented in her previous writings. While there is little doubt of the timeliness and significance of her approach, the epistemological and pedagogical issues it raises should be addressed to better understand how we might provide more relevant, engaging public school music instruction. When we question how well we have designed music curricula, and how well we have prepared our teachers to implement them (Williams 2007), we must take into account the nature and organization of music learning as it occurs beyond the classroom, and for this perspective we are deeply indebted to Green. Her ideas resonate with the growing support for more creative thinking in the classroom. If we construe creativity as a three-part process of considering expected outcomes, rejecting them, then exploring alternatives (Ackoff and Greenberg 2008), informal learning shows great promise for revitalizing the creative aspects of music education. However, we are yet in the infancy stage of our inquiry, with so many new questions arising from the emergent literature. Therefore, in this chapter I present several problems with informal learning that I have encountered in my own fieldwork—specifically, the new roles for teachers in informal learning, and providing informal learning experiences to students who have substantive skill as formal musicians. These problems are discussed in the context of my experiences with pre-service music educators at the university, and with a rock band at a local urban high school.

# Informal Learning and Musicality

I cannot proceed without first addressing the issue of musicality. How one conceptualizes musicality shapes everything else one does in the profession (Rodriguez 2004). I find increasing acceptance of this term in my discussions with peer researchers and educators because it encompasses a broad range of traditional and emergent skills and sensitivities, even while there seems to be some flexibility in its use by these groups (Jaffurs 2004). What it means when we call someone "musical" is rarely the sum of the relatively few factors we can measure accurately, therefore present in the school curriculum. For example, music literacy, in the traditional sense, refers to one's ability to see symbols and convert them into sounds, and to hear sounds and convert them into symbols. However, we expect quite a bit more from the musically literate than these decoding/encoding notational skills, such as extended vocabularies for describing music, stylistic sensitivity across historically and ethnically diverse musical cultures, the ability and willingness to articulate musical preferences, understanding of the multidisciplinary nature of music, a knack for playing instruments and/or singing, some creative facility, and a well-developed conception of the place that music holds in one's life. In the end, music literacy is probably something more than what we typically teach to, and musicality is surely quite a bit more as well.

If I may propose my own conception of musicality: it is one's demonstration of explicit and implicit skills and understandings to communicate musical ideas. I believe Green's proposal of a "critical musicality" is consistent with my conception, in that students develop conscious awareness of their ability to express something of themselves through music. It is a process of extending their personalities through the music—composing and performing in such a way that it identifies the music as uniquely theirs. This process of individualization is not a typical goal of traditional music instruction, so I believe we must look beyond our current teaching practices to more fully develop musicality in students. It has been suggested that there are clear intersections in formal and informal musical learning (Jaffurs 2006), thus we might do well to explore these intersections as means of helping students more fully develop their musicality.

## Teaching for Informal Learning

The more familiar I become with informal learning, the more I recognize its formal qualities. The most basic learning process of listening to and copying recordings becomes more efficient with experience as musicians gradually acquire skill in predicting and remembering changes, audiating through chord progressions without having to play them, and so forth. These thinking skills culminate in the ability to hear the music once and be able to play it, which in turn strengthens the transfer and linkage between mental rehearsal and physical execution. These attainments suggest that there is a system of rules and connections that cumulatively produce sharpened perception, expanded musical memory, and improved dexterity. However, the process is not a pre-ordinate series of steps that is understood separately from the music itself, nor deliberately taught by someone who has already mastered them—thus, perhaps, its nature as informal. It is common of musicians playing by ear, taking its shape from the collective musical materials from which it arises. Informal learning is thus aligned with critical pedagogy in so far as musical attainments are stimulated and mediated by the music itself. This is a hallmark of critical pedagogy—allowing concepts and skills to emerge from engagement in the materials themselves (Abrahams 2005).

However, because informal learning is not algorithmic does not mean that it is not structured. While use of the term "formal" implies that the learning contains hierarchically organized levels of mastery, and is controlled by more experienced participants, these two features may be present in informal learning as well. In formal instructional settings, a pre-ordinate series of instructional steps allows teachers to control learning and efficiently identify problems in the process. In informal learning, the teacher relinquishes this control and enters into a more flexible and dynamic relationship with the learner, yet a plan for instruction must still be negotiated between teachers and students. The activities of copying recordings, improvising, composing, and performing on an instrument (or singing) each invoke steps, even if they happen to be material-, context-, and learner-specific, and even if they are mostly hidden. Experienced teachers naturally desire to bring these steps to the fore. From their standpoint, what does it mean to understand informal learning in music? I believe it means they are cognizant of its sequence of competencies, and are able to re-organize or re-frame these competencies to promote learning. This is what we otherwise train teachers to do, and what we expect them to believe they can do. To repeat a question one of my pre-service music education students asked, why bring informal learning into a classroom if you do not want a teacher to direct the process?

To use a familiar example in children's musical development, we do not really teach children how to learn songs, but we can document what naturally occurs in learning songs by first systematically observing, then describing, then formulating stages in song acquisition (Davidson, McKemon and Gardner 1981; Welch, Sargent and White 1998). We then use these findings to formulate an instructional sequence that teachers use to teach songs to children. This is the functional relationship between research and practice, which permits music educators to believe that they can control and maximize learning—two responsibilities that characterize the American educational system.

However, teachers must make a substantial shift in informal learning, such that they must become experts in helping students make things happen for themselves. Even if this scenario of music teachers and students interacting as co-teachers and co-learners is the hallmark of critical pedagogy (Abrahams 2005), it does drastically redefine what it means to prepare music teachers. When my students are introduced to the concept of informal learning through a series of readings, asked to identify possible points of interaction with formal learning, and then required to present a sample lesson in class, approximately half of them do so with extreme awkwardness, and some even with hostility. These students feel very threatened by the idea that their own education, which has shaped their high musical standards and made them who they are, has somehow been devalued. In my experience, this is a common reaction for in-service teachers as well, even if they do acknowledge the importance of meeting their students' ever-changing needs for musical knowledge and skills. Frustration arises when teachers are not able to accommodate something presumptively a "best practice" into their existing teaching schemas.

## Informal Learning with Formally-Trained Students

Recently, I have experienced joys and concerns observing and assisting a rock band at a local high school. They have "curricular music", meaning that one entire period per day is devoted to practicing to provide accompaniment for the pop vocal ensemble that meets at the same time in a different rehearsal room. The line-up is guitar, bass, keyboard, and drums, and the players are male. We have been working on four new songs. My comments here describe the students trying to learn pre-composed music rather than composing their own.

Each member has been playing violin, cello, or double bass since junior high school, making this group different than others I have observed in an informal learning context. This formal study has been accompanied by their interest in popular music, and while they have each been developing skills in playing by ear on electric guitar, bass, keyboard, and drums, this is the first time any of them has played in a group. I began by asking the music teacher to provide me with CD recordings and scores for each piece. I passed along the recordings to the band members early one week, and then met with them several days later to check on their progress. I was quite surprised to find that they had not even listened to the recordings, but had used the scores to block out their parts. As the bass player, "Josh", described it when I questioned him: "It's so much easier to get the basic part down . . . you know, we just look at the music . . . you can check the key . . . or find out where any changes are . . . then try to remember them as you play." As for the chord progression, Josh was not interested in working on the fingering until he heard the recording, since " . . . the recording tells you how it sounds . . . it's not the same as the music[al score] . . . " So then, what was the score for? "It's just a way to find out how many verses . . . and to look at the cues . . . " Upon further investigation I determined that each player had gone through roughly this same process. In fact, they did it together. We discussed as a group if they could obtain the same information by simply listening to the recording. The guitarist, "David", replied: "It's just too slow . . . you end up listening so many times, and then the song gets really . . . boring."

I watched and listened as the band members copied the CD recordings over several rehearsal sessions. The drummer, "Austen", appeared to have the least experience on his new instrument, and took the most time learning his part. He was not able to develop a sense of how the music went by looking at the score—in his defense, it contained less information for drums than for the pitched instruments—and began listening to the CD recordings before the other members. He expressed resentment over the score-reading stage, but tolerated it since it was something everyone else in the group was doing. I sensed that he complied because he didn't want to fall behind in the learning of the music, and because, for the reason band members are often compelled to act (Inglis 2006), it reinforced his identification with the band.

The protocol described here is quite different from that used by informal learners who do not have developed notational skills. These band members use notation to learn music quickly and efficiently, and are advantaged by very sharp musical ears, no doubt the result of intensive music involvement. Further, their enjoyment of the music, obviously regulated by their familiarity with it (Sluckin, Hargreaves and Colman 1982), is short-lived. Allowed to choose their own path, they attempt to learn the music at a macro-level as quickly as possible, and attend to the various micro-levels later. This trend is the reverse of how Lucy Green and others have observed self-regulated novices approach similar musical tasks, and on this point, Green invokes the developmental theory of Swanwick and Tillman (1986), who support her contention that novice learners are initially "primarily immersed in the immediate sonic qualities of musical materials" (71, footnote).

If the sophistication of one's notational skills mediates one's initial selection of surface or structural aspects to learn music, then informal learning environments are perhaps even more diverse with respect to peer learning and cooperation than it is tempting to assume. We should be prepared for informal learning opportunities to attract former and current band, choir, or orchestra students looking for more creative and flexible music making, as well as students who do not participate in performance ensembles or take private lessons because they dislike the repertory that accompanies these traditions. How might these groups interact, particularly if the pace, style, and organization of learning are determined by students?

The keyboardist, "Julian", is the most accomplished musician in the group, but he is highly introverted, and I question whether he even enjoys playing the raucous pop classics the group was assigned. Considering his behavior, he is a textbook case of an introvert with a lower threshold of arousal, compared to the remaining members, who are all extroverts (Kemp 1996). They admire his more advanced musical skills, but also his freedom and courage to be highly individual in dress, hairstyle, and mannerisms. He certainly does not desire this leadership role.

The song "Do You Want to Dance?" begins with narration as the group, minus drums, plays chords in rhythmic unison. Because they were not together with their timing, I asked Julian to nod his head as he played the chords on the keyboard, for David and Josh to follow. He did so, but with little assertiveness, and it did not bring them together. I demonstrated. He tried again and it really got no better. He was very frustrated since it seemed like it should be an easy task. Julian and I practiced jumping forward from a standing position, in order to feel the anacrusis of the downbeat. He then tried to transfer this feeling to the "head up" motion. The head nodding seemed to work a bit better, but I think he felt self-conscious over the amount of effort it expended. I am continually surprised by how poorly I can predict what tasks will be easy or difficult for us as a working group.

I try to divide my efforts between helping where and how I think they need help, and listening to how they would like me to help them. Josh and David are the best at articulating how they want me to help them. Josh plays me licks he has worked out as embellishments, ostensibly to obtain approval to use them, but I suspect he really just enjoys playing and having me listen. David has very good chops on the guitar, but lacks confidence, so he wants me to create solos for him to imitate. Austen, a bit younger than the rest, continually talks and is not really sure how I might best assist him or the group. Working with all of them at once is exhausting. The foregoing observations demonstrate that my interactions with the group can be unsettling if, despite our best efforts to communicate with each other, my mentoring efforts do not coincide with their mentoring needs.

## Preferences and Technique

Differences in personal taste create obstacles that we must navigate through. One of the songs features a highly syncopated bass line pattern, in the style of "electric funk." In the first run-through, Austen was not playing the kick drum in time with the bass, but was instead kicking on the downbeat, which is a quite natural way for novice drummers to play. The result was a muddy bottom to the sound, with the kick drum and the bass guitar just a sixteenth note apart. I asked Austen to try aligning his right foot with the bass guitar part. He asked why, and I replied that it created a cleaner-sounding bottom and also resolved some tempo problems, i.e., his tendency to drag. He replied that he didn't know what I meant about the "cleaner-sounding bottom" and didn't think he was slowing down while playing. I was tempted to suggest using a click track or strobe to prevail my point, but understood that this was not the best direction to go. To my relief, Josh suggested a click track, which solved the tempo problem but not the muddiness. This episode brought back a memory from several years ago of my daughter playing Zwan's *Mary Star of the Sea,* whose opening song featured a drumming part that I found ludicrous. Using frenetic cymbal and drum combinations in a grandiose style I might have expected in the final few bars, the drummer played in this way relentlessly through the entire song. My daughter commented that the drums were her favorite aspect, because he played with so much passion. I understood that what I had experienced then, and what I was experiencing now, was a difference in what we considered good. I was thus happy to have amended the tempo problem, and let Austen play his drums in the manner he thought best.

To what degree is it beneficial for teachers to attempt to influence the students' personal musical preferences? Perhaps to the degree that they are willing to have their own preferences changed. This perspective is challenging for teachers who believe they are competent by virtue of possessing highly evolved standards for musical thinking and behavior. For now, I am content to let my standards float about the rehearsal space, sneaking them into student-initiated discussions as needed. For example, David could not find out how to get a "1960s rock and roll" sound out of his chording and strumming, primarily because he was playing barred chords in such a way that he was dampening the highest strings, strumming only the inner four strings of the guitar using a mix of neck and bridge pickups, and filtering his signal through an impressively complex maze of compressors, distortion boxes, and master volumes. The resulting sound was characteristic of a style that developed in the 1990s—a very mid-rangy, sustained sound. Together we worked to achieve what guitarist Todd Rundgren called "that kind of dry, upfront, unembellished sound from the pre-pedal days [to] get the effect of being plugged directly into the amp" (Gress 2008, 122). In this case, David was less concerned that I preferred the new sound for the song style, and more interested in the various technical adjustments needed to produce exactly the sound we were searching for.

As a corollary to the previous point, an essential component of an electric musician's craft is tone. I have always worked on my tone as hard as I have worked on my right and left hand technique. So when I, in effect, deconstruct someone else's tone, I consider it a highly personal matter. David's current set-up represents his progress in searching for his sound. Josh appears even more conscious of his choices, typically bringing three basses to practice. Julian has an electronic keyboard that has sampling capabilities, and I hear him exploring its endless possibilities between songs, but he prefers one basic electric piano sound, as if to proclaim that he does not want to orchestrate the music with instruments the group doesn't actually have. Austen is quite impressionable and is searching for his own "voice" on the drums. He is sensitive about his abilities and claims he needs to practice outside of band rehearsal. He currently does not have a favorite drummer. We are collectively quite keen on helping him find one.

## Final Reflection

My experiences with pre-service music educators and high school students generate questions about my future role as an advocate for informal learning. As the primary source of my information and inspiration, Lucy Green makes informal learning seem attractive, timely, and meaningful to our larger aims as music educators. While I am mostly encouraged by the reactions of my students to informal learning experiences, they give rise to the instructional problems I have addressed in this chapter. I find that students engaged in informal learning focus much of their attention on testing and evaluating ways to communicate musical ideas, and while I believe this practice is essential to musicality, it represents a dramatic departure from the purposes and processes of formal music education, so much so that I find myself struggling with the intricacies of moment-to-moment interactions, while I question my role in the formation and appreciation of student preferences. I understand how critical it is to provide the right type of guidance at the right time so as not to constrain their progress. I believe teachers need more concise recommendations on how to provide freedom and direction while remaining compassionate and resourceful leaders, even as longstanding rules for teaching are replaced with newer, mostly untested ones.

My exchanges with high school musicians who have strong formal music backgrounds suggests that informal learning pedagogy requires more flexibility and intensiveness than I had previously imagined. While informal learning environments may provide more accessible and varied musical experiences than traditional music ensembles, students with significant prior notational and practicing abilities tend to bring those skills with them, reducing the informality of the environment. However, because creative decision-making is not a significant part of formal music education, formally-trained students display a heavy reliance on guidelines. They are conditioned to being told what to do, and adopting someone else's ideas of how the music should go, such that they are often not adequately prepared for the individual freedoms informal learning provides. When they are confronted with problems to solve, they often resort to strategies acquired from formal music training, since this is what they know. In this sense, my formally-trained students and I share a similar challenge—to develop new ways to address new problems. One area for future research would be to study the give-and-take of informal and formal learning systems to determine how they can be mutually supportive. To be sure, if we empower students and teachers with greater decision-making power in the content and procedures of learning, we must better prepare them for this challenge and responsibility, suggesting educational changes that reach far beyond music.

# References

Abrahams, F. 2005. "The Application of Critical Pedagogy to Music Teaching and Learning." *Visions of Research in Music Education* 6. http://users.rider.edu/~vrme/special_edition/vision/Abrahams_2005.pdf

Ackoff, R. L., and D. Greenberg. 2008. *Turning Learning Right Side Up: Putting Education Back on Track.* Upper Saddle River: Pearson Education.

Davidson, L., P. McKemon, and H. Gardner. 1981. "The Acquisition of Song: A Developmental Approach." In *Documentary Report of the Ann Arbor Symposium.* Reston: Music Educators National Conference.

Green, L. 2008. *Music, Informal Learning and the School: A New Classroom Pedagogy.* Burlington: Ashgate.

Gress, J. 2008. "Todd Rundgren Returns to the Arena [interview]." *Guitar Player* 42 (10): 116–91.

Inglis, I. 2006. "The Politics of Nomenclature." *Journal of Popular Music Studies* 18 (1): 3–17.

Jaffurs, S. E. 2004. "Developing Musicality: Formal and Informal Learning Practices." *Action, Theory, and Criticism for Music Education* 3 (3). http://act.maydaygroup.org/articles/Jaffurs3_3.pdf

—. 2006. "The Intersection of Formal and Informal Learning Practices." *International Journal of Community Music* Volume D.

Kemp, A. E. 1996. *The Musical Temperament: Psychology and Personality of Musicians.* Oxford: Oxford University Press.

Rodriguez, C. X. 2004. "Popular Music in Music Education: Toward a New Conception of Musicality." In *Bridging the Gap: Popular Music and Music Education*, ed. C. X. Rodriguez, 13–27. Reston: MENC.

Sluckin, W., D. J. Hargreaves, and A. M. Colman. 1982. "Some Experimental Studies of Familiarity and Liking." *Bulletin of the British Psychological Society* 35: 189–94.

Swanwick, K., and J. Tillman. 1986. "The Sequence of Musical Development: A Study of Children's Composition." *British Journal of Music Education* 3 (3): 305–39.

Welch, G. F., D. C. Sargent, and P. J. White. 1998. "The Role of Linguistic Dominance in the Acquisition of Song." *Research Studies in Music Education* 10 (1): 63–74.

Williams, D. 2007. "What Are Music Educators Doing and How Well Are We Doing It?" *Music Educators Journal* 94 (1): 18–23.

# Notes

[1] Previously published in 2009 as "Informal Learning in Music: Emerging Roles of Teachers and Students" in *Action, Criticism and Theory for Music Education* 8 (2): 35–45. Reprinted by permission of the editor.

# CHAPTER EIGHT

# IMPROVISATION AS AN INFORMAL MUSIC LEARNING PROCESS: IMPLICATIONS FOR TEACHER EDUCATION[1]

## PANAGIOTIS KANELLOPOULOS AND RUTH WRIGHT

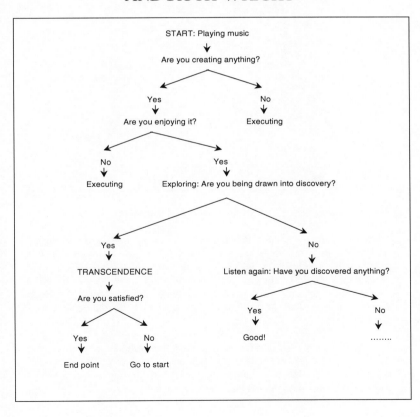

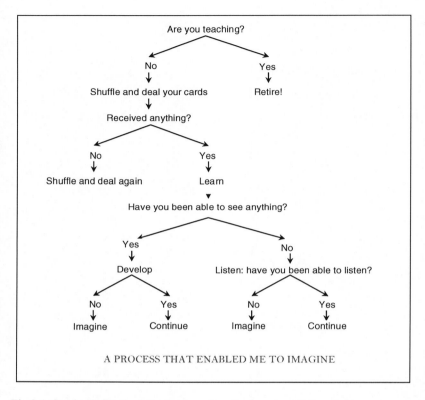

Fig 8-1. Stephen's [student at a music university department] flowchart

I had never thought before that children can create music, not because I underestimate them, not at all, but because I just hadn't thought that this was possible (basically, I did not even believe that I myself could ever play, even the tiniest thing) . . . Now, not only do I know that they are able to play, but I feel quite confident that I know of ways to encourage them to do so. (From the diary of Antonia, student at an early childhood education department)

In searching for sounds and for the responses that are attached to them, and conducting this process within the medium of collective music-making itself, a musician has to remain keenly aware of the human relationships towards both the material and the fellow musicians (Prévost 2004, 84).

# Introduction

The purpose of this chapter is to examine the role of music improvisation in music teacher education. We will present the results of a study conducted in two Greek universities with student teachers, which aimed firstly to investigate the sense in which improvisation might be conceived of as an informal music education process, and secondly the effects of such a course in free improvisation on student teachers' perceptions of themselves as musicians, music as a school subject, and children as musicians. Our study is based on data from the reflective diaries or learning journals of 91 trainee teachers kept as part of their participation in an improvisation university module. We would argue here that improvisation, as a particular type of informal music learning process, has an important role to play in fostering the qualities required of teachers to work with informal pedagogies in music education. Furthermore, we would suggest that such musical experiences might gradually lead to the development of a critical perspective on both music education theories and practices. Improvisation might emerge as a moment and a practice of rupture with the linearity of progress, working against the reification of knowledge and glorification of received information. The findings suggest that improvisation might offer a route for creating an intimate, powerful, evolving dialogue between students' identities as learners, their attitudes towards children and their creative potential, and the interrelationships of the notions of expressive technique and culture, thus becoming "an act of transcendence" (Allsup 1997, 81). Such experiences for pupils and teachers alike might further extend the social and personal effectiveness of informal learning as music pedagogy. We will finally argue that the data collected in this study allow us to support the view that improvisation as a mode of informal music learning in teacher education might be a subversive force against the dominance of the rationalist, performative educational ideology that permeates the training of teachers. Some years ago Ross warned that "The robots *are* coming: a new breed of teachers programmed to deliver art as a business plan, to package culture as a commodity—in short, to consign the children's zest to oblivion" (Ross 1998, 212). As Kushner characteristically observes,

> I've lost count of the number of music performances I have observed with children standing in embarrassed compliance, heads bowed, while public audiences thrill to their private accomplishments. The real object of these tests is the performance of the teacher which is somehow aggregated into the performance of a school which is, itself, aggregated into "performance

league tables" comparing one school with many thousands of others. (Kushner 2004, 207)

Against this context, improvisation might function, after Kushner (2004), as a "petit falsification"—as a transformative experience and a pedagogically subversive mode of action, playing an important role in the education of both music and early childhood teachers.

## The Wider Context

Currently, governments assert the need to reshape conceptions of learning to equip populations with the knowledge, skills and innovative potential required to compete in 21st century knowledge economies (OECD 2007). This has led to the development and implementation of

> new forms of educational capitalism that cultivate a new spirit of enterprise and the enterprise curriculum, give a new emphasis to the entrepreneurial subject, encourage teaching for giftedness and creativity, prioritize accelerated and personal learning, and lend weight to "consumer-citizens" and a new ethic of self-presentation and self-promotion. (Peters 2009, 41)

Against the increasing pressure to view education as a mechanism for the production of "profitable inequalities" and of exploitable human capital, we feel that there is a need to help our students to be able to develop a critical attitude towards the politics of globalization and the "customer-based" societal structure: "Fundamental questions must be raised about what knowledge is produced, by whom, for whose interests, and toward what ends" (Gaventa 1993, 40)—we need, in other words, to be conscious of how capitalist logic exploits openness and child-centered education (which were outcomes of the emancipatory movements of the 1960s), resulting in an *enseignement de l'ignorance*, (see Mishéa 1999). We therefore suggest that it is imperative to work towards modes of research and pedagogical practice that support a democratic school that does not surrender to corporate logic.

The seemingly a-political perspectives put forward by many pedagogic publications, including some in music education, tend to function as discourses that legitimize the currently dominant educational practices and policies. Despite the rhetoric to the contrary, the UK currently appears to be leading Europe in returning to a 19th century model of education, governed by the demands of economic relations and the employment requirements of industry. In Greece, "third way" moderate neo-conservative educational politics dominated the years 1997–2002 (Grollios and Kaskaris 2003; see for example, Ministry of National Education and

Religion Affairs 1997), preparing the way for an even more forceful attempt (from 2004 onwards, intensified to an unparalleled degree as this chapter is being written—December 2010—see Athanasiou 2010; Benveniste 2010; Theotokas 2010) to "rationalize" the education process, rendering Universities accountable to the so-called "needs of the society"—this rhetoric is used to mask the unconditional surrender of education to the rules of the market (see for example, Psycharis 2009). This "restructuring of the schooling and education systems across the world is part of the ideological and policy offensive by neo-liberal Capital" (Hill 2003).

Within this context, there is increasing emphasis on linearity of development and predictability of results, at the expense of creative practice at all levels of the education process (Paynter 2000; Prentice 2000). From a sociological perspective, one could identify an increasing rationalisation of education, whereby the emphasis is upon arriving at absolute efficiency in every field of human activity. Lyotard (1984) and Ball (2003) have spoken separately of this in terms of performativity or the subsumption of education to the efficient functioning of the social system. However, the danger of efficiency technique when applied to education is that we may lose important elements, and they may be those very elements that define our humanity.

## Informal Learning

Awareness has grown during the last 30 years that important learning occurs in situations other than the classroom (Bailey and Doubleday 1990; Colley et al. 2003; Eraut 2000; Rice 1985; Sefton-Green and Soep 2007). Such learning has been described variously as non-formal or informal, drawing a distinction between this kind of learning and formal learning. Formal learning may be described as that which occurs in a traditional pedagogic environment, where clarity of goals and procedures are clearly defined in advance and where learning results in certification or assessment. Non-formal learning occurs outside traditional learning environments, is not the result of deliberation and does not normally result in certification (Eraut 2000). It is important to note here however that aural and oral modes of learning should not automatically be thought of as informal just on the basis of their difference from the formality of traditional western models of learning (Nettl 2007). In his critique of the theoretical rationale that underpins Green's (2008a) study of informal musical learning processes as classroom music pedagogy, Allsup (2008) argued for the need to draw a distinction between "informal learning" and "informalism", emphasised that "researchers must be careful not to make equivalent the notion of informal learning ipso facto with that of popular music" (3) and maintained that informality does not automatically lead to openness and to the transformation of classrooms into spaces for the development of democratic thinking and practice. Folkestad (2006, 135) has also suggested that: "Formal—informal should not be regarded as a dichotomy, but rather as the two poles of a continuum; in most learning situations, both these aspects of learning are in various degrees present and interacting." We suggest that informal learning could be understood as a deliberate attempt to be immersed in intense situations of non-formal learning, and therefore results in the creation of non-traditional social learning environments, combining interactive, non-linear and self-directed processes. Thus, the introduction of informal learning in music education raises interesting questions regarding definition of the term "informal" in pedagogic contexts in music, the extent to which informal learning is or is not linked to particular musical genres, and the potential of informal learning to facilitate openness and democracy in classrooms.

Green's (2002, 2008a) development of a classroom music pedagogy based on informal learning practices of popular musicians has had far-reaching impact upon the practices of music education in schools in England. The core aim of her approach, explained in detail in Green's most recent book (2008a) has been to document and explore the processes through which pupils learn when presented with an approach based on such informal popular music learning practices. Informal learning as the preferred pedagogic modality in music education was the basis of the Musical Futures Hertfordshire action research project. In it Green introduced pedagogy based on the common processes used by some popular musicians in their music making to classroom music lessons (see Green 2002, 2008a). Often referred to as an "informal" pedagogy, it locates production and development of musical knowledge with the pupils themselves. Among its features are that learners choose the music they learn themselves, that it is learnt by listening and copying rather than from notation, and that learning takes place in groups, with skills and knowledge acquired according to individual need, and that the musical areas of performing, composing, improvising and listening are integrated with the emphasis on creativity.

Teachers' roles changed significantly in Green's approach. The first two or three lessons in the first project involved pupils making a cover version of a song they brought in as an audio recording, for which teachers were asked to: "establish ground rules for behaviour, set the task going at each stage, and then stand back and observe what the pupils were doing"

(Green 2008a, 24). This element of Green's work has been taken out of context by some critics who have assumed that such was the role of teachers throughout, yet Green clearly specified that:

> During this time teachers were asked to attempt to take on and empathize with pupils' perspectives and the goals that pupils set for themselves, then to begin to diagnose pupils' needs in relation to those goals. After, and only after, this period, they were to offer suggestions and act as "musical models" through demonstration, so as to help pupils reach the goals that they had set for themselves. (Green 2008a, 24–25)

This led to a new type of pedagogy which involved teaching in a responsive, rather than directive way; metaphorically taking the learners by the hand, getting inside their head and asking "What do they want to achieve now, this minute, and what is the main thing they need to achieve it?" In this way, the teacher sits alongside the learner and is to a large extent a learner herself. (Green 2008a, 34.) Teachers are not intended to disappear from learning contexts but to operate as teacher students, as advocated by critical pedagogues.

This approach may hold significant potential for the extension of openness and democracy in music classrooms, but it also presents significant challenges to the development of teacher education. It may require very different qualities of music teachers entering the profession in the future. In the context of a recent discussion Green (2008b) emphasised the need of prospective music teachers to develop musical skills which will enable them to work intensely and effectively by employing informal music-making strategies, such as "being able to aurally copy music from a recording of any kind of music the students brought in, as well as from the provided curriculum materials; being able to suggest how pupils can improve their instrumental skills, ensemble skills, compositional and improvisational skills; being able to link the informal strategies to the school's formal curriculum" (6). Adding these comments to the issues raised by Green qua the qualities required of teachers to work effectively with her conception of informal pedagogy in music opens a rich field of research. Important questions are raised, which posit the need for further research into how non-traditional modes of musical practice might form an integral part of teacher education.

## Informal Learning and Critical Pedagogy

It is extremely important to note that the notion of informal learning has been used both as a descriptive and as an evaluative term in hugely disparate contexts, informed by different, even conflicting, educational/ philosophical/ideological underpinnings. For example, its use in EU political agenda "is overwhelmingly workplace oriented" (Straka 2004, 5). Informal and non-formal learning, their measurement and quantification, are valued for their potential "to improve economic competitiveness by increasing skills and employability of workers" (5). Thus emphasis is placed upon vocational-related skills, their measurement and development, as well as on the role of the University in this regard.

However, this may not be the only way to look at informal learning. During the 1970s it was associated with "radical social-democratic models of non-formal education in the southern hemisphere that became popular in the North through various (feminist, anti-racist, working class) radical educational projects" and as "the basis of socio-cultural and situated theories of learning" (Straka 2004, 4). Advocates of critical pedagogy have long sought to develop a model in which learning and teaching exist in a dialogic relationship. Based on notions of critical theory derived from the ideas of Marx, Horkheimer and Adorno (Pongratz 2005), Marcuse (1991) and the work of those such as Apple (2005), Freire (1970), Giroux (1983a, 1983b, 1985, 1988a, 1988b, 1988c, 1997, Giroux and McLaren 1994), and McLaren (2006), they acknowledge the value of students' lived experiences to their learning and advocate a commensurate change in the power balance in classrooms. Teachers are to be no longer the sole founts of knowledge in classrooms, their jobs are no longer to fill the empty vessels of their students' minds (following what Freire [1970] described as "a banking model"). Instead, both teacher and students are to be regarded as having something to learn and something to teach. Using that knowledge as a conduit to new learning results in a change of perception for both students and their teachers (Abrahams 2005).

We would argue that the work of Lucy Green (2008a) in the UK, which emphasized students' lived musical experiences as the foundation of their musical explorations and placed teacher and student in a new, more egalitarian and dialogic relationship to previous modes of music education, has much in common with the aims of critical pedagogy. We would further suggest that immersion in improvisation as a core element of music teacher education might do much to prepare teachers to work in such ways with students.

The data we present in the following section of this chapter illustrate the ways in which free improvisation as a significant element of music teacher education might equip student teachers with the skills required to work in such ways in music education. The data also illustrates resonances between Green's identified characteristics of informal learning in music and the practice of improvisation. It is argued here that teachers who have been seriously concerned with the value of improvisation in music education might proceed to develop a teaching approach where deep involvement in improvisatory music-making further demolishes preconceptions according to which children are "fed" with information and skills through a process that is cut off from musical creation and moves further towards dialogic respectful learning situations in music education.

## Introducing the Study

A study was undertaken in two Greek universities (a University Music Department and a University Department of Early Childhood Education) with 91 student teachers during the period 2003–2007. During this period all the students were involved in a free improvisation course designed as part of their teacher education programme. As part of the assessment for the course, the students were required to produce reflective accounts/diaries recording thoughts, questions, impressions and feelings related to their participatory experience in the improvisations made in the class. It was also suggested that they record their possible perceptions of how this experience might influence their ways of thinking as future teachers. Recordings were made of work in progress and some students supplemented their written diaries with illustrations. The form of these journals/diaries was not dictated in advance; hence the data collected took various forms: diary-like regular entries, summative reflective prose, and in some cases cartoon-like representations and conceptual rivers. These different types of written accounts formed the data source drawn upon by the researchers to answer the following research questions:

(1) To what extent can free improvisation be termed an informal music making practice?

(2) What are students' perceptions of the nature and organisation of music making and creativity in this improvisatory setting?

(3) To what extent did this improvisatory music-making facilitate openness and democratic musical practice?

## Methodology

This study adopts a narrative approach to tell the stories of the thoughts and feelings of two groups of student teachers as they experienced a course in improvisation. Narrative is becoming a widely adopted approach to the study of human action, and its value has recently begun to be acknowledged within the field of music education as well (Benedict 2007; Georgii-Hemming 2007; McCarthy 2007). It is an interpretive paradigm used primarily in the social sciences and employs storytelling methodology. It is the story that becomes the object of study, with the aim of understanding how individuals or groups of individuals understand events in their lives (Clandinin 2007). Ethnographic techniques are used to gather data, capturing the subject's story and focusing on how individuals or groups make sense of events and actions in their lives. Situated within a postmodernist stance, the narrative approach emphasises that knowledge is socially constructed, value-laden, and based on multiple perspectives. Thus stories are taken as being constitutive of reality and as such as playing a crucial role in the researcher's understanding of the subject's construction of reality. This is not a kind of research that aims at the advancement of abstract theoretical knowledge, nor does it attempt to provide holistic accounts of "how things are" within a particular setting. Rather, it retains a strong educative component, using a way of data gathering that is at the same time a means for enabling students to actively reflect on their learning experiences (see also Benedict 2007). And, as Maxine Greene has asserted, we are currently becoming increasingly aware of the knowledge potential that inheres in the pursuing of narrative inquiry and also "of the connection between narrative and the growth of identity, of the importance of shaping our own stories and, at the same time, opening ourselves to other stories in all their variety and their different degrees of articulatedness" (Greene 1995, 186).

The diaries were kept as a required assessment element while students were studying the module "Improvisation in Music Education." One of the authors was the module leader. During this course, students were involved in free small and whole group improvisations, semi-structured improvisations, group improvisational composing based on a variety of ideas and stimuli (e.g. the work of John Paynter, see Paynter 1992), and reading and discussion of relevant literature, as well as in ongoing group discussions of the work developed and the issues that emerged.[2] Sometimes children also attended the sessions and improvised alongside the students. This was an attempt to begin working with small groups of young children within the protective environment of the university classroom; these formative experiences were becoming the basis for creating a link between the study of relevant music education literature and the personal experience of creating improvisations. This course did not aim at teaching models for applying improvisation in the classroom. It involved students in a process intended to develop their musical selves and to begin realising the importance of improvisation for their own relationship to music. Asking the students to keep diaries was aiming at creating a place for reflection, through which the students could be able to form and explore their own ideas about their relationship with improvisation and with its educational potential. For only through realising the importance of improvisation for the teacher's own music-making practices could students be able to gradually apprehend the idea that children too might regard improvisation as a valuable musical process. In this context, our study of the students' accounts provides us the opportunity of developing another level of analysis, with the aim of clarifying the role of improvisation in teacher education. The decision to make a collaborative analysis, made by two researchers one of whom was also the course tutor, adds a further dimension to this effort. It denotes our wish to initiate a dialogue between the data, the insider's point of view and theoretical orientations, and a further critical "eye", that of the second researcher, who acted as a critical friend in debating the conclusions drawn from the data and bringing contrasting theoretical perspectives to discussion of the data.

## Data Analysis

In the course of thematic analysis (van Manen 1990) the researchers retained a descriptive interpretive stance, which refrained from extensive coding procedures. An attempt was made to remain close to the data, providing extensive segments-examples that allow the reader to challenge interpretations, preferring "direct interpretation and narrative description" rather than "formal aggregation of categorical data" (Stake 1995, 77). However, Wolcott (1995) argues that, "while the effective story should be 'specific and circumstantial', its relevance in a broader context should also be apparent." The story must transcend its own modest origins: "The case remains particular, its implications broad." (174) Against evidence-based research which "limits the opportunities for educational professionals to exert their judgment about what is educationally desirable in particular situations" (Biesta 2007, 20), this account offers critical observations and interpretations of a particular musical/educational experience. And this is offered as an invitation for dialogue about the "oughts" of music education and the training of teachers, and not as measurable evidence that something "works." Our intention is to offer a research approach that "can provide different understandings of educational reality and different ways of imagining a possible future" (21). In the light of this, when analysing the data we found a number of themes which fall under three main conceptual categories:

- "Autonomy: in search of foundations"
- "Developing the (musical) self"
- "Developing an open attitude towards children and music."

Each of these categories will be explained and elaborated upon in the sections that follow, illustrated by quotations from the students' diaries, musical examples and our reflections upon this material. Translations were made from the original Greek to English by the first researcher. Every attempt was made to preserve the original tone of the diary entries. Students' names have been changed to protect confidentiality.

## Findings

*Autonomy: in search of foundations*[3]

> [I felt] like a person who for the first time in his life tries to speak without a script, or like someone who has just begun to discover the power of difference, and tries to talk about this power, when up to that moment he believed in, or rather, was taught only how to judge better from worse, right from wrong, without being able to think about "difference." [Extract from diary of Vassilis]

In improvisation students began to experience the issue of how to judge difference without having to regress to ready made criteria. For some, this was the beginning of thinking about the power of difference. Initiation into hierarchical modes of thinking about music is seen not only as one-sided, but as leading to closure and exclusion dictated from above. Speaking "without a script" leads students to assuming personal responsibility for developing their judgement.

> A very important facet of improvisation is that it unsettles certainties, upsetting the given. It turns upside down the stereotypes with which you have grown up, and it makes you realize that you have not exercised your ability to be conscious of those stereotypes . . . And maybe the aim of improvisation should always be the development of our ability to judge, and learn to do so in the heat of the moment. [Extract from diary of Paul]

In terms of the role of improvisation as a means of transformative or liberatory education this could be termed the beginning of this student's development of critical consciousness. But this is not an exercise in rational thinking:

> The people in the group should be really present with their whole self and their whole interest in what is happening. What happens there should be

really important to them, and each one of the players should believe in it. [Extract from diary of Kosmas]

Being present means entering in a distinctive realm of musical experience where rational thinking is suspended. At times this experience comes close to that of dreaming:

> Sometimes when I close my eyes and relax I can stop my thinking and a moment comes when I begin to see images; it is as if I am dreaming but without being asleep. The moment I make the slightest thought, everything disappears; it is difficult to remain present . . . in free improvisation there is an element of fleetingness. As long as it lasts, you do not have, but you are. [Extract from diary of Kosmas]

Improvisation leads to the immersion in a form of musical experience that moves beyond the conception of musical knowledge as an object to be mastered. But it also posits the issue of the individual-group relationship in a direct way. Ideally, individuality and group identity are complementary:

> That freedom [experienced in improvisation], is a feeling that isolates but at the same time incorporates one inside the group. You are in a bouquet of flowers, with your own aroma but at the same time you are part of a whole together with the rest equally distinctive flowers. [Extract from diary of Niki]

This sense of creating our own goals is crucial for the development of both individual and collective identity:

> each of the players [should try] to get into the rhythm and style used by the rest of the group. In this way one will be able to follow the melody without being thoroughly absorbed by what one plays . . . but more with answering to the rest of the group and with participating in the dialogue creating one's own answers which, nevertheless fit to the whole melody, resulting in coherence and continuation of the whole thought of the group. [Extract from diary of Peter]

This "whole thought of the group" cannot be dictated and cannot be given in advance. The creation of a heightened sense of presence is a collective enterprise that goes beyond individual rational control, for in free improvisation there is "nothing" to coordinate the musical intentions of the participants. Joint creation of a common musical space where freedom is debated is a valuable educational pursuit:

> Antoine de Saint-Exupèry has noted that to love the other does not mean to look into the eyes of the other; it means that both look towards the same

direction . . . we need to be involved in processes which allow us to realise that we could find common points of (musical) reference, a common, however vague or obscure, goal. [Extract from diary of Georgia]

## Developing the self

One of the most persistent points which was raised by the students was the shortcomings of dominant formal music education training approaches to which they had been subjected. That this was seen as a major obstacle in their development as teachers should be regarded as a source of hope.

I believe that we ourselves have deprived ourselves of the freedom of expression through music. I am terrified of the thought that one day a child will ask me: "What is music?", "How do people make music?", "Can I not make music?" and I will have to give her an answer like this: "I do not know, my dear child. I only take a book full of notes, put it in front of me, and play what's written on it." No! I won't let this happen. [Extract from diary of Alkistis]

But for this to be achieved, student teachers themselves should be given the opportunity to explore how these questions can be given alternative answers. The experience of musical improvisation might be one way forward. But this does not happen automatically:

At the beginning I was systematically avoiding being involved, for I was unable to unlock myself. [Extract from diary of Georgia]

This was a frequent comment read at or near the beginning of students' diaries, for the narrative pattern which described the relationship of improvisation with previous music education often looked like this:

As a child I used to sit at the piano and improvise. When I began taking lessons, I had great difficulties in reading the notes, so I was memorizing the pieces right after listening to them by the piano teacher, and then was pretending that I was reading them . . . When the teacher discovered that I was cheating, he intensified his efforts to get me learn to read. And that was the end of improvisation for me. [Extract from diary of Alan]

Trying to unlock oneself was a continuous process that led to certain peak moments where individual participation in improvisation took the form of a revelation.

And the important thing is that when all this is happening there is no feeling of pressure, no anxiety about what you are doing, because at that moment you are so full that there is no space for anxiety. [Extract from diary of Kosmas]

It was liberating to try and listen to the seemingly random (were they really random?) sounds of the others, or to try to "harmonize" my own ideas with the ideas of the group, to become part of the musical praxis. [Extract from diary of Olga]

The moment of improvisation is a moment of personal and collective responsibility. This experience seemed to have a liberating effect to the ways we approach music-making. Freedom and responsibility emerge as complimentary aspects of the practice of improvisation. Free improvisation might be a way of musical practice that relieves student teachers from the sense of intimidation experienced so often in skill-based competitive musical contexts. In this way it fosters the creation of an intimate relationship with music:

It is amazing how simple are the forms/thoughts that are needed in order to make music. I guess I always favoured simple ideas, but I had never imagined myself working with simple ideas without fear. [Extract from diary of Lisa]

Without fear. That is a theme that kept coming up again and again. And this says something about our ways of educating musicians: elitist, competitive, alienating music education contexts not only ensure "excellence" but also instigate fear. The following comment is characteristic of how the feeling of trusting one's own ideas is as real as it is unexpected:

And the funny thing is that I always wanted to have a xylophone or a metallophone in my hands. From then on, I was playing what I was thinking, and the strange thing is that I wanted to suggest improvements. That was very funny for me indeed! . . . I realised that music does not only mean songs or notes, but also things which you may not be aware that you know, and which now come out in a spontaneous and natural way. [Extract from diary of Natasha]

The process of finding one's personal voice within the improvisation practice often includes heated collaborative discussions about the group's practice. At the beginning discussions were difficult to initiate, for to many students to discuss meant to expose one's shortcomings:

[Initially] I was terrified about the prospect of talking about our music. But I realized that not making judgments about abilities and talents, had a liberating effect in respect to my improvisations. [Extract from diary of Katerina]

And this might lead to a more self-confident relationship between musician and instrument. Not being afraid that one is always "behind schedule" might be important for creating intimate relationships between self and sounds:

> Now I feel much more ready to try and improvise using my own instrument, the flute. Now I love my little flute more, and every musical phrase written or one that comes from my mind fills me up. I always used to listen to a piece and imagine pictures, now I try to turn pictures into music. [Extract from diary of Estelle]

This student had re-engaged with her instrument in a new and more fulfilling way. Her confidence in her own musicality was evidently raised. Involvement in improvisation might then be apprehended as a means of self-development:

> We realised that improvisatory music making can even be a context where one's personality and individuality can be developed: I discover my limits, I'm not afraid to make suggestions, I make room for other people's suggestions, I make use of or I consciously discard certain ideas, I learn something new, I imitate, I become part of, I follow, I provoke, accept the . . . possibility of rejection etc. [Extract from diary of Alkistis]

*Developing an open attitude towards children and music*

Trying to find one's own personal voice within improvisational practice reveals to the student many of the obstacles and the preconceptions that conservatory education may have placed deep down in our thinking. Through involvement in improvisation these obstacles are gradually removed, opening the way for more open approaches to teaching.

> If you don't play the instrument in all kinds of unorthodox ways, how are you going to learn it, to discover it? Through improvisation the child learns the sounds, learns the joy of playing without following rules that are beyond it. Experiment, play, listen, and the forms emerge by themselves. You need only to listen and to be there. [Extract from diary of Lisa]

Notice the important issue that emerges out of the statement "without following rules that are beyond it." This is how the educational potential of improvisation is linked to the project of autonomy. Learning to set the rules through interaction and not through reference to some universal musical norm is what improvisation might offer to education, and this is one way in which music education might be linked to emancipation. Learning with both children and adults would ideally result in a deep sense of respect for children-as-musicians. A sense that emerges out of the following statement where the student-teacher attributes an exceptional sense of value to an improvisation he played with a six-year-old:

> Only a few times was I really present in the improvisation moment. One of those, maybe the one that really stands out, was when I played the metallophone with Katerina. In this improvisation I felt that I was really there with my whole attention and my whole interest in what was happening. [Extract from diary of Kosmas]

We see here emerging mutual respect between the student and teacher, one of the fundamental principles of critical pedagogy. Often the student-teachers-participants of this study documented their efforts to begin forging a personal pathway in their own teaching.

> Finally I would like to say that I tried to get a little girl, whom I teach the piano, into the adventure of improvisation. Despite my lack of substantive experience, I think that this experience, the discussion we had with my pupil and the joy I felt right after this lesson is the most important outcome [of my involvement with improvisation during this university course]. [Extract from diary of Georgia]

Developing the improvisation ethic in the university may well be regarded as the springboard for valuing the constituents of this improvisation ethic for music education itself:

> For now I have learned that . . . even a little primary school child can create wonderful and very clever things when she is given the opportunity, and when you really engage with her. [Extract from diary of Jimmy]

> So I became conscious that when you try to do something without having tons of rules in your mind about what should and should not be done, . . . and when you are given due respect as a human being and as a personality, you can create from the simplest to the most elaborate piece of music. [Extract from diary of Hannah]

Essentially through participation in improvisation one might be led to regard this practice as an ever-present mode of educational action. Learning to develop ways of musico-social relationships, learning to focus on the moment, on the unique qualities of each moment and of the participants, might be important not only in musical but also in interpersonal terms. This was observed by one student teacher as one of the most important things she had learnt from taking part in the module:

Learning to improvise on a variety of musical instruments, but most importantly, learning to improvise in [building] our relationship towards a child/student. [Extract from diary of Donna]

Thus a different pedagogical orientation could be developed, which could allow prospective teachers to begin envisioning a mode of working with music and children that takes informal aspects of music learning seriously:

Using your body for making noises is interesting. You can do something by yourself and you can create new instruments from your body. We should do that kind of thing more in schools too. We don't always need "real" instruments to create music. We could also use anything around us: tables, woods, stones, kitchen pans etc. That's actually the how children create music when nobody is teaching them. [Extract from diary of Mat]

## Discussion

Green (2008a) suggests that there is a strong correlation between the pedagogy experienced in music education and student success and/or persistence in studying music. We suggest here that the three analytical categories identified as arising from our data (autonomy, developing the self, and developing an open attitude towards children and their music) indicate three important areas in which involvement in free improvisation might contribute positively to the pedagogic preparation of teachers. Furthermore, the comments of the students whose journals we studied seem to indicate potential fruitful linkages between improvisation and the development of the qualities of empathy, mutual respect, willingness to take risks, and openness to new conceptions of music and musicking necessary for music teachers to be able to work with new approaches to music education such as Green's. The development of such qualities could moreover be crucial for such approaches to develop their potential to function as critical pedagogy, working towards musically and possibly even socially transformative practice.

Viewed as a core means of educating prospective teachers (both music specialists and generalist teachers), improvisation allows for a direct confrontation of learning as a search for self-transformation. Learning how to build our relationships with children and music: this is maybe the most fundamental value of learning through improvisation. This belief rests on an apprehension of the improvisation process as an exemplary case of situated learning (Lave and Wenger 1991). In this way improvisation becomes a means for unsettling dominant conceptions of music learning and for engaging with informal learning practices. Improvisation not only offers a way of active engagement with music, but also is situated in a presentational epistemology, that is, in an epistemology that does not regard knowledge as "an accurate representation of a pre-existing reality" (Biesta and Osberg 2007, 16) but emphasises the situatedness of knowledge construction as a form of creative socio-cultural praxis. Following Lave and Wenger (1991), we suggest that learning through improvisation should be seen as a constituent feature of participation in communities of improvisation practice. This leads to a change of relationship between children and music, to a move away from music as a given, towards music as an emergent. It further contributes to a move away from apprehending learning as a cognitive process, towards regarding learning, thinking, and knowing, as "relations among people in activity in, with, and arising from the socially and culturally structured world" (Lave and Wenger 1991, 51). Regarding learning as participation places emphasis on how children, through interaction, define their ways for making music, and assign particular meanings to their activities. Moreover, it goes far beyond knowledge as comprised of entities waiting to be internalised:

> Learning is a process that takes place in a participation framework, not in an individual mind. This means, among other things, that it is mediated by the differences of perspective among the co-participants . . . Learning is, as it were, distributed among co-participants, not a one-person act. (Hanks 1991, 15)

Two of the most important tenets of the situated learning approach are the acknowledgement of context as an essential aspect of learning and secondly, the value of implicit knowledge.

> The perceptions resulting from actions are a central feature in both learning and activity. How a person perceives activity may be determined by tools and their appropriated use. What they perceive, however, contributes to how they act and learn. Different activities produce different indexicalized representations, not equivalent, universal ones. And, thus, the activity that led to those representations plays a central role in learning. (Brown et al. 1989, 36)

Moreover, many aspects of learning to act within a particular musical practice need to remain implicit. Talking specifically about conceptual representations and their development from the perspective of situated learning, Brown et al. (1989) argue that "indexical representations gain their efficiency by leaving much of the context underrepresented or implicit" (41).

Thus we propose that the issue of connecting informal learning and improvisation might be resolved by regarding improvisation as an exemplary case of creating a communicative context where most representations/conceptualisations/struggles to solve problems are left implicit. Through the perspective of situated cognition and the importance it gives to leaving things implicit, we could arrive at a solid conceptualisation of the value of improvisation as a mode of learning. Thus its value as a learning resource might be formulated in the following manner: creating a context where implicitness is deeply valued, recognised but not analytically pursued, leading to sustained engagement with the workings of musical structuring and communication from the "inside": "Authentic activity . . . is important for learners, because it is the only way they gain access to the standpoint that enables practitioners to act meaningfully and purposefully" (Brown et al. 1989, 36). Table 1 presents a possible set of links that could be made between the process of learning through improvisation and Lucy Green's vision of informal pedagogy. It aims to show the links between informal learning as espoused by Green, and the concepts of autonomy, self-development, and openness, developed in our chapter as categories describing student-teachers' experience of music improvisation:

**Table 8-1. Learning through improvisation as informal pedagogy**

| Green's informal pedagogy | Learning through improvisation |
|---|---|
| Learners choose the music they learn themselves. Gradually learners become aware of other musics, of other possibilities outside their own experience and express a wish to explore these. | Learners create their own music collectively. Gradually various ideas found in other musics are brought into the class, offered to the students as means for enriching their own improvised music. |
| It is learnt by listening and copying, rather than from notation, learning takes place in groups. | Learning through listening to each other, avoiding copying but encouraging influence. |
| Pupils empowered with control over their learning. Their identity as autonomous learners is strengthened. | Pupils encouraged to consciously render their collective music-making a site of learning, through discussion and further experimentation which gives way to new improvisations. |

| Much of the power and control over pacing and sequencing of learning is devolved to the learners. | Experimentation is encouraged in ways that counter pre-decided sequential learning. |
|---|---|
| Teacher only intervenes when requested by learners to do so. Dialogic learning a feature. Power distributed more equally between teacher and learners. | Teacher responds to what is offered through improvisation, transforming it into an avenue for new learning. Actively plays with students as their partner. Acts against domination, but does not hesitate to become fully involved. |

Repeated engagement with improvisation and borrowing ideas by attending to other people's improvisations are the means by which improvisation generates its own future. All musical, structural and expressive problems are created and solved within it. The heuristic aspect of improvisation (Prévost 1995) is, essentially, its driving force. Intensive and prolonged engagement of the participants of the present study with improvisation should be seen as a case of practising spontaneity, which is regarded as a vital source of knowledge of the workings of musical spontaneity and as a "tool" for student teacher engagement in musical dialogues with their future students. Improvisation emerges as a mode of practice that redefines creativity, through rejecting its individualistic perception as a "problem-solving" process that has dominated the concept of creativity through its appropriation by psychological research.[4]

Improvisation creates a musical context where inventiveness and responsiveness always get their meaning in situ, in the course of emerging ways of working together, and of drawing on different aspects of musical cultures and musical practices. The balance between inventiveness and responsiveness cannot be predefined, or pre-decided. Attending and listening closely to the generation of improvised music is constitutive of the meaning of the music-making process itself. It contributes to its transformation from an exploratory activity to a communicative one, from a private enterprise to a public event. It brings into the musical experience a vital ingredient: the exploration of the listener's response. Improvisation might be a powerful means in which to forge future teachers' identities through action and reflection that might help them be more open and responsive to their future students. Learning and accumulation of experience is the result of identifying important issues that pertain to music making, which were then tackled and worked upon in subsequent improvisations.

Another perspective that emerges from the data and their analysis leads us to begin realizing the value of a political/cultural conception of creativity, emphasizing the role of imagination in creating difference, and thus cultivating autonomy (in Castoriadis' sense of the term). For Castoriadis (1987, 108),

> the problem of autonomy immediately refers to, is even identified with, the problem of the relation of one subject to another—or to others; . . . the other or others do not appear as external obstacles or a malediction to be suffered . . . but instead as constituting the subject, the subject's problem and its possible solution.

An educational culture that connects its work to the project of autonomy results in the self-constitution of practices, to the creation of values and meanings without reference to some superior authority or system of values, and to practices which lead to self-institution and constant positing of the question of the value of these self-instituted practices. Improvisation might be an artistic practice that operates on the basis of autonomy, allowing for both creation *and* doubt.

Improvisation might be a way of placing musical imagination at the centre of the educational process, and to proceed to modes of musical practice that address issues of being and thinking together, thus becoming a form of socio-musical and thus political practice. It might be a way of going beyond Maxine Greene's (1995) thesis that "the role of imagination is not to resolve, not to point the way, not to improve. It is to awaken, to disclose the ordinarily unseen, unheard, and unexpected" (28). To be able to go a step beyond this is to be able to apprehend musical practice as a social locus for the development of distributed imaginative practice, and thus as an active mode of critique of the current state of affairs through imagining possibilities and actively searching for how to realize them musically. Improvisation permits students to become agents of musico-social action. Through processes of sound organisation students are actively engaged in the construction of social relationships.

Thus musical creativity and musical creation might be regarded as analogous to the processes of social creation of autonomous forms of social organisation. There are strong links here with Castoriadis' (1991, 1997) notion of autonomy as a project of radical democracy: "autonomy is the ability to call the given institution of society into question—and that institution itself must make you capable of calling it into question, primarily through education" (Castoriadis 2007, 176). (Musical) autonomy should therefore be understood as the deliberate process of searching for and reflecting upon the rules of musical practice. Free musical improvisation is a musical context that allows the unlimited questioning of its very practice, thus becoming a way of pursuing the project of autonomy in musical terms.

Herein lies the political significance of free improvisation, which "neither resides in the political commitment of improvisers, nor in their declarations of intent, but it is revealed through the aesthetics that their practice confers" (Saladin 2009, 148). Saladin argues that its openness does not lead to an "anything goes" stance but is a consequence of its "lack of identity" (148): "This constituting lack is not a gap which should be bridged within free improvisation; on the contrary, this lack is the empty space which allows it to exist. This empty space manifests itself both in the absence of rules which would come to outline its contours and in the absence of a right required to practice it" (148). In this chapter we have argued that this empty space provides a way for re-searching foundational aspects of what it means to create music, with important consequences for personal development and for building an open attitude towards children's musical potential. Such a musical practice creates a very particular mindset which, we argue, is especially valuable from an educational perspective. For it does not distinguish between levels of ability but between levels of commitment. Drawing on the work of Jacques Rancière (2004a, 2004b), Saladin argues that

> Free improvisation does not pre-exist, but is only a practice. So it cannot take count of the people coming into it, or to say this more explicitly in the terms of Jacques Rancière, it cannot mark out a clear and definitive boundary between those who can take part in it and those who cannot. This does not mean that it can be some sort of pure openness, but rather, that its empty space supposes an indefinite plurality. (Saladin 2009, 148)

Enabling prospective music teachers to pursue, through both practice and reflection, the question of how to create musical contexts that address these issues, seems to be an invaluable and much-needed project.

# References

Abrahams, F. 2005. "Critical Pedagogy for Music Education: A Best Practice to Prepare Future Music Educators." *Visions of Research in Music Education* 6. http://www-usr.rider.edu/~vrme/v7n1/visions/ Abrahams%20CPME%20Best%20Practices.pdf

Allsup, R. E. 1997. "Activating Self-Transformation through Improvisation in Instrumental Music Teaching." *Philosophy of Music Education Review* 5 (2): 80–85.

—. 2008. "Creating an Educational Framework for Popular Music in Public Schools: Anticipating the Second-Wave." *Visions of Research in Music Education* 12.
http://www-usr.rider.edu/~vrme/v12n1/vision/1%20AERA%20-%20Allsup.pdf

Apple, M. W. 2005. "Making Critical Pedagogy Strategic—on Doing Critical Educational Work in Conservative Times." In *Critical Theory and Critical Pedagogy Today: Toward a New Critical Language in Education*, ed. I. Gur Ze'ev, 95–113. Haifa: University of Haifa Press.

Athanasiou, A. 2010. "Η κριτική την εποχή της κρίσης, ή η απαξίωση των κοινωνικών και ανθρωπιστικών σπουδών. (Παρέμβαση στην ημερίδα για τις ανθρωπιστικές και κοινωνικές επιστήμες, του περιοδικού *Ιστορείν*, Αθήνα 13.ΧΙ.2010) [Critique in an Era of Crisis, or the Devaluation of the Humanities and the Social Sciences]." http://historein-historein.blogspot.com/2010/11/blog-post_18.html

Bailey J., and V. Doubleday. 1990. "Patterns of Musical Enculturation in Afghanistan." In *Music and Child Development: Proceedings of the 1987 Denver Conference*, eds. F. R. Wilson and F. L. Roehmann, 88–99. Missouri: MMB Music.

Ball, S. J. 2003. "The Teacher's Soul and the Terrors of Performativity." *Journal of Education Policy* 18 (2): 215–28.

Benedict, C. 2007. "On the Narrative of Challenged Assumptions." *Research Studies in Music Education* 29: 29–38.

Benveniste, R. 2010. "Ρίκα Μπενβενίστε—lingua reformationis universitatis (LRU) ή Πειθάρχηση και Τιμωρία: Η γένεση της Α.Α.ΔΙ.Π και η μετεξέλιξή της σε Α.Α.ΑΞΙ. ΠΙΣ.Χ. (Παρέμβαση στην ημερίδα για τις ανθρωπιστικές και κοινωνικές επιστήμες, του περιοδικού *Ιστορείν*, Αθήνα 13.ΧΙ.2010) [Lingua Reformationis Universitatis (LRU) or Disciplining and Punishment: The Implementation of Independent Authority for Quality Control to and Its Transformation to Independent Authority for Evaluation, Certification and Funding]." http://historein-historein.blogspot.com/2010/11/lingua-reformationis-universitatis-lru.html

Biesta, G. 2007 "Why 'What Works' Won't Work: Evidence-Based Practice and the Democratic Deficit of Educational Research." *Educational Theory* 57 (1): 1–22.

Biesta, G., and D. Osberg. 2007. "Beyond Re/presentation: A Case for Updating the Epistemology of Schooling." *Interchange* 38 (1): 15–29.

Brown, S. J., A. Collins, and P. Duguid. 1989. "Situated Cognition and the Culture of Learning." *Educational Researcher* 18 (1): 32–42.

Castoriadis, C. 1987. *The Imaginary Institution of Society.* Cambridge: Polity Press.

—. 1991. "Power Politics Autonomy." In *Cornelius Castoriadis— Philosophy, Politics, Autonomy: Essays in Political Philosophy*, ed. D. A. Curtis, 143–74. New York: Oxford University Press.

—. 1997. "Phusis and Autonomy." In *Cornelius Castoriadis—World in Fragments*, ed. D. A. Curtis, 331–41. Stanford: Stanford University Press.

—. 2007. "Psyche and Education." In *Cornelius Castoriadis—Figures of the Thinkable,* ed. W. Hamacher, 165–87. Stanford: Stanford University Press.

Clandinin, J. D., ed. 2007. *Handbook of Narrative Inquiry: Mapping a Methodology.* London: Sage.

Colley, H., P. Hodkinson, and J. Malcom. 2003. *Informality and Formality in Learning. Report to the Learning and Skills Research Centre from the Lifelong Learning Institute at the University of Leeds.* London: Learning and Skills Development Agency.

Devine, N., and R. Irwin 2006. "Autonomy, Agency and Education: He tangata, He tangata, He tangata." In *Postfoundationalist Themes in the Philosophy of Education: Festschrift for James D. Marshall*, eds. P. Smeyers and M. A. Peters, 11–24. Oxford: Blackwell.

Eraut, M. 2000. "Non-Formal Learning and Tacit Knowledge in Professional Work." *British Journal of Educational Psychology* 70 (1): 113–36.

Fizimons P. 2002. "Neoliberalism and Education: the Autonomous Chooser." *Radical Pedagogy* 4.
http://radicalpedagogy.icaap.org/content/issue4_2/04_fitzsimons.html

Folkestad, G. 2006. "Formal and Informal Learning Situations or Practices *vs.* Formal and Informal Ways of Learning." *British Journal of Music Education* 23 (2): 135–45.

Ford, C. C. 1995. "Free Collective Improvisation in Higher Education." *British Journal of Music Education* 12 (2): 103–12.

Freire, P. 1970. *Pedagogy of the Oppressed.* New York: Continuum.

Gaventa, J. 1993. "The Powerful, the Powerless and the Experts: Knowledge Struggles in an Information Age." In *Voices of Change: Participatory Research in the United States and Canada*, eds. P. Park, M. Bryndon-Miller, B. Hall, and T. Jackson. Westport: Bergin and Garvey.

Georgii-Hemming, E. 2007. "Hermeneutic knowledge: Dialogue between experiences." *Research Studies in Music Education* 29: 13–28.

Giroux H. 1983a. *Theory and Resistance in Education: A Pedagogy for the Opposition*. South Hadley: Bergin and Garvey.

—. 1983b. "Rationality, Reproduction, and Resistance: Toward a Critical Theory of Schooling." In *Current Perspectives in Social Theory*, ed. S. McNall, 85–118. Greenwich: JAI Press.

—. 1985. "Teachers as Intellectuals." *Social Education* 49 (15): 376–79.

—. 1988a. "Literacy and the Pedagogy of Political Empowerment." *Educational Theory* 38 (1): 61–75.

—. 1988b. "Schrag Speaks: Spinning the Wheel of Misfortune." *Educational Theory* 38 (1): 145–46.

—. 1988c. "Hope and Radical Education." *Journal of Education* 170 (2): 91–101.

—. 1997. *Pedagogy and the Politics of Hope: Theory, Culture, and Schooling*. Oxford: Westview.

Giroux, H., and P. McLaren. 1994. *Between Borders: Pedagogy and Politics in Cultural Studies*. New York: Routledge.

Green, L. 2002. *How Popular Musicians Learn: A Way Ahead for Music Education*. London: Ashgate.

—. 2008a. *Music, Informal Learning and the School: A New Classroom Pedagogy*. London: Ashgate.

—. 2008b. "Response to Panel: Beyond Lucy Green: Operationalizing Theories of Informal Music Learning Panel Presentation." *Visions of Research in Music Education* 12.
http://www-usr.rider.edu/~vrme/v12n1/vision/Green%20Response.pdf

Greene, M. 1995. *Releasing the Imagination: Essays on Education, the Arts, and Social Change*. San Francisco: Jossey-Bass.

Grollios, G., and I. Kaskaris. 2003. "From Socialist-Democratic to 'Third Way' Politics and Rhetoric in Greek Education (1997–2002)." *Journal for Critical Education Policy Studies* 1 (1).
http://www.jceps.com/index.php?pageID=article&articleID=4

Hanks, W. F. 1991. "Introduction." In *Situated Learning: Legitimate Peripheral Participation*, authored by J. Lave, and E. Wenger, 13–24. Cambridge: Cambridge University Press.

Hill, D. 2003. "Global Neo-Liberalism, the Deformation of Education and Resistance." *Journal for Critical Education Policy Studies* 1 (1).
www.jceps.com/?pageID=article&articleID=7

Kushner, S. 2004. "Falsifying Schooling: Surrealism and Curriculum." In *The Social Context of Music Education*, ed. J. L. Arostegui, 203-18. Champaign: Center for Instructional Research and Curriculum Evaluation, University of Illinois.

Lankshear, C. 1982. *Freedom and Education: Towards a Non-Rational Philosophy of Education*. Auckland: Milton Brookes.

Lave, J., and E. Wenger. 1991. *Situated Learning: Legitimate Peripheral Participation*. Cambridge: Cambridge University Press.

Levinson, M. 1999. *The Demands of Liberal Education*. Oxford: Oxford University Press.

Lyotard, J. F. 1984. *The Postmodern Condition: A Report on Knowledge*. Minneapolis: University of Minnesota Press.

Marcuse, H. 1991. *One-Dimensional Man* (2nd edn). London: Routledge and Kegan Paul.

Marshall, J. D. 1996. *Michel Foucault: Personal Autonomy and Education*. Dordrecht: Kluwer Academic Publishers.

McCarthy, M. 2007. "Narrative Inquiry as a Way of Knowing in Music Education." *Research Studies in Music Education* 29 (1): 3–12.

McLaren, P. 2006. *Life in Schools: An Introduction to Critical Pedagogy in the Foundations of Education* (5th ed.). Boston: Pearson Allyn & Bacon.

Ministry of National Education and Religion Affairs [YPEPTH]. 1997. *Εκπαίδευση 2000. Για μια Παιδεία Ανοιχτών Οριζόντων* [*Education 2000. Towards a Paedia of Opened Horizons*]. Athens: YPEPTH.

Mishéa, J. C. 1999. *Enseignement de l'Ignorance, et ses Conditions Modernes*. Paris: éditions Climats.

Nettl, B. 2007. "Interlude: An Ethnomusicological Perspective." In *International Handbook of Research in Arts Education*, ed. L. Bresler, 829–34. Dordrecht: Springer.

Organisation for Economic Cooperation and Development (OECD). 2007. "Activity on the Recognition of Non-Formal and Informal Learning (RNFIL). Pan-Canadian Overview". Council of Ministers of Education, Canada (CMEC). http://www.oecd.org/dataoecd/19/46/41829243.pdf

Olssen, M. 2006. "Foucault, Educational Research and the Issue of Autonomy." In *Postfoundationalist Themes in the Philosophy of Education: Festschrift for James D. Marshall*, eds. P. Smeyers and M. A. Peters, 57–79. Oxford: Blackwell.

Paynter J. 1992. *Sound and Structure*. Cambridge: Cambridge University Press.

—. 2000. "Making Progress with Composing." *British Journal of Music Education* 17 (1): 5–31.

Peters, M. A. 2009. "Education, Creativity and the Economy of Passions: New Forms of Educational Capitalism." *Thesis Eleven* 96: 40–63.

Pongratz, L. 2005. "Critical Theory and Pedagogy: Theodor W. Adorno and Max Horkheimer's Contemporary Significance for a Critical Pedagogy." In *Critical Theories, Radical Pedagogies, and Global Conflicts*, eds. G. E. Fischman, P. McLaren, H. Sünker, and C. Lankshear, 154–63. Lanham: Rowman & Littlefield.

Prentice, R. 2000. "Creativity: a Reaffirmation of Its Place in Early Childhood Education." *The Curriculum Journal* 11 (2): 145–58.

Prévost, E. 1995. *No Sound is Innocent: AMM and The Practice of Self-Invention. Meta-Musical Narratives. Essays*. Essex: Copula.

—. 2004. *Minute Particulars: Meanings in Music Making in the Wake of Hierarchical Realignments and Other Essays*. Essex: Copula.

Psycharis, S. 2009. "Επάγγελμα . . . ; [Editorial: Occupation. . . ?]" *To Vima* 25 (1). http://www.tovima.gr/opinions/article/?aid=252132

Ranciére J. 2004a. *The Politics of Aesthetics*. New York: Continuum.

—. 2004b. *Malaise dans l'Esthétique*. Paris: Galilée.

Reich, R. 2002. *Bridging Liberalism and Multiculturalism in American Education*. Chicago: Chicago University Press.

Rice, T. 1985. "Music Learnt But not Taught: The Bulgarian Case." In *Becoming Human through Music,* D. P. McAllester (project director), 115–22. Reston: MENC.

Ross, M. 1998. "Herbert Read: Art, Education, and the Means of Redemption." In *Herbert Read reassessed*, ed. D. Goodway, 196-214. Liverpool: Liverpool University Press.

Saladin, M. 2009. "Points Of Resistance and Criticism in Free Improvisation: Remarks on a Musical Practice and Some Economic Transformations." In *Noise and Capitalism,* 133–149. Kritika. (This book is intended as a non-copyrighted material and is available at: http://www.arteleku.net/audiolab/noise_capitalism.pdf)

Sefton-Green, J., and E. Soep. 2007. "Creative Media Cultures: Making and Learning Beyond the School." In *International Handbook of Research in Arts Education*, ed. L. Bresler, 835–54. Dordrecht: Springer.

Stake, R. E. 1995. *The Art of Case Study Research*. Thousand Oaks: Sage.

Straka, G. A. 2004. *Informal Learning: Genealogies, Concepts, Antagonisms and Questions*. Forschungsberichte 1, Bremen: Institut Technik und Bildung (ITB), Universität Bremen.

Theotokas N. 2010. "Οι φανατικοί του νεοφιλελευθερισμού διαλύουν το Δημόσιο Πανεπιστήμιο και καταλύουν το Σύνταγμα [Neo-Liberal Fanatics Destroy Public Universities and Demolish the Constitution]." *Avgi*, October 31, 6–10.

van Manen, M. 1990. *Researching Lived Experience: Human Science for an Action Sensitive Pedagogy*. London: Althouse.
Walduck, J. 2005. "Collaborative Arts Practice and Identity: The Role of Leadership." In *The Reflective Conservatoire*, eds. G. Odam and N. Bannan, 301–31. London: Ashgate.
Wolcott, H. F. 1995. *The Art of Fieldwork*. Walnut Creek: AltaMira.

# Notes

[1] This chapter is an extended version of an article previously published in 2010 as "Informal Music Learning, Improvisation and Teacher Education" in *British Journal of Music Education* 27 (1): 71–87. Reprinted by permission of the publisher Cambridge University Press.

[2] There has been a growing interest in the role of free improvisation and collaborative composition in higher education, as evidenced by a conference recently organised by the University of Surrey on "Collaborative Processes in Music Making: Pedagogy and Practice" (see http://78.158.56.101/archive/palatine/events/viewreport/1577/index.html)—for important documentation of such approaches, their rationale and theoretical justification, see Ford (1995) and Walduck (2005).

[3] As you will see in what follows the notion of autonomy as used here has a very different meaning from the way it is used by mainly liberal philosophers of education as an advancement towards independent rationality (e.g. Levinson 1999; Reich 2002) (for critiques of the liberal conception of autonomy as an exercise of rational thinking and free choice see Devine and Irwin 2006; Fitzsimons 2002; Lankshear 1982; Marshall 1996; Olssen 2006).

[4] For an analysis of the uses of the notion of creativity in education and a critique of the political neutrality of psychological versions of creativity, see Peters (2009).

# PART IV

# CHAPTER NINE

# INFORMAL LEARNING AND AURAL LEARNING IN THE INSTRUMENTAL MUSIC LESSON: A RESEARCH-AND-DEVELOPMENT PILOT PROJECT

## LUCY GREEN[1]

## Introduction

*Parvesh (clarinet) lesson 3*

Parvesh comes in on the right note, stumbles, makes a few more attempts and eventually plays correctly along with the music. It's interesting that he, as with many kids, gets one note right followed by a wrong note; then next time it comes round he gets two notes right; then three. This seems to be a pattern.

*Edward (piano) lesson 7*

Kate (teacher): It's also actually, it's hearing, can you actually hear what's actually happening in the left hand, which is slightly more complex, but what's actually happening in terms of the layers of sound, can you just see—
Edward: I know there are chords, but I'm not sure—
Kate: Yes, just, listen to the left hand and just see what you can hear. (We all listen.)
Edward: It's like before each chord there's a lower note that it goes up to that it kind of starts from, but, because that note's played at the same time as the right hand, it's kind of hard to work out.

*Katie (cello) lesson 8*

"Eleanor Rigby" starts . . . Katie plays along . . . and she now has the final arpeggio. She plays well with a few places where she loses it but picks up again quite quickly, often right in the middle of a phrase.

Above are three extracts from observations and recordings of 104 instrumental lessons, in which pupils aged 10 to 17 attempted to learn aurally by playing along with a recording, in an approach based upon the informal learning practices of popular musicians. This chapter gives an overview of the project's background and rationale; research methods; pedagogic strategies and materials; the different approaches to learning adopted by the pupils; how pupils progressed; the pedagogy and the roles of the teachers; and finally the views of the participants. As the chapter goes along, I will mention some areas that differed from those in another related project that took place in general music classrooms, and will close by raising some topics that might be of interest for future development and research.

## Background and Rationale

The rationale for the work was that many children and young people who fail and drop out of formal music education, are often far from being either uninterested or unmusical. Rather, many of them pursue alternative, informal methods of music learning in the popular music sphere (and other alternative spheres), where their approaches to acquiring musical skills and knowledge are associated with high levels of enjoyment, and can lead to the development of advanced musicianship emphasising aural, improvisatory and creative aspects. The development of such skills has tended to be relatively overlooked in both the instrumental training of classical musicians, and in traditional music curricula and pedagogy in schools.

Nowadays there is nothing surprising about finding popular music firmly embedded in the school curriculum of many countries. However, it is only recently that the informal learning practices of the musicians themselves have been recognised or adopted as teaching and learning strategies in classrooms. Between 2002 and 2006, I conducted a curriculum research-and-development project in the UK. The aims were to adapt aspects of the informal learning practices used by young pop and rock musicians, and bring them into the secondary school classroom. The project then investigated to what extent the adapted informal learning practices could increase pupils' performing, listening and composing skills; raise their levels of motivation, enjoyment and group cooperation; and extend their skills and appreciation in relation to a range of music going beyond the popular sphere, including classical music. The project became part of a national UK music education initiative called "Musical Futures", and since its initial research phase has been taken up by over

1,000 schools in the UK and other countries.[2] In other schools, universities, and countries similar work has been ongoing, and classroom strategies derived from popular musicians' informal learning practices, or those of other vernacular and/or aural musicians, are being used in a range of contexts.[3]

Drawing from my own and others' previous research,[4] I divided informal popular music learning practices into five central characteristics, each one differing in various ways from formal music educational approaches, as follows (Green 2008, 10):

- With informal popular music learning practices, the music is self-selected by the learner.
- The main learning practice involves aural copying from a recording.
- The learning is self-directed and peer-directed, usually in the absence of adult supervision or guidance.
- The skills and knowledge tend to be acquired holistically, according to whatever music is being played, rather than according to a pre-designated order going from simple to complex.
- There is a high integration of listening, playing, composing and improvising throughout the learning.

These characteristics were then adapted for the secondary school music classroom. Pupils were asked to get into friendship groups, choose their own music, select instruments, and attempt to play the music by ear from a recording, whilst largely directing their own learning. The role of the teacher was different from the usual instructional mode; the teachers were asked to start out by observing, then diagnosing pupils' needs. At that point they started to offer guidance and respond to requests for help in a range of ways. These included demonstrating and acting as musical models, explanation, giving technical advice, helping pupils to listen to parts, assisting in making arrangements, and many more such activities. To cut a long story short, the findings of the project have been overwhelmingly positive, with high levels of motivation, group co-operation, inclusivity and skill-acquisition being reported.[5]

During the classroom project, many instrumental teachers asked us, and continue to ask us, whether popular musicians' informal learning strategies might or might not usefully be adapted for the very different, specialised context of the instrumental lesson. In response to this and a range of other factors, I started a project whose objectives were to adapt informal music-learning practices in similar ways to the classroom project, but this time apply them to the instrumental lesson and evaluate what happened. Whereas many instrumental teachers have backgrounds in popular and other aurally-transmitted musics, and many already use a range of aural learning techniques and recordings in their lessons, I especially wanted to develop strategies that might be useful to classically-trained teachers who might not be inclined to adopt informally-based approaches. At the time of writing I have completed a substantial pilot study, which is the focus of the current chapter. The main study began in September 2011. At the time of writing, in December of that year, we have inducted over 100 teachers into the project and are on the point of starting to implement the strategies and collect data. [6]

One of the differences between the instrumental project and the classroom project is that the instrumental one involved mainly one-to-one teaching. From a research point of view, this meant that I could observe every lesson and focus on each individual child in more detail than was possible in the classroom, where up to 30 pupils were working in small groups simultaneously. Thus some detailed findings concerning how individual learners approached the task came to light. Further differences between the two projects concern the ways in which each was set up. The different teaching-and-learning contexts demand different pedagogical approaches; the instruments involved in the instrumental project, apart from the piano, were mostly not used at all, or used only by a small number of pupils at the very end of the classroom project; the pupils in the current project already had varying degrees of proficiency on their instruments, which was only the case for a small minority in the classroom project; and the current pupils had all been learning to play their instrument through notation and formal teaching, which was again barely the case in the classroom. In fact, in the classroom most of those pupils who did receive specialist instrumental lessons chose to work on instruments that were just as new to them as to the rest of the class (see e.g. Green 2008, 138, 161–162). Therefore, in the current project some pedagogical considerations had to be made, and some findings emerged which were not relevant to, or did not surface in the classroom project. As mentioned earlier, in general I will focus on those issues in the current chapter.

## The Research Sample

The project involved 15 pupils, mostly aged 13 to 15, with one 10 year-old and one 17 year-old. One pupil took part in an informal pre-pilot study; the other 14 took part in the pilot study proper. There were 6 boys and 9 girls. Ten of them were white, 4 Asian, and 1 mixed-race. Two had special educational needs. Between them they played the piano, clarinet, saxophone, trumpet, euphonium, trombone, violin and cello. They had been learning their instruments for varying periods of time from 8 months to 12 years. Most of them were around Grade 2 standard, the highest grade being Grade 6 (using a well-known grading system in the UK).[7] All but one was attending a state comprehensive school in West London; the youngest pupil was attending the neighbouring primary school.

Four instrumental teachers were involved, all women. Between them they taught the piano, woodwind, brass and strings respectively. The piano teacher worked at home, and the other three worked as peripatetic teachers in the school. Three of them had received traditional, classical conservatoire training. Of these, the string and brass teachers particularly said they felt in "foreign territory" to use their term, in the realms of popular music, ear-playing and improvisation. The piano teacher had professional experience of playing by ear and improvising, particularly in theatre bands, and described herself as self-taught in these areas. The woodwind teacher's training was in jazz and light music, and she had more experience of ear-playing and improvisation than the others. All but one of the pupils had 6 to 8 project lessons, each lasting 10–15 minutes, once a week.[8] Altogether 104 project lessons took place. Most of the pupils followed three different project-stages, but in three cases only one stage was taken. All the lessons were individual, apart from one case where two pupils took their weekly lesson together.

## Research Methods

The research methods were qualitative, and included participant-observation in all 104 lessons. As participant-observer I took the role of both researcher and teacher; meanwhile, the normal instrumental teacher acted as a critical observer and co-teacher. Each lesson was audio-recorded then transcribed and annotated. The transcriptions and annotations were combined with any field-notes that I had made straight after each lesson, as well as observations of gestures, facial expressions or other factors taken from memory. At the end of the project I conducted individual semi-structured interviews with the students and teachers; a questionnaire with the students; and recorded and transcribed an end-of-project teacher meeting in which I presented and discussed the initial findings with three of the four teachers (the piano teacher had moved away but I discussed the findings with her informally). The data were analysed by hand using an iterative coding method, and the findings were allowed to emerge in the manner of grounded theory.

There are obvious disadvantages as well as advantages of such research methods. There is likely to be a halo effect for both teachers and pupils, produced from knowing that one is participating in a research project, or from having a stranger in the room, a colleague with whom to share ideas, a new teacher from whom to get positive feedback, and so on. Researcher-bias is wont to creep in, as the researcher may be inclined to ignore data that threatens the success of the strategies or detracts from the coherence of the findings. Such issues are well-rehearsed in the literature, and naturally I attempted to reduce all of them as much as possible. The benefits of participant-observation and qualitative research are equally well-known. In this case, the research methods enabled me to try out the teaching strategies in the role of teacher myself, and thus get an insider's view of the teacher's role; to make detailed observations of the responses and behaviours of each pupil; to exchange views with the teachers as we went along; and to involve the teachers as co-observers. The observations, perspectives and opinions of the pupils as well as the teachers formed a vital part of the project, and are triangulated with my own observations and conclusions.

## The Pedagogic Strategies and Materials

The primary aim of the pedagogy was to enable pupils to *learn a new approach to learning* through developing their listening skills in a way that is modelled upon the aural informal learning practices of popular musicians. This can be broken down into the following aims, which were to:

- introduce pupils to a way of playing by ear which they may not otherwise have come across;
- enhance aural skills and aural understanding, especially the ability to pick out and reproduce pitches by ear;
- help pupils to develop a skill which they could build on in their own time, thus developing learner-autonomy;
- give pupils the means to approach a range of music, arrange it for their own instrument, and play it creatively in a way that pleases them;
- introduce pupils to a way of learning which they find enjoyable, and thus increase motivation;
- give teachers opportunities to observe this kind of aural learning

taking place, and to encounter ways of teaching as well as learning which were likely to be new to them.

The project was not intended in any way to either replace existing traditional or notation-based methods, nor to challenge existing instrumental pedagogy in the popular or any other musical field. Rather, the intention was to add something to traditional notation-based approaches, particularly for those classically-trained teachers who lack confidence in aural or improvisatory realms. As mentioned, the strategies took up only 10 to 15 minutes per week, and normal work was resumed during the rest of the lesson.

The teaching-and-learning strategies were organised in three stages, as follows:

## Stage 1: Funk Track, "Link Up"

The first stage involved a specially-prepared instrumental track in a pop/funk style (see Ex. 9-1). Firstly each pupil listened to the opening of the full piece, then to the opening of a track in which the bass riff is played on its own, and repeated over and over for two minutes. (I will refer to such tracks as being "looped", although they were not technologically looped but were played live to avoid a mechanical quality.) Pupils were then asked to attempt to find the pitches of the riff on their own instrument, transposed up or down an octave as they wished. The role of the teacher, which is described in detail later on in this chapter, was to stand back as much as their professional judgement allowed; however various types of help were offered if needed and these will be discussed later. Once the riff had been learnt, this was followed by learning two to five more riffs in the same way. After this the pupils played along to the recording, using any riff they knew, and playing the riffs in any order and combination that they liked. This therefore brought in a certain amount of improvisation. For pianists it meant playing with two hands and, in some cases, playing chords. As well as, or instead of playing along to a recording, the riffs could also be played in a duet with the teacher, or in groups of any number of instrumentalists playing any instruments, during lessons or extra-curricular activities.

Ex. 9-1. "Link Up"

Figure A: Link Up

## Stage 2: Classical music, with isolated, repeated parts

Stage 2 began around the third lesson for most pupils. The task was to listen to the openings (at least) of six pieces of classical music, and choose one. The pieces were:

- Mozart, *Eine Kleine Nachtmusik*, 1st movt, arranged for string quartet
- Beethoven, "Für Elise", for piano
- Clara Schumann, *Piano Trio*, 1st movt, for piano, violin and cello
- Handel, *Flute sonata*, Minuet and Trio, for flute, harpsichord and cello
- Brahms, *Symphony no. 1*, fourth movement theme, arranged for string quartet with synthesiser for brass/woodwind
- Bach, "Minuet" from *Anna Magdalena notebook*, played on harpsichord

As with the funk track, each piece was presented first in its complete instrumentation, then each melody or bass line was presented in just two parts, sometimes a little simplified, then the *first phrase* of each melody or bass line was repeated (or "looped") over and over again for two minutes, then the next phrase, and so on.

*Stage 3: Self-chosen music*

Stage 3 began in most cases around the fifth or sixth lesson. The pupils were requested to listen to their own music at home, choose any piece, which could be in any style and for any instrument/voice or combination of such, and teach themselves to play any part of it that they wished, by ear. They then brought a recording of it to the next lesson, and showed what they had done. In this case there was of course no pre-prepared "looped" material to help them.

In devising the strategies, I took into account some of the main characteristics of informal learning as used in the classroom project mentioned above. These characteristics were adapted for the instrumental lesson, but in ways that could be accommodated within this setting:

- The main learning practice was aural copying from a recording.
- The pupils did not choose their own music at first, but after around 5 or 6 lessons.
- A teacher (and a researcher) was present during the lesson, so the self-directed aspect of informal learning was not present. However the pupils moved gradually towards more self-directed learning as the project went on.
- To begin with the skills and knowledge were structured through set pieces and the isolated and repeated riffs or melodies, with some built-in progression. However, after 4 or 5 lessons, the learners chose their own "real" music to work on.
- As well as playing, the task involved a high level of listening and a certain amount of improvisation.

Therefore at first the emphasis was more on *aural* learning than *informal* learning, moving in the direction of informal learning after four or five lessons.[9]

In the CD tracks for Stages 1 and 2 of the project, the keys were not too demanding, the tempi not too fast, and the phrases not too long.[10] In addition, the materials were slightly graded, starting with shorter riffs in the pop/funk piece and moving towards longer phrases in the classical pieces. However, overall the work was based on the principle of differentiation by outcome. In other words, we gave the same materials to each learner regardless of their level of ability, achievement, or the instrument they played. After the first few lessons, when pupils chose their own pieces to work on, any pedagogic systematisation or control over the demands of the piece chosen was of course relinquished.[11]

## A Brief Summary of the Pupils' Initial Approaches to the Task: the Emergence of Potential "Learning Styles"

None of the pupils had previously attempted to find pitches by ear from a recording during a lesson; and in interviewing them at the end of the project, I found that only 4 of the 15 pupils had been confident in the knowledge that music could be learnt entirely by ear before the project started. Another four had never attempted to play by ear before. Nine said they had tried some ear-playing at home, but not by playing along with a recording, and they reported a feeling that they had not had much success. Only one pupil, Tom, regularly played along to recordings at home: "when I'm bored, I pick up the clarinet to play, when I'm listening to some music, I just play along with it." He, however, said that the project strategies had given him "a more rounded kind of information type thing."

As I worked through the data, one area that unexpectedly began to emerge was that there seemed to be four distinct ways in which the pupils approached the task. I conceptualised these as four different "learning styles."[12] By "learning styles" I mean an approach to learning which seemed to come about spontaneously rather than as a result of practice or teaching. At the end-of-project teacher meeting I explained how I was viewing each learning style, presented the criteria on paper, and played one audio-excerpt of each to the teachers. The audio-excerpts were the recordings of the very first moments in which the pupil had attempted to aurally copy the very first notes within the project. I then played further excerpts of first attempts, one from each pupil, and asked the teachers to independently categorise each one according to the same criteria, acting in the manner of judges in an expert panel. I also asked them to note whether they felt the audio excerpts fitted none of the criteria, or would be more accurately described in a different way than the criteria allowed. There was a 100 per cent agreement with my own categorisation in all cases but one, where one teacher classed one pupil differently from how I and the other two teachers categorized her. The four categories are summarised below.

### 1. The "impulsive" style

After listening to only one rendition of the bass riff, Fred started to play his trumpet loudly and apparently with enormous confidence. He played the rhythm with exact precision, but mainly all on one note (not one of the correct notes, and slightly out of tune); then he switched to another note and stuck on that. On his second attempt he started dead on the first note, straight after the two-bar drum introduction, and again played with a great deal of rhythmic accuracy, but on a set of pitches that bore only some similarity to those on the track. By the end, with only encouragement and no specific advice from the teacher, he had settled on his own two-note version of the riff. I called his approach the "impulsive" learning style, because: he started to respond to the music so quickly that he had hardly any time to listen to it first; he played loudly and with seeming confidence; showed no concern for whether his pitches matched those on the recording; and kept going without stopping to make corrections, ask questions or assess progress. Fred was the only pupil we placed in this category; the reason being simply that his approach seemed quite distinct from that of any other pupils.

## 2. The "shot-in-the-dark" style

Seven of the 15 pupils were placed in this category. In contrast with Fred, these young people approached the task with great hesitation, seeming to harbour doubt and even fear of making a mistake. They would start by listening for several bars, sometimes up to a minute or longer, then when they tried out notes, they would play very quietly. Quite often they would wince or grimace as soon as they had played a note, regardless of whether it was a correct one or not. Even if they happened to play a correct note, they did not usually show any signs of recognising it as such. In most cases, and with a great deal of teacher-encouragement and some guidance (as outlined below), these pupils were able to play the whole of one riff by the end of the first 10 to 15-minute session, and in some cases part of another riff; but with some hesitation and quite a few mistakes. I called this the "shot-in-the-dark" approach.

## 3. The "practical" style

Five of the 15 pupils were placed in this category. Rather than holding back and stabbing at notes in the manner of the "shot-in-the-dark" pupils, they seemed quite pragmatic, and started off by *playing* their instrument. In that sense, their approach was similar to that of Fred, the "impulsive" pupil. However, in another sense, they took a more applied, strategic approach than Fred, in that they spontaneously broke down the task into components. These components may have been short phrases, but were not always identifiable as such; for example, they may have been just three notes from within the middle of a phrase, or an outstanding interval or a scalar passage. Another approach they had in common was to play their instrument quietly, which was both unlike Fred, and unlike the quiet, hesitant way identified amongst the "shot-in-the-dark" pupils. Rather, playing quietly enabled them to listen carefully to the CD without drowning its sound with their own playing. Another strategy was to play up a scale until a note in the riff was hit, at which point the player would usually immediately recognize it as one of the correct notes, use it as an anchor, and work out the other notes from there. Another approach was to do something I later called "dwell and catch up", which was to dwell on a few notes and practice them a couple of times, even though the music on the CD track was still moving forwards through time, then to catch up with the CD music by leaving out the next few bars, and do the same thing the next time the same notes came around. In this way they would fill in the missing notes, not necessarily by following the order in which the notes come on the recording, but by starting perhaps in the middle of the riff and working backwards and forwards. In most cases, by the end of the very first attempt, these pupils had got the whole, or almost the whole riff correct with very little teacher-input, enabling them to move straight on to the next riff.

## 4. The "theoretical" style

Two pupils were placed in this category. They seemed more inclined to ask questions than to play notes. One of them was William, who had been playing the violin for 4 years. Immediately after I had explained the task and we had listened to the full instrumental track of "Link Up", he said:

*William (violin), lesson 1*

William: Which part are we going to be playing, since there were several instruments?
LG: They were indeed. Yes. There were several.
William: So which one are we going to be playing? Or are we playing all of them?

No-one else asked this question, or indeed any question at this point. Other comments and questions he proffered over the course of the project include those below, which the reader might otherwise assume were made by myself or his teacher.

- It's only playing three notes I think. Three different notes.
- Because the chords, the top chord, the middle chord, and bottom chord were the same rhythm, just different notes.
- It was third finger on the D string wasn't it?

- The top notes are chords.
- So it just goes second finger, second finger and then first finger, right?
- So it's just the same three notes that just keep on, that they are going to repeat . . . So it just keeps on going on. D-C-D, D-C-D.
- It just goes like third finger, second finger, third finger and then it repeats that once and it goes third finger, first finger on the E and then back.
- I think it starts somewhere around the E string, but I'm not sure.

Both William and Liz, the other pupil who was placed in this category, seemed to have an analytical, theoretically-orientated approach to the task. They listened with concentration, but instead of trying notes on their instruments, they would ask questions, and seemed to want to conceptualise how the music was structured, and/or to work out each note in theory before trying to play it. Unlike Fred's "impulsive" style of learning, and the "practical" style of five of the pupils, but rather like the "shot-in-the-dark" style of seven pupils, they seemed reluctant to play. However, as with the "shot-in-the-dark" pupils, by the end of the first lesson, with encouragement and guidance, all but one could play at least one riff either correctly, or with the correct rhythm and contour, if not total pitch accuracy. The exception was the youngest pupil, Joelly, who achieved this at the end of her second session.

*An overall picture of the four learning styles*

Table 9-1 gives an overall picture of which pupils were placed within each style-category, including their age, instrument, and number of years of taking lessons on that instrument.

**Table 9-1. Categorisation of the pupil's learning styles**

| Impulsive | Shot-in-the-dark | Practical | Theoretical |
|---|---|---|---|
| Fred (14) trpt 4 yrs | Oliver (13) trom 2 yrs<br>Shilpa (15) sax 4 yrs<br>Evie (13) vln 5 yrs<br>Molly (14) euph 8 mnth<br>Raksha (14) cello 3 yrs<br>Joelly (10) pf 2 yrs<br>Parvesh (13) clar 3 yrs | Tom (13) clar 4 yrs<br>Edward (17) pf 12 yrs<br>Ruby (14) pf 5 yrs<br>Jessica (15) pf 7 yrs<br>Katie (15) cello 8 yrs | William (12) vln 4 yrs<br>Liz (13) pf 2 yrs |

Clearly there will be much to be discovered with a larger sample. One issue would be the extent to which these four learning styles are replicated, confirmed or contravened with greater numbers of pupils and a bigger expert panel. Others would be the extent to which historical variables such as the type of instrument played, or previous experience of learning might affect the outcomes. Then there are pre-existing psychological differences between pupils, such as personality traits; musical ability differences such as the prior possession or not of "perfect pitch"; social group factors such as age or gender; and a range of other issues which may or may not influence the validity and reliability of the claims about learning styles made here. These are areas that we will aim to investigate to some extent in the main study, although it will not be possible to test for all of them. I will pick them up again briefly at the end of this chapter.

## "Learning Style", "Learning Strategy" and Pupils' Progress beyond the Initial Stages

Above I have suggested that the pupils' initial, spontaneous approaches to the task can helpfully be regarded as a type of "learning style." The concept of "learning style" can be distinguished from that of "learning strategy" (of which claim there is more detailed discussion in Green 2010, and see Note 12). How "style" and "strategy" differ is, basically and briefly, as follows: "style" arises spontaneously, prior to or free from any influences derived from being taught, observing others carrying out the task, or practicing the task; "strategy" develops gradually and appears to be the result of teaching, observation or practice. Here I will give a very brief overview of some of the ways in which pupils progressed, and some of the learning strategies (as distinct from learning styles) that they adopted for themselves as the project went on. Many of the issues are rich, and could probably form the focus of an article on their own. However owing to space I am only able to indicate the overarching areas.

In all cases improvement was noted by myself, the teacher, and the pupil, in the sense that without exception pupils became increasingly able to accurately identify and play pitches by ear as the project went by, as well as gaining in confidence. Those who had been identified as in the "practical" category outlined above maintained basically the same approaches as the task went by, only becoming faster, more accurate and more confident. However, in some cases other pupils seemed to progress *through* different learning styles. For example, Evie's initial approach was classed as "shot-in-the-dark" but she moved towards a "practical" approach as the lessons went by; and Oliver, initially a "shot-in-the-dark" pupil, moved towards a more "theoretical" approach. It may be that there is a natural progression between the learning styles, with the "practical approach" being the most effective. In other words, what for some pupils starts out as a spontaneous learning style, becomes for others a learnt strategy.

For example, one strategy that has already been mentioned in connection with the "practical" pupils was what I called "dwell-and-catch-up." This approach was adopted immediately and spontaneously by all five pupils in the "practical" category, but began to be observable towards the end of the project in the case of at least two others.

Working through the recordings and transcripts, it became possible to identify a number of other strategies that were gradually developed by all or many of the pupils, and which cut across the learning styles. What might be called "deep listening" was a primary one, as pupils began to identify parts within the texture. This is evidenced by statements such as:

> Katie (cello): I was trying to pick out bits of the cello parts but it's really hard to . . . so, I just, kind of focused on the main tune . . . There was one little bit of cello part that I picked out as well . . .

> Shilpa (saxophone): I did the Little Mermaid song, but I really got like a really random part . . .

Pupils also began to listen more structurally, as evidenced by statements including "Which part of the melody do you think would be good to learn?" and "Does it just, is it just the same notes twice? . . . Is it the same notes three times?" In the post-intervention interviews, 14 pupils were asked the question: "Have you noticed any changes in the way you listen to music in general since you've been doing the task? If so, can you explain how?" Five pupils said "no"; four said "some" and five "yes." There is no space here to quote their exact words, which were in fact very similar to how pupils in the classroom project discussed this issue (see Green 2008, Chapter 4).

Another strategy is related to a tendency amongst many pupils to do what I later called "edge forward." That is, after having practiced a short part, say four or five notes long, they would then have a stab at the next note or couple of notes almost impulsively. At least 11 instances of this were recorded as independent events that occurred amongst seven of the pupils, and a further pupil talked about having had this experience in her interview. One example was cited at the beginning of this chapter:

### Parvesh (clarinet) lesson 3

Parvesh comes in on the right note, stumbles, makes a few more attempts and eventually plays correctly along with the music. Note that he, as with many kids, gets one note right followed by a wrong note; then next time it comes round he gets two notes right; then three. This seems to be a pattern.

Singing the notes that were being sought was another strategy which three pupils in particular spontaneously adopted, one a brass player, one a pianist and one a cellist. This also connects with a teaching strategy, which I will mention later.

There were many instances where pupils were able to play more-or-less the correct pitch *contour* but without getting the exact pitches. This would normally precede finding the exact pitches. Pupils also often spontaneously harmonised, sometimes playing fourths or fifths and sometimes thirds. This lead into what can be seen as spontaneous improvisation, which for all the pupils except Tom was a novel experience. As an example:

### Edward (piano) lesson 6

At the end something very interesting happens—he reaches for a big chord to finish with, misses it, tries again and misses, then tries again, and says:

Edward: Oh! (Tries again) That's how I wanted to end it, but I haven't practiced that before, it just came to me that I should end it on a high note. (Plays the chord he was aiming for again.)

Along similar lines, some pupils developed the ability to fluently turn a mistake into something that could be considered an improvisatory variation.[13]

Connected with the concept of improvisation, I also observed many instances where pupils appeared to be "in flow", and this was confirmed by the interviews and discussions with participants. The concept of "flow" as it was first put forward in Csikszentmihalyi's well-known study (1990) refers to a combination of certain types of activity, of which music is one, with an individual's attitudinal state. "Flow" arises when the activity is thoroughly engaging and continuously rewarding, and the individual is wholly and undistractedly wrapped up in carrying out the activity. Here, however, I am not only referring to the concept as a psychological experience of the individual, but also as a quality of the *musical product* itself; in other words, the performance was heard to "flow" or to be more fluent than is normally expected in a novice player learning a new piece.

This finding was also confirmed in the interviews, as a view shared by both pupils and teachers. Again, the presence of "flow" was comparable with its presence in the classroom project (Green 2008).[14]

There were some interesting differences between pupils within the present project, in the ways they approached the task when it involved music that they were unfamiliar with, and also music that they were familiar with. It goes without saying that the task of aurally copying an unfamiliar piece of music is more challenging than copying a familiar piece. It is also—as pupils in both the classroom and the current project told us—far more enjoyable when the piece is familiar as well as well-liked. Most pupils expressed quite strong opinions about which music they wanted to choose, both when they were asked to choose between the six classical pieces in Stage 2, and when they were given free choice in Stage 3. Their choices represented a more diverse range of styles than the choices that had been made by pupils in the classroom project.[15] Some selected what they regarded as "suitable" choices which were played either on the instrument they were learning, or that were otherwise suited to it (for example the trumpeter Fred chose the opening of the first movement of Mozart's *Eine Kleine Nachtmusik*, played by a string quartet but eminently suitable for trumpet too in relation to its arpeggiated "hunting call" nature). By contrast, some went for pieces which they said they thought would be a challenge for their instrument. Some were concerned to pick music that they liked regardless of what instrument it was for; some were concerned to pick music that was easy enough for them to play (this was a consideration which came later to the pupils in the classroom project); and some displayed a mix of these approaches. Two pupils independently of each other picked a piece which happened to be in a very difficult key for them; but which without guidance, and working at home, they both spontaneously learnt to play in a key that they could manage. This was facilitated, of course, because they already knew and liked the tune.

## The Pedagogy and the Roles of the Teachers

As explained earlier, at the outset of the project teachers were asked to stand back rather more than usual; this meant saying less, and giving pupils more time than they might normally do to tackle and achieve a task. During her induction session Kate, the piano teacher, responded to this notion with:

> Marvellous! My only worry is as a piano teacher I shall become completely redundant!

The fear that highly skilled and dedicated music teachers could become redundant in a teaching situation where they allow learners more autonomy than usual is understandable and has been voiced by others; however, it is exceedingly far from the case.[16] By the end of both the classroom and the instrumental project such fears were dispelled, as evidenced by Kate's view in her end-of-project interview below:

> . . . I have really enjoyed it. I found it on occasions as I said, you know an exquisite torture . . . because you know I am terribly difficult keeping my mouth shut at best of times, but it has been a fantastic learning experience for me and so an enriching thing for me that hopefully I can fit back into my work with my pupils.

In what follows I wish to briefly illustrate and discuss the kinds of roles and teaching strategies that the four teachers and myself took as the project went on.

One primary strategy was not dissimilar to strategies often used when teaching from notation. This was to encourage pupils to "keep going." However, the quality of "keeping on going" is different when one is playing along to a recording, especially one that is "looped" as in Stages 1 and 2 of this project, compared with when one is playing from notation. With a recording as a model, whatever the pupil plays or fails to play, the recording carries, moving and changing on through time, whereas the score is a spatial object which remains static and unchanged. Thus, particularly when the recording is "looped", the pupil is able to pick up after a mistake, or wait until the same part of the melody returns in the loop (termed "dwell and catch up", as above), without losing the sense of the musical flow of time. Encouraging pupils to keep going therefore frequently enabled them to learn how to recover from or "play through" any inaccuracies or mistakes (see Note 13). It was easily done, simply with using encouraging words such as "don't worry, just keep going" at appropriate moments; and by ensuring that pupils knew mistakes were allowable and that playing through them was both expected and appropriate. In addition, as discussed above in relation to the concept of "flow", and as the teachers indicated in the post-project interviews, playing along with a recording tended to help pupils play more fluently in a number of ways.

Connected with encouraging pupils to keep going was the strategy of encouraging them to "make their own version" of the piece being copied. Their "own version" may not have been a fully intentional product, however, but could arise willy-nilly, due to a number of causes. These include the fact that the pupil may have not have been technically competent enough to play the original piece accurately according to its recorded form; or that whilst they may have been technically competent enough, their aural skills were not up to the job; or that they made mistakes in relation to their own intentions (regardless of whether their intentions were accurate or not). Often, in most aurally-based musics, a "mistake" can be—intentionally or unintentionally—played through, then repeated, so that it comes to be "played in"; the player can at some point in that process make a decision to treat the mistake as an intentional alteration. As we saw earlier with an example from Edward, through such processes the pupils began to engage in intentional embellishment and improvisation. As mentioned earlier, and as touched on in Note 13, the issue of what is correct and what is a mistake, and where the boundaries between these two notions lie in relation to musical creativity and performance, is complex and fascinating.

The notion of "musical sketching" might be helpful here, where the role of the teacher can be understood as encouraging the pupils to make a "musical sketch" rather than a "correct" realisation. As teachers we had to use our judgement about when to offer guidance designed to "correct" what we perceived to be a "mistake", or what we considered the pupil to have perceived to be a "mistake", and when to accept an alternative realisation as a potentially valuable, or intentional, variation. Alternatively the opportunity can also be taken to demonstrate the "correct" notes.

Guiding the pupil's listening was a major strategy. One approach was to ask questions about what was being heard, another was to ask the pupil to listen again and notice small details. Sometimes pupils could respond by playing what they heard, sometimes by describing it in words, or sometimes by simply confirming that they had heard it, even if they were as yet unable to either play it back, or use words to describe it.

Another much-used method was to sing the pitches to the pupil. This enabled us to slow the music down, stop in the middle to wait whilst the pupil found the note, and/or sing a note and allow the pupil to seek it whilst we held onto it. This usually took place either after the pupil was already able to play the broad contour of the melody, or where no progress had been made. Sometimes, if singing was not enough, we gave the name of one or two notes, from which point the pupils could work out the rest by themselves. The next stage was to show the pupils where a note was on the instrument, or how to play it. This was particularly necessary on instruments where notes are less immediately visible, such as the violin or trumpet; or where fingering has many possibilities such as the saxophone or clarinet. Strangely the brass players seemed to need less help with this than I and the brass teacher expected. (An interesting issue emerged concerning how pupils approached embouchure or "lipping" on brass instruments, which I will mention below as it arose without teacher-intervention.)

Strategies that directly involve modelling by showing pupils how to play whole phrases or pieces were also used, but only after the pupil had already had time to work out pitches autonomously to as great an extent as possible. Demonstration allows the pupil to learn by watching as well as listening, linking sound to eye, and observing a range of physical aspects of playing such as posture, gesture and instrumental technique. Such modelling was also particularly helpful, and described as enjoyable by all parties, when the teacher played along with the pupil as a duet. Another helpful way to model was to occasionally seek pitches ourselves in front of the pupil. The teachers decided not to familiarise themselves in advance with the given CD tracks, and we did not know what music the pupils would bring to the final lessons. In this way, the teachers chose to put themselves in the same position as the pupils. We felt this was both eye-opening and ear-opening for pupils, and for two of the four teachers it was described as challenging and interesting.

Another strategy was to adopt the "theoretical" approach that two of the pupils had spontaneously adopted for themselves, as discussed earlier. Examples of this included asking pupils to listen, as illustrated above, and in this case, to name or describe aspects of the music that they could hear, such as note-names, how many beats were played, whether the harmony was the same or different, what scale or key was being used, how many notes were in the chord, whether the key is major or minor, and so on.

As a useful way of helping pupils to find notes, and to connect the teaching to theory, we also found it helpful to link the piece to scales that the pupils already knew, and clearly opportunities can also be taken to show pupils a new scale, or ask them to work out a new scale for themselves. In addition, the teacher could often find an opportunity to connect the learning to other pieces or other activities that had taken place or were about to take place in other parts of the lesson, with or without notation. Of course teachers also took the opportunity to teach many aspects of instrumental technique, musicianship and musical interpretation—fingering, breathing, intonation, phrasing, dynamics and so on. Such teaching tended to occur at later stages once the pupils had found pitches and gained confidence in playing fluently.

## The Pupils' and Teachers' Views

In the post-intervention interview I asked the pupils: "When I first played you the very first CD and said you were going to learn it by ear, without notation, what did you think about that?" Ten of them said they expected it to be difficult or impossible, using words such as: "I thought I am not going to be able to do this"; "it might be a bit hard"; "I thought I wouldn't be able to do that at all, truthfully. I didn't know how to tackle it"; and "panic!" However, after the project all except Tom, the only one who had previously done aural learning by himself at home, reported that it turned out to be easier than expected. Surprisingly perhaps, given their initial reactions and expectations, all the pupils reported that they found it enjoyable, with three-quarters ticking the "very enjoyable" box. Words used to describe the experience, often by several pupils independently of each other, included "fun", "really good fun", "enjoyed it a lot", "really interesting", "brilliant", "something new and interesting to learn", and others. All the pupils said that given a choice between learning only by notation, only by ear, or both, they would choose both.

The teachers were often surprised by how well pupils tackled and progressed at the task, and found that pupils could make leaps which exceeded normal expectations. Examples of this fell into two categories which I will treat below, the first regarding technique, and the second regarding what I will refer to as musical expression.

Firstly, I asked teachers the question: "How much do you feel the pupils' technique—e.g. fingering, embouchure and so on—was affected or not affected by the approach, and if relevant, in what ways?" Examples picked out by teachers included: producing a note that the pupil had not known how to play previously; in the case of brass players, this included "lipping" which was something they did spontaneously and had not been shown how to do; for string players, it might be moving their hand into a new position that they had not previously come across; for all instruments apart from the piano it involved playing with better intonation, and/or making a better sound than normal; for pianists it could be playing a hands-together syncopation that would have been beyond them using notation. In general, it involved most pupils, at some point in time, playing phrases or pieces that the teacher would have thought were beyond them.

As illustrated by the string teacher below, the issue of technique was not without its frustrations, but these also had some compensations, some of which relate to the issue of musical expression:

Susanna: Well the whole thing of technique, I thought featured quite largely in my mind, because there were times when they were doing things or trying to do it and I was very aware of the fact that they couldn't get the notes they wanted to, because they didn't really know about certain aspects of technique, and actually there was a certain frustration inside me at the time . . . but yes, I think they would, they were learning bits of technique in a much more musical way than if it was just in a scale book; or as I say as you are reading notation, sometimes, it can come out so the notes are all there but it's not remotely phrased how it should be. So in that sense you are starting from the *musical* point of view, so that was good I think, yes; and they were copying things that they heard in their recording, perhaps a short bass stroke or, whereas if they were doing that from the notation you'd have to *tell* them.

As Sarah, the brass teacher said on more than one occasion: "You'd need a thousand words to get that out of them."

Secondly, then, regarding musical expression, I asked: "How much do you feel the pupils' musicianship—e.g. phrasing, dynamics, articulation, touch—was affected or not affected by the approach, and if relevant, in what ways?" In this area there was quite strong agreement that the approach elicited a number of valuable and unexpected outcomes, as the example below indicates:

Kate (piano): I would say that's some of the, I mean obviously there was a couple of slips, but that's some of the most sensitive playing I've ever heard [Edward] do! . . . [He] I think played better when he wasn't having to read music, because he was able to listen to what he was doing . . . I think he achieved a more musical, he was playing more musically at an earlier stage. Because you wouldn't have that extra level of hand-to-eye co-ordination, your brain to page, back to brain and then to fingers, you know all that kind of stuff, they are all little stumbling blocks to playing musically.

As with the classroom project, teachers were unanimous in the view that the foremost skill developed by the strategies was listening. For example:

Kate: . . . they are beginning to actively listen to music as opposed to passively hear it, which is something that I am trying to incorporate in all my lessons . . .

For those instruments other than the piano, another area where improvement was noted, was that of intonation:

Susanna (strings): I think it [the pupils' intonation] is definitely better. Because the thing with the notation, they're playing the right, what they think is the right thing so they think it must be right, you know, because they've actually forgetting to listen. They're just reading the note and thinking, you know, that's a high 2 and putting the finger there; and, it's actually out of tune. But they're just thinking, "I've got my finger in the right position, so it's right." Whereas when we took the music [score] out of the way and they're actually focusing on [listening to] the music, they knew instantly it wasn't right because they were copying and matching.

All four teachers, without prompt, said they felt the task increased pupils' confidence and also linked this to the ability to take ear-playing towards improvisation and in some cases, composition.

The above findings concerning the quality of pupils' performances and/or confidence correlate with findings by other research studies, which systematically investigated the results of aural versus notation-based learning. In a study by Watson (2010) a jazz improvisation task was given to 62 college students; half of them received instruction primarily through aural imitation, and the other half received instruction primarily through notated exercises. In a study by Woody and Lehmann (2010), an aural learning task was carried out by two groups of 12 musicians. The members of one group had backgrounds in formal training and classical music only; whilst those in the other group had backgrounds in both formal training and aural, informal, vernacular music-learning. Findings in both studies were deduced from systematic observation, expert judgement and/or the reported perceptions of the players themselves. Participants who had learnt by ear felt more confident, played more fluently, "musically" or expertly and/or had a more fluid relationship with their instrument. For example, in Woody and Lehmann's study, in unprompted responses to open questions, out of 12 formally-trained participants, 5 mentioned that they had found the aurally-learnt melody problematic or unpredictable; meanwhile, none of the vernacular musicians made such a comment, but on the contrary, 6 of them mentioned that they had found the melody predictable and typical. Whereas 9 of the formal musicians reported having been conscious of fingering or other actions on their instrument during the task, only one of the vernacular musicians did so.

Back to the current project, there was agreement amongst the teachers that, although many of us found it difficult to stand back at the outset of the project, this was indeed necessary; and also that as in all teaching, one has to carefully judge the moment when it is necessary to step in and offer help. It is perhaps worth citing two examples at some length:

Kate (piano): Sometimes I found it absolutely agonising to stand back and watch whilst their fingers hover over the right notes, and you want to say "Yes, that's it, go for it" but you know I see why it is better to let them find the notes themselves . . . I think that it's got to be determined by each particular teacher and how they work best, and how they relate to each different pupil. I think the role has got to be facilitative, if that word exists, rather than telling; because what you could find yourself doing and what I would be tempted to do, because I tend to be quite hands on, is say: "Yes there is your start note, there it is, look at it, that's how it is." I can see that's not always helpful, although I think you have to do it on a case-by-case, pupil-by-pupil basis. But I absolutely take [the project's] point and I've learnt from that, sometimes you just have to learn to sit back and let them sink or swim, but hopefully you are not going to let them drown . . . and what I will take from it is giving them the tools to do it for themselves . . . So there is no point in just showing them, but I think as a teacher you have to accept the point at which we reached a block, a stumbling block at which there is a danger that this is all going to fall apart. So I think you have to approach it on a pupil-by-pupil basis.

Sarah (brass): . . . from my point of view I thought it was really good because you didn't know [inaudible] anyway. The less you would say to them kind of was the better, so if you just explained what you want and then left them to their own devices to try and work it out, and then from my point of view just giving a helping hand, explaining how they could use their instruments to help them do what they were doing, either different positions or using their valves or using their lip, just little technical things that helped them to get their notes. I think that worked best. And just really sort of leaving them to work it out themselves.

All the teachers indicated that they felt they had learnt from being involved in the project, and that the approaches would be likely to influence their future teaching, not necessarily through an exact replication of the materials and strategies, but in more general ways. To end with a quote from each teacher:

Kate (piano): . . . I am finding this absolutely fascinating; and it's already having an effect on the rest of my teaching too, just in a general way; and it's reminding me that there is more than one way to learn, you know, what a middle C is . . . I think it has reminded me that a holistic approach to teaching is very important. And I think I will incorporate the aural tradition, if you like, your teaching methods, on a daily basis . . .

Susanna (strings) [in an unsolicited email sent after the project]: I found taking part in the whole project really interesting and rewarding. It gave me new insights into how people learn and has given me new ideas which I will definitely incorporate into future lessons.

Sarah (brass): It's been a real eye-opening experience . . . at the time I thought, "Oh, I am not sure how it's going to work or how it's going to fit in with our lessons and our timetables and things with the exams around", but it's been really good for the kids and they've all enjoyed it. So I mean, I thought some of them might come to me the next week and say, "I really don't like it", or "I am really not getting on." But nobody said anything.

Lynne (woodwind): . . . the [pupils] that did it thought it was fun, and if you can make learning fun, then that's just the best way to do it. So I think that really it should be incorporated into every lesson, to be perfectly frank, if you can . . . I think it was a resounding success. That's my comment. It really was! All the teachers enjoyed it and all the pupils enjoyed it.

## Issues for Further Research and Development

This project was a small-scale investigation in an area which seems to contain much potential for further work concerning a range of issues confronting music educators today. Such issues are by no means tied to the particular pedagogic strategies involved in the current project, but relate to a number of approaches currently being developed in which informal, aural learning practices, or learning practices that have generally been associated with the informal sphere, are being taken more seriously and adapted within formal music education (see Note 3). Here I will briefly indicate some of the areas which seem to me to bear potential fruit. I have restricted my comments to those which could arise directly from the project under consideration in this chapter, but of course they have a wider potential application in relation to other similar projects.

One thing is clear: we would need to study the learning processes involved in the project over a longer period of time, and with much larger numbers of pupils and teachers, before we could produce any thoroughly robust findings. In the main study, due to start in September 2011, that will be possible to some extent, and some of the questions and issues which I have identified above and below will be investigated. However it will by no means be possible to address them all. Issues for further development can be considered to fall under two broad categories. One concerns the practical development of the project's pedagogy, and the other concerns the theoretical and methodological development of the research.

One way in which to extend the pedagogic approach would be to introduce further stages. For example, a fourth stage could be added to the current three-stage model, focussing more directly on improvisation; a fifth stage could focus on composition, a sixth stage on group-learning or peer-directed learning, and another one on the development of musical leadership skills. After the project had ended, the teachers put together a performance for the school concert involving 35 pupils who had learnt the music by ear in sectional rehearsals. Susanna, the string teacher, adapted the strategies for her adult string class, which involved a teacher-directed, group session, and went on for a whole academic year.

The pedagogy involved in facilitating group learning by ear is necessarily rather different from that involved in individual learning. This is particularly so because the individual can choose when to start and stop the recording, and can focus their ear on the recording itself without the distraction of others playing at the same time. But with more than one person learning at a time, the decision about when to stop the recording has to be taken either by the teacher, or an appointed member of the class acting as musical leader; and the other members of the class may be playing any notes—accurate, inaccurate, improvisatory, or whatever—as the music goes on. There are a number of implications concerning the pedagogic strategies, including for example how to manage the needs of everyone in the group; how to build in a higher level of visual learning as the group will watch the teacher modelling at the same time as they are attempting to copy; the use of peer-direction, and many more. Such extensions to the model would obviously also contain implications for extending the research.

Regarding other possible extensions to the research, as distinct from the pedagogy, there are many possibilities. For example I would hypothesise that—despite the fact that both the project pedagogy and notational pedagogy involve the replication of a pre-composed piece and largely require no necessary improvisation—learners would be in a better position to improvise after they had followed the first three stages of the project (or other similar approaches), than if they had learnt to play the same pieces by notation. Such a hypothesis, and many others, could be investigated by the use of a matched control group, with both quantitative and qualitative measures of ability and achievement taken before, during and after the intervention.

In the present research, the teaching and research team formed an "expert panel" which made judgements about outcomes. These included, for example, the proposition that pupils were displaying different learning styles as discussed earlier, and they included judgements about skill and knowledge-acquisition, quality of playing, and other issues. The use of a larger independent panel of experts to judge such matters could confirm, invalidate, and/or throw further light on them.

There are many questions to be explored regarding both individual and social-group differences between the pupils, which would again require larger numbers of participants in order to be investigated. As mentioned earlier, individual differences would concern areas such as ability and motivation, whereas social differences would concern membership of different social groups. Regarding the former, clinical tests of pitch-sense, for example, could be administered before, during and after the intervention. It would also be interesting to observe whether pupils who display signs of "perfect pitch" before the project adapt different approaches to the task; for example, would it be the case that those with perfect pitch are more likely to adopt what I earlier called the "practical" approach? Age-differences are also likely to have an effect on both the approach to learning and the ability to undertake the task. An application and investigation of the project strategies, or other similar strategies, across different age-groups could throw new light on child-development in relation to musical ability and understanding.

As mentioned earlier, it is likely that different instruments will be connected with different approaches to aural learning, and different outcomes. More knowledge and understanding of the capacities or affordances of different instruments in these respects could be of vital interest to music educators, as they may carry implications for which instruments are most likely to be of help at different levels, ages, or for different individuals.

There are also potentially interesting questions about whether complete beginners would display the same approaches to learning as those who had been taking lessons for varying lengths of time. So far, there are indications that our normal grading systems may not apply to learning and teaching using aural-copying approaches: some learners who are graded as beginner in the traditional structure may be better at this particular task than those graded as more advanced, and vice versa; and some pupils who have been designated as having high ability may be less good at this task than those who have been designated as having low ability, and vice versa. There are also questions to be explored concerning aural learning in relation to assessment, inclusion, and special educational needs.

Many music teachers and researchers are today committed to the expansion of the styles of music that are included and valued within education, and a broadening of concepts concerning how to teach music and how to both facilitate and direct musical learning. The bibliography given at the end of this chapter represents only a small proportion of the work being done. The work is not, and should not be, restricted to any one style of music; nor should we risk losing the time-honoured, and often very differing traditions of music-teaching that have kept alive highly specialist educational practices, from the Western classical to the Indian classical styles and beyond. But there is much which remains to be done in attempting to return the enjoyment of music-making to what I believe most music-educators agree is its rightful place—a participatory aspect of what it is to be human.

# References

Allsup, R. E. 2004. "Of Concert Bands and Garage Bands: Creating Democracy Through Popular Music." In *Bridging the Gap: Popular Music and Education*, ed. C. X. Rodriguez, 204–23. Reston: MENC.
—. 2008. "Creating an Educational Framework for Popular Music in Public Schools: Anticipating the Second-Wave." *Visions of Research in Music Education* 12. http://www-usr.rider.edu/~vrme/v12n1/vision/1%20AERA%20-%20Allsup.pdf
Bailey, D. 1992. *Improvisation: Its Nature and Practice in Music.* New York: Da Capo Press.
Bayton, M. 1997. *Frock Rock: Women Performing Popular Music.* Oxford: Oxford University Press.
Bennett, H. S. 1980. *On Becoming a Rock Musician.* Amherst: University of Massachusetts Press.
Berkaak, O. A. 1999. "Entangled Dreams and Twisted Memories: Order and Disruption in Local Music Making." *YOUNG—Nordic Journal of Youth Research* 7 (2): 25–43. http://logic.itsc.cuhk.edu.hk/~b114299/young/1999/articleOdd%20Are%20Berkaak99-2.htm
Berliner, P. F. 1994. *Thinking in Jazz. The Infinite Art of Improvisation.* Chicago: University of Chicago.
Björnberg, A. 1993. "'Teach You to Rock'? Popular Music in the University Music Department." *Popular Music* 12 (1): 69–77.
Boespflug, G. 2004. "The Pop Music Ensemble in Music Education." In *Bridging the Gap: Popular Music and Education*, ed. C. X. Rodriguez, 190–203. Reston: MENC.
Byrne, C. 2005. "Pedagogical Communication in the Music Classroom." In *Musical Communication*, eds. D. Miell, R. MacDonald, and D. Hargreaves, 301–19. Oxford: Oxford University Press.
Byrne, C., and M. Sheridan. 2000. "The Long and Winding Road: the Story of Rock Music in Scottish Schools." *International Journal of Music Education* 36 (1): 46–58.
Campbell, P. S. 1995. "Of Garage Bands and Song-Getting: The Musical Development of Young Rock Musicians." *Research Studies in Music Education* 4 (1): 12–20.
Clawson, M. A. 1999. "Masculinity and Skill Acquisition in the Adolescent Rock Band." *Popular Music* 18 (1): 99–114.

Clements, A. C. 2008. "Escaping the Classical Canon: Changing Methods Through a Change of Paradigm." *Visions of Research in Music Education* 12. http://www-usr.rider.edu/~vrme/v12n1/vision/3%20AERA%20-%20Clements.pdf

Cohen, S. 1991. *Rock Culture in Liverpool: Popular Music in the Making.* Oxford: Clarendon.

Coffield, F., D. Moseley, E. Hall, and K. Ecclesonte. 2004. *Learning Styles and Pedagogy in Post-16 Learning: a Systematic and Critical Review.* London: The Learning and Skills Research Centre.

Cope, P. 1999. "Community-Based Traditional Fiddling as a Basis for Increasing Participation in Instrumental Playing." *Music Education Research* 1 (1): 61–73.

Csikszentmihalyi, M. 1990. *Flow: The Psychology of Optimal Experience.* New York: Harper and Row.

Cutietta, R. A. 2004. "When We Question Popular Music in Education, What is the Question?" In *Bridging the Gap: Popular Music and Education*, ed. C. X. Rodriguez, 242–47. Reston: MENC.

Davis, S. 2005. "That Thing You Do! Compositional Processes of a Rock Band." *International Journal of Education and the Arts* 16 (6). http://www.ijea.org/v6n16/index.html

Downey, J. 2009. "Informal Learning in Music in the Irish Secondary School Context." *Action, Criticism and Theory in Music Education* 8 (2): 47–60. http://act.maydaygroup.org/articles/Downey8_2.pdf

Dunbar-Hall, P. 1996. "Designing a Teaching Model for Popular Music." In *Teaching Music*, ed. G. Spruce, 216–26. London and New York: Routledge in association with the Open University.

Dunbar-Hall, P., and K. Wemyss. 2000. "The Effects of the Study of Popular Music on Music Education." *International Journal of Music Education* 36 (1): 23–35.

Emmons, S. E. 2004. "Preparing Teachers for Popular Music Processes and Practices." In *Bridging the Gap: Popular Music and Education*, ed. C. X. Rodriguez, 158–73. Reston: MENC.

Evelein, F. 2006. "Pop and World Music in Dutch Music Education: Two Cases of Authentic Learning in Music Teacher Education and Secondary Music Education." *International Journal of Music Education* 24 (2): 178–87.

Feichas, H. 2010. "Informal Music Learning Practices as a Pedagogy of Integration in Brazilian Higher Education." *British Journal of Music Education* 27 (1): 47–58.

Finnegan, R. 1989. *The Hidden Musicians: Music-Making in an English Town.* Cambridge: Cambridge University Press.

Finney, J., and C. Philpott. 2010. "Student Teachers Appropriating Informal Pedagogy." *British Journal of Music Education* 27 (1): 7–19.

Folkestad, G. 2006. "Formal and Informal Learning Situations or Practices *vs* Formal and Informal Ways Of Learning." *British Journal of Music Education* 23 (2): 135–45.

Gatien, G. 2009. "Categories and Music Transmission." *Action, Criticism and Theory in Music Education* 8 (2): 95–120. http://act.maydaygroup.org/articles/Gatien8_2.pdf

Georgii-Hemming, E., and M. Westvall. 2010. "Examining Current Discourses Of Music Education In Sweden." *British Journal of Music Education* 27 (1): 21–33.

Green, L. 2001. *How Popular Musicians Learn: A Way Ahead for Music Education*. Aldershot: Ashgate.

—. 2008. *Music, Informal Learning and the School: A New Classroom Pedagogy*. Aldershot: Ashgate.

—. 2010. "Musical 'Learning Styles' and 'Learning Strategies' in the Instrumental Lesson: Some Emergent Findings From a Pilot Study." *Psychology of Music* (currently available as on online article; paper version to appear in due course).

Hallam, S., A. Creech, C. Sandford, T. Rinta, and K. Shave. 2008. *Survey of Musical Futures: a Report from Institute of Education University of London for the Paul Hamlyn Foundation*. Paul Hamlyn Foundation Project Report. http://media.musicalfutures.org.uk/documents/resource/27229/IOE_M usical_Futures_report.pdf

Heuser, F. 2008. "Encouraging Change: Incorporating Aural and Informal Learning Processes in an Introductory Music Education Course." *Visions of Research in Music Education* 12. http://www-usr.rider.edu/~vrme/v12n1/vision/4%20AERA%20-%20Heuser.pdf

Horn, K. 1984. "Rock Music-Making as a Work Model in Community Music Workshops." *British Journal of Music Education* 1 (2): 111–35.

Humphreys, J. T. 2004. "Popular Music in the American Schools: What History Tells us About the Present and the Future." In *Bridging the Gap: Popular Music and Music Education*, ed. C. X. Rodriguez, 91–106. Reston: MENC.

Jaffurs, S. E. 2004. "The Impact of Informal Music Learning Practices in the Classroom, or How I Learned How To Teach From a Garage Band." *International Journal of Music Education* 22 (3): 189–200

Jones, P. M. 2008. "Preparing Music Teachers for Change: Broadening Instrument Class Offerings to Foster Lifewide and Lifelong Musicing."

*Visions of Research in Music Education* 12. http://www-usr.rider.edu/~vrme/v12n1/vision/2%20AERA%20-%20Jones.pdf

Karlsen, S. 2010. "BoomTown Music Education and the Need for Authenticity: Informal Learning Put into Practice in Swedish Post-Compulsory Music Education." *British Journal of Music Education* 27 (1): 35–46.

Kirshner, T. 1998. "Studying Rock: Towards a Materialist Ethnography." In *Mapping The Beat*, eds. T. Swiss, J. Sloop, and A. Herman, 247–68. Oxford: Blackwell.

Lebler, D. 2007. "Student as Master? Reflections on a Learning Innovation in Popular Music Pedagogy." *International Journal of Music Education* 25 (3): 205–21.

—. 2008. "Popular Music Pedagogy: Peer Learning in Practice." *Music Education Research* 10 (2): 193–213.

Lilliestam, L. 1996. "On Playing by Ear." *Popular Music* 15 (2): 195–216.

Lines, D. 2005. "Improvisations and Cultural Work in Music and Music Education." In *Music Education for the New Millennium: Theory and Practice Futures for Music Education and Learning*, ed. D. Lines, 65–74. Oxford: Blackwell.

—. 2009. "Exploring the Contexts of Informal Learning." *Action, Criticism and Theory in Music Education* 8 (2): 1–7. http://act.maydaygroup.org/articles/Lines8_2.pdf

Mans, M. 2009. "Informal Learning and Values." *Action, Criticism and Theory in Music Education* 8 (2): 80–94. http://act.maydaygroup.org/articles/Mans8_2.pdf

Marsh, K. 2008. *The Musical Playground: Global Tradition and Change in Children's Songs and Games*. Oxford: Oxford University Press.

Martin, P. 1996. "Improvisation in Jazz: towards a Sociological Model." *Manchester Sociology Occasional Papers* 45.

Monson, I. 1996. *Saying Something: Jazz Improvisation and Interaction*. Chicago: University of Chicago Press.

Negus. K. 2000. *Music Genres and Corporate Cultures*. London: Routledge.

O'Flynn, J. 2006. "Vernacular Music-Making and Education." *International Journal of Music Education* 24 (2): 140–47.

Riding, R., and S. Raynor. 1998. *Cognitive Styles and Learning Strategies*. London: David Fulton Publishers.

Rodriguez, C. X. 2004. "The Broader Perspective." In *Bridging the Gap: Popular Music and Music Education*, ed. C. X. Rodríguez. Reston: MENC.

—. 2009. "Informal Learning in Music: Emerging Roles of Teachers and Students." *Action, Criticism and Theory in Music Education* 8 (2): 36–47. http://act.maydaygroup.org/articles/Rodriguez8_2.pdf

Schmeck, R. R., ed. 1988. *Learning Strategies and Learning Styles*. New York and London: Plenum Press.

Seddon, F., and M. Biasutti. 2009. "Participant Approaches to and Reflections on Learning to Play a 12-bar Blues in an Asynchronous E-Learning Environment." *International Journal of Music Education* 27 (3): 189–203.

—. 2010. "Strategies Students Adopted When Learning to Play an Improvised Blues in an E-Learning Environment." *Journal of Research in Music Education* 58 (2): 147–67.

Siefried, S. 2006. "Exploring the Outcomes of Rock and Popular Music Instruction in High School Guitar Class: a Case Study." *International Journal of Music Education* 24 (2): 168–177.

Sternberg, R. J., and L.-F. Zhang, eds. 2001. *Perspectives on Thinking, Learning, and Cognitive Styles*. Mahway: Lawrence Erlbaum Associates.

Suzuki, S. 1986. *Nurtured by Love: The Classic Approach to Talent Education* (2nd ed.). Miami: Suzuki Method International.

Väkevä, L. 2006. "Teaching Popular Music in Finland: What's Up, What's Ahead?" *International Journal of Music Education* 24 (2): 126–31.

—. 2009. "The World Well Lost, Found: Reality and Authenticity in Green's 'New Classroom Pedagogy'." *Action, Criticism and Theory in Music Education* 8 (2): 8–35. http://act.maydaygroup.org/articles/Vakeva8_2.pdf

—. 2010. "Garageband or GarageBand®? Remixing Musical Futures." *British Journal of Music Education* 27 (1): 59–70.

Watson, K. E. 2010. "The Effects of Aural Versus Notated Instructional Materials on Achievement and Self-Efficacy in Jazz Improvisation." *Journal of Research in Music Education* 58 (3): 240–59.

Wemyss, K. L. 2004. "Reciprocity and Exchange: Popular Music in Australian Secondary Schools." In *Bridging the Gap: Popular Music and Education*, ed. C. X. Rodriguez, 141–57. Reston: MENC.

Westerlund, H. 2006. "Garage Rock Bands: a Future Model for Developing Musical Expertise?" *International Journal of Music Education* 24 (2): 119–25.

Woody, R. H., and A. C. Lehmann. 2010. "Student Musicians' Ear-Playing Ability as a Function of Vernacular Music Experiences." *Journal of Research in Music Education* 58 (2): 101–115.

Wright, R., and P. Kanellopoulos. 2010. "Informal Music Learning, Improvisation and Teacher Education." *British Journal of Music Education* 27 (1): 71–87.

Zhang, L.-F., and R. J. Sternberg. 2006. *The Nature of Intellectual Styles*. Mahwah and London: Lawrence Erlbaum Associates.

# Notes

[1] I am deeply grateful to the teachers, Sarah Dias, Kate Edgar, Lynne Hobart and Susanna Wilson, all of whom went beyond the call of duty in their participation, and beyond my expectations in their enthusiastic and perceptive professional input. The 15 pupils impressed me with their commitment, their musical abilities, and the thoughtful and insightful ways in which they talked to me about their experiences of the project. I am deeply grateful to them all, and it was a pleasure to work with them. I would also like to thank the Head of Department and the school where I worked, for their interest, warm welcome and support. The project was funded by the Esmée Fairbairn Foundation, to whom I remain extremely grateful. I would also like to acknowledge the initial support of the Paul Hamlyn Foundation "Musical Futures" project in undertaking the background to this research, and the Institute of Education, University of London.

[2] The Musical Futures project www.musicalfutures.org is funded by the Paul Hamlyn Foundation. A detailed discussion of the strategies and research findings is available in Green (2008), and the background to the project is in Green (2001). The project's teaching strategies and materials themselves, along with a range of related materials which have since been developed by teachers, are available on the website at www.musicalfutures.org.uk/c/Informal. A range of Musical Futures informal learning initiatives are now taking place in Australia, the USA, Canada, Brazil and other countries. The first year and other aspects of the project were funded by the Esmée Fairbairn Foundation with the support of the London University Institute of Education.

[3] For current projects and commentaries concerning the adaptation of informal music learning practices within the formal realm, see for example: Allsup (2004), Boespflug (2004), Byrne (2005), Byrne and Sheridan (2000), Cope (1999), Cutietta (2004), Downey (2009), Dunbar-Hall (1996), Dunbar-Hall and Wemyss (2000), Emmons (2004), Evelein (2006), Feichas (2010), Finney and Philpott (2010), Folkestad (2006), Gatien (2009), Georgii-Hemming and Westvall (2010), Green (2001, 2008), Heuser (2008), Humphreys (2004), Jaffurs (2004), Jones (2008), Karlsen (2010), Lebler (2007, 2008), Lines (2009), Mans (2009), Marsh (2008), O'Flynn (2006), Rodriguez (2004, 2009), Seddon and Biasutti (2009, 2010), Siefried (2006), Väkevä (2006, 2009, 2010), Watson (2010), Wemyss (2004), Westerlund (2006), Woody and Lehmann (2010), Wright and Kanellopoulos (2010). This list is not exhaustive and there are many other excellent references on this topic to be explored.

[4] For examinations of popular musicians' informal learning practices see e.g. Bayton (1997), Bennett (1980), Berkaak (1999), Björnberg (1993), Campbell

(1995), Clawson (1999), Cohen (1991), Davis (2005), Finnegan (1989), Green (2001), Horn (1984), Kirshner (1998), Lilliestam (1996), Negus (2000).

[5] This is explored in Green (2008), but for an independent evaluation report see Hallam et al. (2008).

[6] This study is funded by the Esmée Fairbairn Foundation with the support of the London University Institute of Education.

[7] The grade system is run by a range of boards in the UK, and exported to many other countries. Two of the most well-known boards are the Associated Board of the Royal Schools of Music, and Trinity Guildhall. The grades run from 1 to 8. Usually (but not always) a minimum of a distinction in Grade 8 would be expected for a first-study entrant to a conservatoire, with a pass in Grade 8, or in some cases, Grade 6, being acceptable for an entrant to a music degree at a university.

[8] One girl, Liz, had only two lessons because she had to go into hospital during the project; however she and her mother agreed that she should nonetheless participate in the interviews, and I have included data from her lessons and interview along with the others.

[9] The relationship between aural and informal learning both inside and outside formal education contexts is of course fascinating, although there is no space to enter into it here. See e.g. Folkestad (2006), Green (2001, 3–7, 2008, 10), and various texts in Note 3 for discussions.

[10] How exactly the word "too" was measured here, was based on long experience of music teaching, and on the practice-based findings of the classroom project. Basically the principles were to use: keys of no more than two accidentals, a high proportion of step-wise movement, intervals of no more than a fifth, phrases of usually no more than four bars, rhythms consisting of mainly quavers, crotchets and minims (although with some syncopation at times), and moderate tempi.

[11] There are a number of similarities between this approach and the Suzuki method (Suzuki 1986), particularly the system of giving pupils recordings to copy aurally. However there are also differences which are quite deep-rooted. These arise partly from the different ways in which the two approaches came about. Whilst the Suzuki method is based on observing how children learn their native tongue, the approach of this project is based on observing how novice popular musicians learn aurally and informally. Another difference is that, unlike in Suzuki, here, each piece is not specially designed for the pupil's particular instrument, and not systematically graded according to an organised trajectory of pupil-progress. Rather, the attempt is to open the world of music to the pupils in a different way, by helping them to realise that they can adapt a wide range of musical styles, played by any instrument or combination of forces, and arrange it for their own instrument. After the first few lessons, the child is given free choice about what music to play. In Suzuki, differentiation is built into the strategy, since different tasks and materials are given to the learners at different ability levels or stages of development, and specially designed for different instruments; whereas here as mentioned above, differentiation is by outcome. Another difference is in the role of the teacher and parent: in the Suzuki method there is a high level not only of progressive structure, but also adult and expert guidance. Here, the teacher is asked

in the first instance, to stand back and make observations about how the pupil goes about the learning, and only later on to offer guidance, suggestions and demonstration. Parents were not involved. Finally, as mentioned earlier, the aim of the project strategies was to enable pupils to adopt a particular, aural approach concerning *how* to learn, rather than primarily to enable them to achieve mastery over *what* is learnt.

[12] The notion of "learning styles" and all the findings discussed in the present sub-section of this chapter are the focus of more detailed discussion in Green (2010). For overviews of work on the concept of "learning style" generally, not related to music, see e.g. Zhang and Sternberg (2006), or Coffield et al. (2004). Riding and Raynor (1998) provide a useful overview of work up to that date. Schmeck (1988) and Sternberg and Zhang (2001) offer anthologies with chapters by many of the core authors in the field. Within music education some interesting detailed studies on ways in which learners approach tasks and the identification of different strategies or approaches have also been carried out. See for example Seddon and Biasutti (2009, 2010), who identified five distinct learning activities amongst pupils engaged in improvisation.

[13] The place where improvisation begins, and making a mistake ends, is not always clear-cut, nor should it be (as discussed in Green 2001, 41–45). For a range of discussions see Bailey (1992), Berliner (1994), Lines (2005), Martin (1996), or Monson (1996). I will pick up this thread again briefly below in the section on the role of the teachers.

[14] In the instrumental setting pupils were less likely to play for extended periods of time, whereas in the classroom setting groups of up to 8 pupils (at the most) were seen to be "in flow" for periods of over five minutes at a time. However there was a case in the instrumental lesson where myself, the woodwind teacher and a clarinet pupil played through "Stand By Me" together, and this went on for several minutes, resulting in the teacher saying she had never heard the pupil play so fluently before. No doubt the differences were more to do with the presence or absence of other musicians to play with than anything intrinsic about the nature of the task.

[15] When they first carried out the task, the classroom pupils chose almost entirely current charts pop songs. When they repeated the task later in the year, their choices broadened out to include "classic" songs, often taken from their parents' collections. However this range was still less diverse than that represented by the choices of the instrumental pupils in the current project. Few classroom pupils and none of the 15 instrumental pupils selected music that reflected any ethnic minority. However this could change if they did the task over a longer period, and further research on this topic could be interesting.

[16] See Allsup (2008) and Clements (2008), and also my response (Green 2008). There is further advice about the role of the teacher in the classroom project on www.musicalfutures.org

# CONTRIBUTORS

## Editors

Sidsel Karlsen, Ph. D.
Professor of Music Education
Hedmark University College, Norway

Lauri Väkevä, Ph. D.
Professor of Music Education
Sibelius Academy, Finland

## Other Writers

Randall Everett Allsup, Ed. D.
Associate Professor of Music and Music Education
Teachers College, Columbia University, USA

Ann C. Clements, Ph. D.
Associate Professor of Music Education
The Pennsylvania State University, USA

Greg Gatien, M. Mus.
Assistant Professor
Chair of Applied Studies
Brandon University's School of Music, Canada

Eva Georgii-Hemming, Ph. D.
Professor and Subject Representative of Musicology
Örebro University, Sweden

Lucy Green, D. Phil.
Professor of Music Education
University of London, Institute of Education, UK

Panagiotis A. Kanellopoulos, Ph. D.
Assistant Professor of Music Education
University of Thessaly, Greece

Nathaniel J. Olson, M. Mus.
Doctoral Student
Teachers College, Columbia University, USA

Carlos Xavier Rodriguez, Ph. D.
Associate Professor and Chair of Music Education
University of Michigan, USA

Maria Westvall, Ph. D.
Senior Lecturer in Music Education
Örebro University, Sweden

Ruth Wright, Ph. D.
Chair of Music Education
The University of Western Ontario, Canada

# INDEX